# 1001 HELPFUL FAMILY HINTS

**Editor-in-Chief**
**DONALD D. WOLF**

**Illustrator**
**JAMES E. BARRY**

**Design, Layout
and Production
MARGOT L. WOLF**

elair
Consolidated
new york
A DELAIR PUBLISHING COMPANY

# Contents

HIGH BLOOD PRESSURE  7
THE DRUGS YOU TAKE  29
A FITNESS PROGRAM FOR ADULTS  51
FIRST AID  73
THE FOOD YOU EAT  95
FOOD AND COOKING TIPS  117
HOW TO ENTERTAIN  139
BASIC TOOLS  161
INTERIOR HOME REPAIRS  179
EXTERIOR HOME REPAIRS  197
CREDIT  215
BUYING INSURANCE  235

Written by
MARTIN SHARP

# High Blood Pressure

# Contents

**WHAT IS BLOOD PRESSURE?** . . . . . . . . . . . . . . . . . . . . 9
Why High Blood Pressure Is Dangerous . . . . . . . . 9
A Silent Killer . . . . . . . . . . . . . . . . . . . . . . . . . . . . . 10
Who Can Tell You If You Have High Blood
Pressure? . . . . . . . . . . . . . . . . . . . . . . . . . . . . . . . . 11

**THE CARDIOVASCULAR SYSTEM** . . . . . . . . . . . . . 12
Systole and Diastole . . . . . . . . . . . . . . . . . . . . . . 13
The Arteries . . . . . . . . . . . . . . . . . . . . . . . . . . . . . . 14
The Veins . . . . . . . . . . . . . . . . . . . . . . . . . . . . . . . . 15
The Heart as a Pump . . . . . . . . . . . . . . . . . . . . . . 15
The Rise and Fall of Blood Pressure . . . . . . . . . . . 16
How the Body Regulates Blood Pressure . . . . . . . 16
What Is Normal Blood Pressure? . . . . . . . . . . . . . 17
How Blood Pressure Is Measured . . . . . . . . . . . . . 18

**WHAT CAUSES HIGH BLOOD PRESSURE?** . . . . . . 19
Hardening of the Arteries and High Blood
Pressure . . . . . . . . . . . . . . . . . . . . . . . . . . . . . . . 20
Who Develops High Blood Pressure? . . . . . . . . . . 21
How to Tell Whether You Have High Blood
Pressure . . . . . . . . . . . . . . . . . . . . . . . . . . . . . . . 22
Suppose You Do Have High Blood Pressure . . . . 24
High Blood Pressure, the Pill, and Pregnancy . . . 24

**TREATMENT PLANS** . . . . . . . . . . . . . . . . . . . . . . . . 24
Medication . . . . . . . . . . . . . . . . . . . . . . . . . . . . . . . 25

**LIVING WITH HIGH BLOOD PRESSURE** . . . . . . . . 26
Can You Still Use Stimulants? . . . . . . . . . . . . . . . . 27

**SOME FINAL ADVICE** . . . . . . . . . . . . . . . . . . . . . . . 28

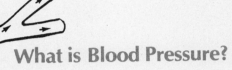

## What is Blood Pressure?

Everyone has blood pressure. It is the force of the blood against the walls of the blood vessels—the arteries and veins —in your body. Without blood pressure, the blood could not circulate. How and why the blood circulates and what creates the pressure is explained later.

In all human beings, blood pressure varies from day to day and from moment to moment. It goes up when we are excited, and it goes down when we are at rest or asleep. Changes in blood pressure such as these are normal. It is *not* normal when blood pressure goes up and stays up. This condition is called *high blood pressure,* and it is a definite chronic illness that may have very serious consequences such as stroke, heart failure, and kidney failure.

The plagues of the past, cholera, bubonic plague, and tuberculosis, have been almost wiped out. In modern life, these mass killers of human beings have been replaced by a new kind of plague: high blood pressure. The old-time plagues were contagious diseases that spread from person to person, raging through whole continents and killing millions of people. Today, millions of people have high blood pressure and millions die from its consequences, although high blood pressure, unlike the plagues, is not contagious.

About one out of every five adults has high blood pressure, and one out of every five deaths of persons below the age of 65 is caused by its consequences.

## Why High Blood Pressure Is Dangerous

When blood pressure is high, the heart has to pump harder to circulate the blood within the blood vessels, which are resisting its flow. After a period of years the heart muscle tires, and failure of the heart can result. Also, continued high pressure against the walls of arteries can eventually cause them to leak and burst. The damage to the arteries of the heart causes a heart attack; of the kidneys, kidney failure; and of the brain, stroke. Persons with high blood pressure have twice the chance of having a fatal stroke or heart attack as do those with normal blood pressure.

## A Silent Killer

High blood pressure is a chronic, lifelong, usually incurable disease which, however, can nearly always be controlled with proper and continuing treatment. Few if any symptoms are noticeable until the blood pressure has been high for a long time, often many years, and has caused damage to major organs of the body such as the heart, brain, or kidneys. The lack of symptoms for so long a time while damage is being done has caused high blood pressure to be called "the silent killer."

People are aware of diseases that produce discomfort or pain. Silent diseases that require preventive action based on knowledge of the disease rather than physical pain do not

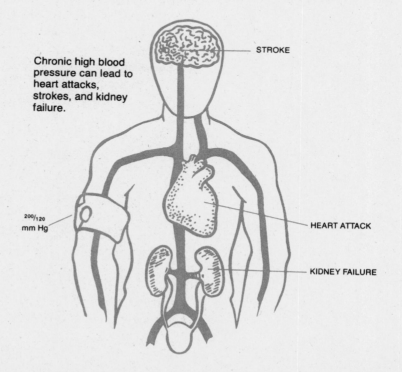

Chronic high blood pressure can lead to heart attacks, strokes, and kidney failure.

STROKE

200/120 mm Hg

HEART ATTACK

KIDNEY FAILURE

attract the average person's attention. Yet if those who have high blood pressure can be made aware of its consequences and be convinced that it can be controlled, a large drop in the number and severity of cases of heart attack, stroke, and kidney disease will follow.

Too many people believe that high blood pressure is only a moderately important disease and are reluctant to accept, or are unaware of, its serious consequences. A patient who goes to a specialist for the treatment of an acute disease or a surgical problem and is told that he or she also has high blood pressure may ignore the warning.

## Who Can Tell You If You Have High Blood Pressure?

Since, as we have seen, high blood pressure does not produce dramatic symptoms until it has caused severe damage to vital organs, an untrained person cannot tell if he or she has high blood pressure. The only way to find out is to have your blood pressure measured by a physician or other medically trained professional. Measurement of blood pressure is painless and takes only a few minutes, but it may save your life or prevent years of disablement.

High blood pressure is found in all groups of society, but the incidence is higher in blacks (and more often in black women than in black men), in overweight persons, persons living on an income of less than $5,000 a year, people over 65 years of age, or people who have a family history of high blood pressure. If you belong to one of these groups, have your blood pressure checked regularly. This does not mean, however, that anybody outside these groups should not do the same.

Though high blood pressure is called the silent killer, there are some symptoms that should not be overlooked. Among them are persistent headaches, fatigue, dizziness, and feelings of tension. Also, persons with high blood pressure may experience shortness of breath because of the additional work their hearts must do. The absence of these symptoms is in no way a reason to be careless.

There is much you can do to prevent any of the disastrous consequences of high blood pressure, once you have learned that you have the disease. The first step is to see a doctor, who will give you a schedule of things you must do in order to bring your blood pressure down to normal limits, or at least to a level that will keep it from damaging your heart, brain, or kidneys. What the doctor will ask you to do will be painless and will not require much time or effort: have your blood pressure measured at regular intervals, make the prescribed changes in your diet and living habits, and take medicine exactly as ordered. These simple measures should control your blood pressure and enable you to lead a normal and productive life.

## The Cardiovascular System

The blood flows through the heart, arteries, and veins. These and the brain center and nerves that control the beating of the heart are called the *cardiovascular system*.

The heart is a muscle about the size of a fist. It has four chambers, two on each side. The upper chambers are called *auricles* (or *atria*); the lower are *ventricles*. Blood enters the heart through a large *vein* called the *vena cava,* which opens into the right auricle (or atrium). This blood has come to the heart from all parts of the body through a network of veins. From the atrium the blood flows through a one-way valve, composed of muscle, to the right ventricle. The ventricle has thick muscular walls that contract and force the blood out of the heart through large arteries called the *pulmonary arteries*. These arteries conduct the blood to the lungs, where the red blood cells take on oxygen from the air in the lungs. Blood then goes back to the heart through the *pulmonary veins,* entering the left atrium. Again it passes through a valve, flowing down into the left ventricle. As the left ventricle contracts, it pumps blood into a large artery called the *aorta*. This artery carries the blood, via a network of smaller

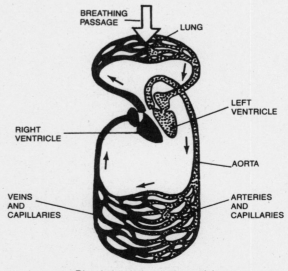

Blood circulation (schematic).

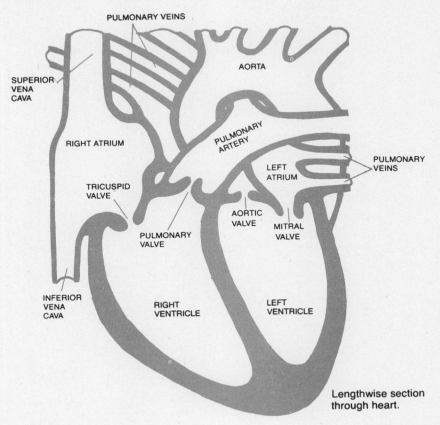

PULMONARY VEINS

AORTA

SUPERIOR
VENA
CAVA

RIGHT ATRIUM

PULMONARY
ARTERY

LEFT
ATRIUM

PULMONARY
VEINS

TRICUSPID
VALVE

AORTIC
VALVE

MITRAL
VALVE

PULMONARY
VALVE

INFERIOR
VENA
CAVA

RIGHT
VENTRICLE

LEFT
VENTRICLE

Lengthwise section
through heart.

arteries, to all parts of the body. The path of the blood in your body, then, is: veins—heart—lungs—heart—arteries—veins, around and around. This continual movement is called the *circulation* of the blood. Each contraction of the ventricles is a heartbeat. A normal heart beats 60 to 90 times each minute when the body is at rest.

## Systole and Diastole

When the left ventricle contracts, it pumps a jet of blood into the arteries. The blood flows through the arteries as a wave, or *pulse*. When a doctor or nurse "feels your pulse," it is this wave of blood that he or she feels passing beneath the fingertips held on your wrist. The wave of blood causes a temporary increase in the amount of blood in the part of the artery through which it passes. This increases the pressure of the blood on the walls of the artery. The momentary increase is called *systole*. As we shall see, it is important when measuring blood pressure. After the ventricles contract, they rest for a little less than a second while blood flows into them from the atria. During this resting time, which is called *diastole*, blood pressure is lowest.

## The Arteries

The blood vessels that carry blood from the heart to all parts of the body are called *arteries*. In addition to carrying blood, arteries also regulate the pressure and amount of blood that goes to the organs.

There are two main kinds of arteries: elastic and muscular. The elastic arteries are made up of rings of elastic fibers. As we have seen, the pumping of the heart sends out the blood in pulses at regular intervals, not as an even flow. The elastic arteries, because they can expand and contract as pulse waves of blood enter them and then leave, can smooth out the blood flow. By the time the blood reaches the smaller arteries, it is flowing in a smooth stream, instead of pulses.

The elastic arteries not only smooth out the flow of blood, but, by expanding as a pulse of blood reaches them, they also lessen the pressure of the blood on the walls of the arteries. If anything causes these arteries to lose their elasticity, it creates a condition known as "hardening of the arteries." In this condition, the arteries cannot expand sufficiently when a pulse of blood passes through them. The result is a rise in the pressure of the blood.

The muscular arteries, at the periphery of the arterial system, have walls of muscle tissue. These arteries can expand (or dilate) and contract as their muscles expand or contract. As they expand or contract, they help the heart to move blood to those parts of the body that need it most at any time.

The smallest muscular arteries are called *arterioles*. They branch into even smaller ones, the *capillary arteries,* which bring oxygen and food to the tissues of all the organs of the body.

If the muscular arteries do not expand and contract in rhythm with the pulses of blood flowing through them, they can offer considerable resistance to the flow of blood. This may raise the pressure of the blood. The resistance of all the arterioles and capillary arteries is called *peripheral arterial resistance* and is an important factor in the level of blood pressure in the arterial system.

By far the most important cause of hardening of the arteries is *atherosclerosis*. In this condition, fatty deposits form on the inner walls of arteries. These deposits may eventually become so thick that they fill the whole artery, completely choking off the flow of blood through it. The fatty deposits cause the artery to lose its suppleness and become "hard."

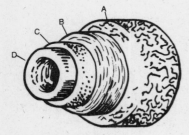

Section through artery:
A. Fat, longitudinal muscle and elastic fibers.
B. Circular muscle.
C. Elastic membrane.
D. Thin lining (endothelium).

The cause of fatty deposits is an excess of blood fats, which are called *lipids*. The two most dangerous of these substances are cholesterol and triglycerides. Cholesterol is found in many foods, such as fatty meats, sausages, shellfish, egg yolks, and inner organs such as liver and brains. The body converts carbohydrates such as sugar, flour, bread, and bread products into fats called triglycerides.

Once an artery has developed a deposit of blood fat, it is almost impossible to remove it. However, a diet low in cholesterol, triglycerides, and other fats will go a long way toward preventing hardening of the arteries.

## The Veins

The blood vessels that carry blood from the tissues back to the heart are the *veins*. Blood begins its return journey to the heart in the capillary veins, which gather carbon dioxide and waste materials from the cells that make up the tissues. The capillaries unite with larger veins, and these in turn unite with still larger ones. Finally, the veins merge into two very large ones, called the *venae cavae*. Blood returning from the head, neck, and arms to the heart passes through the *superior vena cava;* blood returning from the trunk and legs flows through the *inferior vena cava*. Both these large veins carry blood to the right atrium of the heart.

The walls of veins are much thinner than those of arteries, and the pressure in the veins is very low—almost unnoticeable.

CORONARY ARTERIES

CORONARY ARTERIES

## The Heart as a Pump

With each heartbeat, the left ventricle sends into the arteries a measurable amount of blood, and the number of heartbeats is easily counted. Thus we can calculate the amount of work the heart does. When the heart is beating at a normal rate, 60 to 80 beats per minute, it pumps 3 to 5 quarts of blood per minute. This amount of blood can increase greatly when one does strenuous work. This remarkable pump works year after year with no time out for repair. It gets its energy from nutrients in the blood—not directly from the blood passing through the atria and ventricles, but rather from its own set of blood vessels. They bring to the heart muscle fuel to furnish energy and oxygen to burn the fuel, and muscle material for repair. They carry away the waste and are essential for the life and activity of the heart. These *coronary arteries* branch out from the base of the aorta just as it leaves the left chamber of the heart and just above the valves that separate the aorta from the ventricle. They and the network of vessels branching from them come down over the top of the heart like a crown (corona). They are the most important blood vessels in the body, and leakage, blockage, or bursting of weakened coronary blood vessels almost surely leads to death.

## The Rise and Fall of Blood Pressure

In normal, healthy persons, blood pressure is constantly rising and falling. When you are lying down, especially when asleep, blood pressure is lowest. When you sit up, certain muscles need more blood, and the heart pumps harder and faster to supply this blood. As a result, your blood pressure goes up. When you stand up, more muscles need increased amounts of blood, and blood pressure goes higher. Walking, climbing stairs, running, and other strenuous activities raise the blood pressure even higher. Certain emotions, such as anger, fear, anxiety, or elation, also cause the blood pressure to rise. The rise of blood pressure due to emotions causes more blood to flow to the brain and makes the person more alert and responsive.

In a normal person, when physical exercise is over or strong emotions subside, the blood pressure returns to its normal level. If your heart and blood vessels are in healthy condition, the temporary rise in blood pressure does no harm. It is when pressure remains higher than normal, causing damage to the blood vessels, that a sudden rise in blood pressure can be dangerous and even fatal.

## How the Body Regulates Blood Pressure

The body must constantly adjust the pressure and distribution of blood in the arteries to meet the changing demands of the organs for blood. To accomplish this, the body has a *feedback system,* comparable to that of many electrical and electronic devices.

How does this blood-pressure feedback work? The walls of certain large arteries, especially the aorta and the kidney arteries, are lined with cells that are sensitive to pressure. These act as tiny gauges, measuring the pressure of the blood that passes through the arteries. The pressure-sensitive cells are connected by nerves to that part of the brain which controls blood circulation. "Messages" about the level of blood pressure in the arteries are continually passing along the nerves to the brain. The circulation center in the brain collates the bits of information it receives from the arteries. Another part of the nervous system connects the circulation center with the heart and the muscles of the arterial walls. If more blood is needed in any part of the body—for example, in a muscle—a message is sent from the brain to the adrenal gland. This organ then secretes a powerful hormone, *noradrenalin,* into the bloodstream, which causes the arterioles and capillary arteries to contract. It also causes the heart to beat harder. With a more powerful heartbeat pumping blood through narrowed arteries, the pressure must rise.

If the messages from the pressure-sensitive cells tell the brain that the increased blood pressure exceeds the need for it, the circulation center stops the secretion of noradrenalin, the narrowed arteries relax and widen, and the blood pressure soon lowers to normal.

## What Is Normal Blood Pressure?

Blood pressure, as we have seen, varies from moment to moment. It also varies with age, often becoming higher as a person grows older. Furthermore, as we have also learned, blood pressure increases at systole, when the left ventricle is pumping blood into the arteries; and pressure lowers at diastole, when the ventricles are filling with blood. Thus, a single measurement is not enough. However, if we measure the pressure both at systole (systolic pressure) and at diastole (diastolic pressure), we get two useful measurements.

Blood pressure measurements are reported in millimeters of mercury, usually abbreviated as "mm Hg." (Hg is the chemical symbol for mercury). The mercury is contained in a narrow glass tube, and the level of the column of mercury rises and falls as blood pressure rises and falls. Thus, a pressure of 120 mm Hg means that the height of the column is 120 millimeters.

Millions of blood pressure measurements have established that a normal range of blood pressure is systolic 160 mm Hg and diastolic 90 mm Hg. These are usually reported as 160/90, and are read as "160 over 90." It is possible to have slightly higher pressures than these and still be healthy, but 160/90 are the standards for comparing pressures.

When a physician or nurse measures blood pressure, he or she wraps a cloth-covered rubber cuff around your arm just above the elbow. The cuff is actually a bag from which two rubber tubes project. The free end of one tube is connected to a rubber bulb. The free end of the other tube connects with a glass tube that is partially filled with mercury, or it may connect with a hollow metal container that has a numbered dial and a needle that moves over the numbers. This instrument is called a *sphygmomanometer*.

In a thorough job, your blood pressure is measured three times: when you are lying down, sitting, and standing; but sometimes the last of these is omitted.

To begin the measurement, the doctor or nurse tightens a knob on the rubber bulb. This causes the air that is pumped from the bulb by squeezing it to move through the rubber tube to the cuff. As the cuff fills with air, it presses on the artery that runs to your hand. Eventually, it presses hard enough to stop the flow of blood in the artery. The air entering the cuff also pushes up the column of mercury in the glass tube. Next to the glass tube is a scale of marks, one millimeter apart. The cuff is pumped until the column of mercury rises to a level even higher than it would be in a case of high systolic blood pressure. Then a stethoscope is placed on your arm at the bottom of the cuff and in line with the artery.

Next, the knob on the bulb is loosened to allow air to escape from the cuff. This lessens the pressure in the cuff. As the pressure goes down, the level of the column of mercury in the tube also goes down. When the pressure in the cuff is low enough to let blood flow again in the artery, the doctor begins to hear the pumping of the heart as it moves blood through the artery. At this point, he or she notes the height of the column of mercury. This is the systolic blood pressure—the pressure at the time the heart is pushing blood out of the left ventricle.

As air continues to escape from the cuff, the heart sounds grow louder and then begin to fade away. At the moment when the sounds can no longer be heard, the height of the column of mercury is again noted. This is the diastolic blood pressure—the pressure when the heart is resting and filling with blood.

A person suffering from high blood pressure can measure his or her own blood pressure at home. There are good and quite inexpensive sphygmomanometers on the market today. Most are the type with a numbered dial and needle to indicate millimeters of mercury. Some are electronic and automatically display the pressure in illuminated numbers. You can easily learn to use one of these instruments. It will be useful when the doctor has brought your blood pressure down and your visits to his office are at longer intervals. During these intervals, you yourself can check your blood pressure.

## What Causes High Blood Pressure?

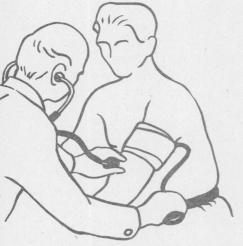
Measuring blood pressure with a sphygmomanometer.

There are two main kinds of high blood pressure, or *hypertension*. They are *malignant hypertension* and *benign hypertension*.

The cause of malignant hypertension is not known. It occurs more often in young people than in old. In this disease, the pressure is very high. The patient's vision is usually affected. His or her kidneys function poorly and decline rapidly. He or she may have spells of breathlessness. At one time a patient died within months or at most a year after malignant hypertension was diagnosed. Currently this disease can be controlled successfully, and patients can look forward to useful lives of normal length.

Benign hypertension is certainly a misnomer. In medicine, *benign* means mild or harmless; and a disease that disables and kills as many people as high blood pressure does is not harmless. Still the name persists. Benign hypertension, unlike the malignant form, progresses slowly. For many years it may create no symptoms: no dramatic loss of vision, no breathless spells, no sudden kidney failure. Nevertheless, benign hypertension slowly damages the heart and the arteries, paving the way for heart failure, stroke, and kidney failure.

In more than 90 percent of people who have benign hypertension, no physical cause can be found. This kind of hypertension is called *essential hypertension,* or *primary high blood pressure*. If the small arteries become narrowed and stay that way, blood pressure rises and stays up. Why this happens is still not completely understood.

Experts who have studied essential hypertension report that a tendency toward the condition is often inherited. They believe that inherited high blood pressure does not reveal itself until middle age. The degree of the rise of blood pressure is higher if both parents suffered from the disease. If the tendency toward hypertension is not inherited from either parent, blood pressure will rise very little as a person grows older.

Eating large amounts of salt may cause high blood pressure, but not everybody who eats large amounts of salt

**19**

develops the disease. Some investigators believe that persons who inherit the tendency toward high blood pressure are more likely to develop the disease from eating large amounts of salt.

There is evidence that people who live in areas where the water is soft (lacking dissolved calcium and magnesium) are more susceptible to high blood pressure than those who live in areas where the water is hard (containing calcium and magnesium). Another suspected chemical cause is the element cadmium in soft drinking water. Hard water coats water pipes with calcium, thus preventing the dissolving of tiny amounts of cadmium in the water. Cadmium is suspected because persons with hypertension have higher then normal concentrations of cadmium in their kidneys.

A 30-year continuing study of the blood pressure of thousands of the citizens of Framingham, Massachusetts, has led to the conclusion that obesity and overweight greatly increase the risk of developing hypertension. A decrease in blood pressure was observed in persons who lost weight.

As mentioned earlier, strong emotions such as fear and anger cause stress, or tension. Studies have shown that when blood pressure rises because of stress, it usually lowers again when the tension eases. This is usually the case even when the stress lasts for months or a few years. In some persons, however, the pressure does not go down when stress ends.

Some people respond to life situations with more anxiety —stress—than others. The blood pressure of these people is continually being raised as they meet daily situations. Eventually the pressure may remain high. Investigators say that these people have a "hypertensive personality."

In only about 10 percent of high blood pressure cases, a definite cause is known. Infection of the kidneys is one such cause. Another is damage to the adrenal glands that lie atop the kidneys. An obstruction in the artery that carries blood to the kidneys also can cause hypertension. So can a constriction of the aorta, the large artery feeding the heart. When any of these conditions is corrected, the hypertension usually disappears.

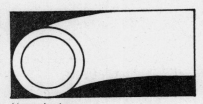
Normal artery.

Fatty streaks in artery.

Partial occlusion of artery.

Almost complete occlusion of artery.

## Hardening of the Arteries and High Blood Pressure

We frequently hear people talk about "hardening of the arteries" as being a cause of one or another kind of illness. Hardening of the arteries, which physicians call *atherosclerosis,* is a condition in which the arteries become "hard" or less elastic. This happens because the inner walls of an artery become coated with a fatty deposit, which not only hardens the artery's wall but also narrows its diameter. A narrowed artery carries less blood than a healthy one. Also, the fatty deposits create on the artery walls a rough surface that holds back the flow of blood. As a result of these conditions, the heart has to pump harder to move blood through the arteries, so the pressure of the blood rises.

## Who Develops High Blood Pressure?

Anyone can have high blood pressure. There are no age limits, and the disease attacks anyone of any race, income, occupation, or place of residence. However, certain groups —in the United States and some other industrialized countries—have a greater risk of developing high blood pressure.

Older people have more high blood pressure than younger ones. Since the outward symptoms of high blood pressure may take a long time to appear, the higher incidence of the disease in older people probably means that many had the disease when younger but did not know it. Not all older persons have high blood pressure, so the disease is not caused simply by growing old.

In the United States, more black people have high blood pressure than whites and people of other races. Since high blood pressure is a silent killer, it is hard to say just how many people in any group have the disease. But a government survey found that only 22 percent of whites, compared with 34 percent of blacks and 25 percent of other minorities, have ever been told that they had high blood pressure.

In blacks, the high blood pressure occurs at an earlier age and is more severe. Also, black women have higher pressure than black men. It cannot be said definitely what is the reason for the racial difference in hypertension, but there is some reason to believe that it is connected with the greater social pressures under which most blacks live. Those with low income and little education usually live under higher tension than those who are better educated and earn more money. As stress can create high blood pressure, the uneducated low-income group are more likely to suffer from the disease.

For the better educated person, the pressure of family and the need to succeed in work are most likely to be felt between the ages of 35 and 49. A government survey pointed to the possibility that the stress of not making a financial success may have an effect on high blood pressure.

Among men, the number of those with hypertension increases with age up to the age of 50 but then levels out. The leveling begins somewhat earlier for blacks than whites.

**21**

Among women, the number with high blood pressure increases continuously with age. At each age level, without exception, black women have higher levels of hypertension than do white women. As a group, more women have high blood pressure than do men. Among whites, there is little difference between men and women in the incidence of hypertension in each group up to the age of 65. At that age, the number of women with hypertension increases much faster than the number of men. Among blacks, women have higher levels of hypertension than do men of each age group.

A study of men found that the more active ones were less likely to have high blood pressure than those who worked less. However, this observation is ambiguous, because men who worked less than 40 hours a week had lower blood pressures than those who worked 40 to 50 hours, and those who worked more than 50 hours had the highest pressures.

As mentioned, overweight and high blood pressure often go together; therefore, fat people are more likely to suffer from hypertension than thin ones.

## How to Tell Whether You Have High Blood Pressure

When you become sick, your body gives certain tell-tale signals. For example, if you contract measles, you develop a rash all over your body; if you have a cold, you cough and sneeze and may have a sore throat; if you have the flu, you run a fever, may have aches in your joints, and may cough. These signals are called *symptoms*. They tell you clearly that something is wrong with the functioning of your body. A very short time after you contract a disease, you can see or feel its symptoms. But, as we have seen, with high blood pressure, the silent killer, it usually takes years from the time the pressure of the blood begins to rise to the appearance of symptoms.

There are some symptoms that appear early, but since they are also symptoms of other diseases, they may not be recognized as being caused by high blood pressure. These,

| COMPLAINT | APPROXIMATE FREQUENCY |
|---|---|
| Chest pains | 26% |
| Depression, lack of drive | 7% |
| Dizziness | 30% |
| Headaches | 23% |
| Nervousness | 35% |
| Palpitation of the heart | 32% |

and the frequency with which they appear, are listed in the chart below.

Young people may have trouble sleeping or digesting their food. They may perspire a lot when it is not particularly hot; they may feel fatigued without having worked hard; or they may become excited for no apparent reason. All these complaints can be symptoms of high blood pressure.

Persons above 45 years of age may complain of general malaise. They cannot concentrate on their jobs and so do not perform well; they tire easily; they cannot endure stress as well as they formerly could; their sexual drive declines. These complaints, too, can be symptoms of elevated blood pressure.

Even if high blood pressure does not make itself known through one of the foregoing signs or symptoms, it is still possible for you to have it, and it is advisable to have regular checkups.

If high blood pressure is not treated for some time, it causes damage that may produce tightness and pain radiating to the left shoulder and down the left arm to the hand. These symptoms are very serious. They can indicate a blockage of the flow of blood in the coronary arteries that supply the heart muscle and can be a forewarning of a heart attack.

Repeat attacks of dizziness, lapses of memory, and inability to concentrate are early symptoms of insufficient flow of blood through the arteries of the brain. These symptoms will be followed by fainting, temporary difficulties in speaking, intermittent weakness of the arms or legs or both, and difficulty in walking, which indicate a slight stroke or warnings of one to come.

Shortness of breath after only a little exercise or physical work, frequent urination at night, and a persistent cough may be warnings of heart failure in the near future. Swelling of the ankles, at first only during the day, but later at night, too, and finally swelling of the entire legs are more specific signs of heart failure.

Another sign of the damage caused by high blood pressure is cramps in one leg at a time or, rarely, both at the same time. The cramps may come while the afflicted person is walking and force him to stop and rest. These symptoms result from a lessened flow of blood in the arteries of the pelvis and legs.

Any of the symptoms described above should be reported to your doctor, because he is the only one who can decide definitely whether the cause of the symptom is high blood pressure or some other disease. In any case, the visit to your doctor may save your life.

### Suppose You Do Have High Blood Pressure

Once your physician has determined that you have high blood pressure, he or she will seek to find out three basic things: (1) how far the disease has gone and what organs it may have damaged; (2) what is causing it; and (3) what else you may be doing that could worsen the condition.

Your physician will give you a series of examinations that will determine what damage, if any, has taken place in your heart, arteries, kidneys, and possibly your brain.

The doctor will try to find a cause, or perhaps more than one, for your elevated blood pressure. It is simple common sense that unless the cause of the high blood pressure is eliminated, treatment of the condition is impossible. It may turn out that the cause can be entirely eliminated by surgery (a tumor on the adrenal gland) or by medication (infection of the kidneys). If this can be done, the blood pressure will return to normal.

Since a number of people have hypertension for which no clear-cut cause can be found, it is important that the physician look for factors that may be aggravating the disease. Among these, called *risk factors*, are overweight, smoking, stress, diabetes, and a diet high in cholesterol, triglycerides, or salt.

### High Blood Pressure, the Pill, and Pregnancy

High blood pressure is a rare side effect of the use of birth control pills. A survey of 600 women in inner-city Washington showed that 7 percent who had no history of elevated blood pressure before taking the pill developed high blood pressure while taking it. But it is not known how many of these women would have developed high blood pressure anyway. This is an important question, because most of the women were black and it is known that blacks—especially black women—have a higher rate of elevated blood pressure than whites.

## Treatment Plans

When the doctor has determined what damage high blood pressure has done to a patient, what the cause of the ailment is, and what, if any, risk factors are present, he or she must decide on a plan of treatment. Different findings require different kinds of treatment. High blood pressure caused by a tumor on an adrenal gland requires immediate surgery. If a patient is young, is of a nervous disposition, and is under stress in school or work, and if the blood pressure is much above normal, the doctor may simply monitor the blood pressure at regular intervals. If, when the stressful condition no longer exists, the patient's pressure does not lower, then the doctor may prescribe medication.

If a physician finds that a young black woman has a slight rise in blood pressure, is of nervous disposition, and is under stress in school or work, a different course of treatment is called for. The woman's race provides the high risk that her slightly increased blood pressure will develop into a severe chronic condition. Therefore the physician immediately prescribes medication to lower the pressure.

If a man in his 60's has high blood pressure because of atherosclerosis which raises his systolic pressure to between 170 and 180 and also has a high blood-fat level, the doctor may not prescribe any medication. In this case medicine will not cure the atherosclerosis nor extend the patient's life expectancy, but proper diet will help to keep the atherosclerosis from increasing rapidly.

These three examples show that not all cases of high blood pressure can be treated in the same way. It is important to realize this and to maintain confidence in your doctor, even if a friend or relative, also suffering from hypertension, is treated differently. There is no standard overall treatment that can be used for all who suffer from the disease.

Confidence in the physician and mutual understanding and respect are even more necessary in the treatment of essential hypertension, as the patient must remain under doctor's care for life.

## Medication

Many laymen believe that, since high blood pressure may be due to stress, tranquilizers and sedatives should be used to combat it. However, these two types of drugs are not effective.

The cornerstone of most treatment programs is a diuretic agent. This is a type of drug that eliminates excess sodium (usually found in salt) from the body. Some of these (with their trade names in parentheses) are chlorothiazide (Diuril), hydrochlorothiazide (Esidrix, Hydrodiuril, Oretic), benzoflumethiazide (Naturetin), chlorthalidone (Hygrotin), furosemide (Lasix), and methyclothrozide (Enduron). Since all these drugs perform the same function, the doctor will probably prescribe the one with which he is most familiar and to which the patient reacts most favorably.

If the use of a diuretic does not succeed in bringing the blood pressure down to normal, the doctor may add other drugs to his treatment program. Among the more effective drugs that might be added are the ones derived from reserpine, a chemical compound, which itself is derived from a group of plants called *Rauwolfia serpentina*. Some of these and their trade names are alpha methyldopa (Aldomet), propranolol (Inderal), hydralazine (Apresoline), guanethedine (Ismelin), clonodine (Catapres), and prazosin (Minipres). These drugs relax the narrowed arteries, which lowers blood pressure. But the lowering takes place only while the drug is in the bloodstream. Therefore, its use can never be stopped, even after the blood pressure has been lowered. This may mean taking the drug for the rest of the patient's life. These drugs usually are combined with a diuretic in a single pill, so that the number of pills to be taken in a day can be reduced.

If you are taking any of these drugs, your doctor must watch their effects on your blood pressure. Since some persons react to some drugs by developing unwanted symptoms, called *side effects*, the doctor must know about these, too. Some side effects are headache, dizziness, nausea, pains in the joints, drowsiness, fever, and diarrhea. You must continue to visit your doctor often—at least until your blood pressure is brought under control. Then you may visit him or her less often, but this is a decision for the doctor, not the patient, to make.

Since each person is an individual with his or her own life history and reactions to drugs, a doctor may have to try several drugs before the right one is found—the one that lowers the blood pressure and has the fewest side effects.

## Living With High Blood Pressure

Once you learn that you have high blood pressure and your doctor has brought the pressure down to acceptable levels, you must accept the fact that you will have to live with your ailment for the rest of your life. At first this may seem frightening, but you will soon learn that your life can be quite normal—even, in some ways, better than before.

In addition to giving you medicine, your doctor will prescribe a sodium-free diet. Actually, most foods in their natural state contain very little, if any, sodium. Foods that must be avoided usually contain sodium in the form of salt that was added in the commercial preparation of the foods; frankfurters are an example. All in all, you will find that it is quite easy to have tasty meals that are very low in sodium content.

Take your medicine regularly.

Stick to your diet.

Don't smoke.

26

Learn to relax.

Play.

Mix play with work.

Take a vacation every year.

The one strict rule in the diet will be that you must not add table salt (sodium chloride) to your food either when cooking or eating it. Fortunately, there is another kind of salt, potassium chloride, that is available in supermarkets and other food stores. This kind of salt is not as salty to the taste but is a good substitute for table salt. Furthermore, you can soon learn how to use spices and herbs to make your food tasty.

We have seen the harmful effect of overweight on blood pressure, so if you are overweight, you will have to go on a reducing diet in addition to the low-sodium one. You definitely should avoid any kind of crash diet, but rather lose weight gradually and sensibly. Your doctor will help you with your reducing problems and might also prescribe a diet low in cholesterol and triglycerides, even if your weight is normal.

Since high blood pressure is a very serious matter, you should set a routine for yourself and stick to it. Your routine should consist of the following:

Take your medicine regularly.

Stick to your diet.

Don't smoke.

Learn to relax and play, and alternate these activities with work. Take at least one vacation a year.

Get enough sleep to feel rested.

Exercise moderately.

See your doctor regularly for checkups.

You may have to change your work habits. You may have to choose between a coveted promotion or income level and continuing to remain alive. Reevaluate your goals and slow down.

### Can You Still Use Stimulants?

Get enough rest.

Exercise moderately.

High blood pressure patients may drink coffee, tea, and cocoa in moderate amounts. However, since the stimulants (caffeine, aminophyllin, and theobromine) in these beverages may cause the drugs the patient is taking to produce undesirable side effects, the doctor may forbid drinking one or another of the beverages. On the other hand, the stimulants may help the patient to overcome the drowsiness that some antihypertensive drugs cause. Again,

Have regular checkups.

27

the doctor must decide whether you can make this use of coffee, tea, or cocoa.

A glass of wine or beer after a day of work is not forbidden a high blood pressure patient. But alcohol can intensify the fatigue produced by some blood pressure drugs. This could be a hazard to the patient who drinks an alcoholic beverage before driving, since it may make him or her too drowsy to drive safely.

## Some Final Advice

Don't be frightened or depressed by high blood pressure. It can be treated effectively.

Follow the orders your doctor gives you. Simple measures such as faithfully taking diuretic pills produce good results.

Persons who are taking blood pressure medication should carry in their purse or wallet an identification card that states the type and dosage of the medicines, their most recent blood pressure reading, and the address of their doctor. Your physician can give you one of these ID cards.

Don't run from one doctor to another, looking for a quick and easy miracle drug. Stick to one reliable doctor or one good clinic, and follow the plan of treatment given you.

If your doctor does prescribe drug treatment, be patient; don't stop taking the drugs because they produce annoying side effects. Tell your doctor about these effects.

Give yourself a chance to adjust to the action of a blood pressure drug. It may take weeks to act, but the end results will reward your persistence.

Modern treatment of hypertension may be complicated and may require much time, patience, and understanding by both patient and physician. It is annoying to take pills and experience unpleasant side reactions when you may have felt well before treatment—but remember, you were *not* well; the silent killer was at work. Don't be discouraged if you must continue treatment for the rest of your life. All your effort is less than it would be if you let the complications of high blood pressure set in. Most high blood pressure cases respond to treatment, and most patients whose blood pressure is being successfully treated live long and *normal* lives.

Written by
**MARTIN SHARP**

# The
# Drugs
# You
# Take

# Contents

MILLIONS OF DOLLARS FOR MEDICINES ....... 31

OVER-THE-COUNTER AND PRESCRIPTION
  DRUGS .................................... 31
  When Should You Take Medicines? ............ 32
  Buying OTC Drugs ......................... 33
  Pharmacists Can Help You ................... 34
  How to Buy Prescription Medicines ........... 34
  Choosing a Pharmacy ...................... 35
  Using and Storing Medicines ................ 36
  You Can Help ............................. 38
  Generic Drugs: How Good Are They? ......... 38
  Drug Development ......................... 39
  Mixing Medicines .......................... 41
  Food and Drug Interactions .................. 42
  Painkillers: Their Uses and Abuses ............ 43
  Sleep Aids ................................ 44
  Laxatives: What Does "Regular" Mean? ....... 45
  Tranquilizers: Use, Abuse, and Dependency .... 47

DRUGS AND PREGNANCY .................... 48

LAETRILE: THE FATAL CURE .................. 49

DRUGS AND YOU .......................... 50

## Millions of Dollars for Medicines

Almost everyone in the United States takes drugs of some kind. Even healthy persons have an occasional muscle pain or headache, for which they take aspirin or another painkiller. The prescriptions for medicines written by physicians are counted in the billions every year. American consumers spend about $9 billion each year for medicines.

The science of medicines, pharmacology, has progressed further in the past 30 years than in the previous 30 centuries. Many medicines available today had not even been discovered 40 years ago.

Although a great amount of money is spent on medicines, it does not always buy good health. People sometimes take medicines to wake up, to get to sleep, to relax from everyday tensions, to stimulate or reduce appetite. Health can actually be harmed by continual taking of medicines for these purposes. The misuse or excessive use of medicines is a major drug problem in America.

This does not mean that you should not take medicines when you need them, but you should know when and how to use them. You can protect your health, prevent accidents or illness or even death, and save a lot of money by knowing the best ways to buy and use medicines.

## Over-the-Counter and Prescription Drugs

For the consumer, there are two types of medicine: over-the-counter (OTC) and prescription ($R_x$) drugs.

*Over-the-counter medicines* are also known as patent medicines or home remedies. They include such common drugs as aspirin, laxatives, and antacids. If you use these drugs according to the directions on the label, they are relatively safe. This means that you must not take them oftener or in larger doses than is indicated by the label. You can buy OTC drugs without a prescription in any drugstore and in many supermarkets.

*Prescription drugs* (which bear the symbol $R_x$) can be ordered or prescribed only by a doctor and can be sold only by a registered pharmacist. $R_x$ drugs are generally more powerful than OTC drugs and are more likely to cause side effects such as rashes, nausea, dizziness, shortness of breath, and others.

## When Should You Take Medicines?

You should not always reach for a medicine when you don't feel good. Feeling tired, a little tense during the working day, or perhaps a bit nauseated are parts of everyday living. A little extra sleep and time out for relaxation may cause most of these symptoms to disappear.

Newspaper or magazine advertisements or broadcast commercials may make you think you have a condition that is described. Then you reach for, or go out and buy, the medicine the sponsor is selling. It would be better to wait a while and see if the symptom you think you have does not go away without medication.

Many OTC and $R_x$ medicines relieve pain, nasal stuffiness, or a headache without curing the condition that brought on these, and other, symptoms. A cold remedy may make you feel more comfortable by reducing sniffles and sneezes, but your cold will last as long as if you had taken no medicine at all.

When you take a medicine that relieves unpleasant or painful symptoms, you naturally will want to take it again if the symptoms return. However, you should not do this for very long. If pain, fever, headache, or other symptoms persist, it is important for you to see a doctor about them. They may be the symptoms of a serious disease.

All medicines affect the way your body functions. OTC medicines generally affect you less than $R_x$ medicines because they are less powerful.

A medicine that is safe and effective for most people may cause problems for others who have unpleasant or allergic reactions to certain drugs. Some people get a skin rash if they take even one aspirin.

Many medicines decrease or increase in strength as time passes. This points to the fact that buying the large, economy size of a drug may not be economical if it remains in your medicine cabinet unused for a long time. On the other hand, many $R_x$ drugs are so expensive that it may pay to buy in large quantities. If you must take an $R_x$ drug, ask your doctor or pharmacist how long it will keep its proper strength; then you will know whether or not to buy a large quantity.

Buying OTC Drugs.

Before you buy any OTC drug, ask yourself if you really need it. Do you feel you should buy it because you were persuaded by a TV commercial, a friend who said it helped him or her, or an article in a newspaper or magazine? If you feel tired, should you buy a medicine to relieve the tiredness or should you relax frequently or get more sleep? Or should you see your doctor?

If you feel that you do need an OTC medicine, ask your pharmacist's advice and be sure to read the label. You may change your mind.

On the labels of OTC drugs you will find certain information that federal law requires all manufacturers to give:

• The name of the medicine and the name and address of the manufacturer, packer, or distributor.

• The active ingredients. This information will help you to avoid any allergic reactions or other sensitivities that you may have to certain ingredients. Also, this information can save you money, because many OTC medicines contain exactly the same ingredients and differ from each other only in brand name. Knowing that two medicines are identical should keep you from buying both.

• Directions for safe use. For example, certain drugs cause drowsiness and should not be taken if you are going to drive a car or operate certain kinds of machinery soon after you have taken them. Others should not be taken by people with high blood pressure. The label may warn you not to take the drug for too long or in larger than recommended amounts; for example, "Do not take more than two tablets in four hours or more than six in 24 hours." The label may contain the warning, "If symptoms persist more than 24 hours, see your doctor."

## Pharmacists Can Help You

Pharmacists are well-trained professionals who can help their customers to understand how to buy and use drugs. Pharmacists are not allowed to prescribe R$_x$ drugs.

Your pharmacist can explain to you the meaning of terms on labels. He or she may be able to recommend a lower-priced brand of drug than the one you chose.

Don't be afraid to ask a pharmacist for help; your health is at stake, and the pharmacist will be glad to help.

## How to Buy Prescription Medicines

When you see your doctor, besides telling him the symptoms that brought you to his office, tell him of any bad experience you have had with taking medicines and of any allergies you may have. This information will enable him or her to avoid giving you a medicine that will cause such side effects.

Don't expect the doctor to prescribe medicine every time you see him; often he won't find it necessary to prescribe any. When a medicine is prescribed for you, make sure you know the answers to these questions before leaving his office:

*What is the name of the medicine?* Since the names of medicines are not common words, write down the name of the one you are given. You may need to tell another doctor about it later.

*When and how often should I take it?* If the doctor tells you to take the medicine three times a day, ask whether it should be taken before or after meals. Some drugs taken on an empty stomach may cause you to feel upset; others should be taken only on an empty stomach.

*Can the least expensive brand of the medicine be prescribed?* Many medicines are very expensive, so you should not be afraid to ask your doctor for the least expensive brand that will be effective. Ask if you can be given a prescription for the generic name of the medicine rather than the brand name. Drugs bought by generic name are usually cheaper. If the doctor will not prescribe a particular medicine by generic name, he probably feels that a brand-name medicine will help you more.

*Can the new medicine be taken with others?* If you are

taking other medicines, you should have told your doctor; if you haven't, tell him before he writes your prescription. This knowledge will help the doctor to prescribe properly.

*What reactions, or side effects, can I expect?* In some people, certain medicines may cause drowsiness, nausea, vomiting, dizziness, nervousness, or other reactions. These are unfortunate but unavoidable. If the side effects become severe, tell the doctor, who will probably prescribe another medicine.

*What precautions should I take?* As with OTC drugs, you should be warned not to engage in certain activities soon after taking a dose of certain medicines.

*Can the prescription be refilled?* If the medicine is to be taken frequently or for a long time, you may need to have the prescription refilled. If so, ask your doctor about this. When you have taken all the medicine prescribed, the doctor may want to reexamine you to see if you still need that medicine or perhaps a different one; or the doctor may allow a limited number of refills.

*Must I finish all the medicine that has been prescribed for me?* If your symptoms disappear before you finish the medicine the doctor has prescribed, should you stop taking it? Should you continue in order to prevent a recurrence of the illness? Does the doctor want you to check with him after you have taken a certain amount of the prescribed medicine? You should find out the answers to these questions.

If, after leaving the doctor's office, you have more questions or have forgotten some of the answers, don't hesitate to call the doctor.

## Choosing a Pharmacy

When you need a medicine immediately — perhaps for a child running a high fever — you will want to go to the pharmacy that is nearest and gives the quickest service. However, when you are using the same medicine for a long time, you may be wise to shop around and compare prices. On the other hand, you may be using a pharmacy that gives you just the kind of service you want, and you may not want to change. An advantage to buying from the same pharmacy over a long period of time is that the pharmacist has a record of the drugs you and your family have been using. This may enable him to spot undesirable combinations of medicines that you and your doctor may not be aware of.

Before you leave a pharmacy with your newly filled

prescription, look at the label on the medicine. It should contain the following:

• the pharmacy's name, address, and phone number
• the prescription number
• the patient's name
• how often and when to take the drug
• how much to take each time
• special instructions (shake well, refrigerate, etc.)
• the doctor's name
• the date the prescription was filled
• the name of the drug (if the doctor says it should be put on the label)

If any of this information is not on the label or if you think any of it is wrong, ask the pharmacist about it. If you are still not sure, call your doctor.

When you have a prescription refilled, write the date on the label. The pharmacist uses the date the prescription was first filled.

## Using and Storing Medicines

*Directions.* With both $R_x$ and OTC drugs, carefully follow the directions about how much to take and when. Continue taking an $R_x$ drug for the entire time the doctor ordered. If you stop taking it too soon, you may prevent the drug from accomplishing what the doctor prescribed it for —and find yourself sick again.

*Side effects.* As we have seen, some drugs cause unwanted side effects such as rash, nausea, dizziness, or headache. If this happens to you, immediately consult your doctor or pharmacist. The drug may be discontinued, the dosage changed, or another drug may be prescribed.

*Combining drugs.* Always consult your doctor or pharmacist before you take two medicines together. Failure to do this may result in great harm or even death. If you are taking any medicines at all, don't drink alcohol without first consulting your doctor. Failure to do so may result in death.

*Storing drugs.* Always look at the labels of both OTC and $R_x$ drugs for special storage instructions. If the label says, "Keep in a cool, dry place," do not store the drug in the medicine cabinet of a warm, steamy bathroom; store it in the refrigerator.

Clean out your medicine cabinet regularly. Throw out old medicines that may have lost or gained strength or have changed chemically. Throw out a medicine when your doctor tells you to stop taking it.

*Labels.* Keep the label on or in the container. You need it to identify the medicine and to refer to the directions. When you pour liquid medicines, keep the label side on top so that any spilled liquid won't run down the side and blot out the print on the label.

*Don't share drugs.* Your doctor prescribes an $R_x$ drug for you and you alone. Never give the drug to anyone else or let anyone share it because you think his symptoms are the same as yours. Only a doctor can tell whether the symptoms really are the same. Your guess may do serious harm to the other person.

*Look carefully.* Many pillboxes, bottles, and drugs look alike. Don't take a drug until you have read the label on the container. Never take medicines in the dark.

*When you travel.* If you need to take prescription medicines with you on a long trip, be sure to take enough. Carry them in the original labeled containers. Pharmacists may not fill prescriptions written by out-of-state doctors. In an emergency, go to a hospital. If you move to another city, take enough medicine to last until you find another doctor. Also, arrange with your doctor to forward your medical record when you have found a new doctor.

*Precautions with children.* Medicines cause more accidental poisonings among children under five than any other materials in the household. Toddlers like to crawl and climb and get into things. A bottle of medicine can look as inviting to a child as a bottle of soda pop, a bottle of brightly colored pills as interesting as colored candy. And what toddlers can get their hands on, they put into their mouths. All medicines—as well as any other chemicals used in the home—should be kept on a high shelf out of children's reach, or better still, in a locked cabinet.

But this precaution is not enough. Medicines should not

be left in handbags that are then left on chairs, beds, or other low places that a child can reach. Children love to explore pocketbooks.

If the phone or doorbell rings when you are about to take or have just taken medicine, don't walk away from the medicine leaving it where a child can reach it. It takes only a few seconds for a child to imitate you by taking your medicine. The results can be tragic.

To protect children from poisoning by medicines, the Food and Drug Administration (FDA), under the Poison Prevention Packaging Act, requires that all poisonous substances be enclosed in safety packaging. Such packaging is designed to be especially hard for children to open, but it works only if you make sure that you close the package in the correct manner.

When you give children medicine, don't tell them it is candy or something else they like. They may try to get more of it when they are alone.

## You Can Help

If, after buying a medicine, you notice that it does not seem to be the right color or has a different odor, *don't use it*. Return it to the pharmacy. If a medicine packaged by the manufacturer seems to be discolored or otherwise bad, report this fact to the FDA — don't just toss it away. The address of the nearest FDA field office or resident inspection station is in the phone book under U.S. Department of Health, Education, and Welfare; Food and Drug Administration. Or you can write directly to FDA headquarters at 5600 Fishers Lane, Rockville, MD 20852.

## Generic Drugs: How Good Are They?

All drugs, whether they are sold under brand names or their generic names, must meet the same FDA standards for safety, purity, strength, and effectiveness. All drug manufacturers, large and small, are subject to FDA inspection and must follow the FDA's current Good Manufacturing Practice Regulations. That is why the FDA sees no significant difference in quality between brand-name and generic drugs.

The generic name is also called the "official" or "nonproprietary" name. A generic name is assigned to a drug when it appears to be of some use in the curing of disease. Generic names are usually contractions of complex chemical names. The new drug also is given a brand name by its developer or manufacturer. This name is generally short, easy to remember, and often devised to suggest the action of the drug.

It is the brand name that is used to advertise the drug to the medical profession. However, the generic name must also appear in advertising and labeling in letters half as big as those of the brand name. Aspirin is the generic name for the leading OTC painkiller; Bayer and St. Joseph's are brand names for two manufacturers' aspirin. Potassium penicillin, G is a generic name for a kind of penicillin. *Pentids®* is the registered name for the same drug as sold by Squibb Laboratories. The drug with the generic name *reserpine* is used for lowering blood pressure. It is marketed under more than 40 brand names.

It is a popular misconception that brand-name drugs are produced only by large, well-known firms, and generic drugs are made by small, almost unknown companies. This is not a fact. Any drug manufacturer, no matter how small, can put a brand name on its product, and many large manufacturers can and do sell the same product under both a brand name and a generic name.

**Not only must each drug meet FDA requirements, but so must each drug plant — large or small. All drug** manufacturers must register with the FDA; all are subject to periodic inspection; and all must follow FDA Good Manufacturing Practice Regulations that touch on every aspect of making drugs, from plant maintenance to quality control. These regulations apply to all producers and are intended to assure that all drugs meet the same standards of safety, strength, purity, and effectiveness. These requirements were written into the 1962 amendments to the food and drug laws for the very purpose of encouraging physicians to make wider use of generic drugs in order to lower the cost of medical care.

Thus, FDA Commissioner Donald Kennedy could say, "There simply is no evidence to support the notion of serious quality differences between generic and brand-name drugs."

## Drug Development

The development of a new drug is a long and complex process that can begin in many places — a drug manufacturer's laboratory, a chemical company, or a research lab at the National Institutes of Health. The development hopefully will culminate in benefits to all sick persons.

By the time a new medicine becomes available to the

public, it has been thoroughly tested in both animals and humans under carefully controlled conditions, and information has been approved for physicians to help them prescribe the drug correctly.

The Food and Drug Administration is responsible for approving the marketing of all new drugs sold in the United States and for monitoring their use after approval.

The first step in the development of a new drug is research into the chemistry or anatomy of a disease, or the discovery that a chemical has possible use as a drug.

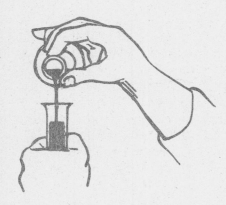

The chemical is subjected to screening tests and to testing in animals. This is done to see whether the drug has the desired effects. If it does, additional testing is done to determine what side effects the drug might have, what dosage amounts are poisonous, what the safe dosage range might be for human beings, and whether there is any reason to test the drug on human beings.

Before the new drug can be used in any way on human beings, it is tested on hundreds or thousands of animals. The FDA does not monitor these tests, but if the animal tests are successful or promising in effectiveness against a disease and the drug seems safe enough to use in human beings, the FDA steps in. The drug is then known as an Investigational New Drug (IND). At this point, the sponsor must submit to the FDA the complete composition of the drug, its source, how it is made, and documented results of the animal tests showing clearly the disease-combating qualities of the drug and proving its safety for testing on human beings.

Human testing is divided into three phases. Phase I is directed at determining the chemical actions of a drug, how it is absorbed into the body, how it should be given (by mouth or injection, for example), and the safe dosage range. These tests usually involve fewer than ten patients. The safety record of such research is excellent. The FDA knows of no volunteer patient who has been permanently harmed as a result of Phase I testing. Some, however, have become ill.

In Phase II testing is done on a limited number of human beings to learn if the drug actually does prevent or cure a specific disease. If Phase II shows that the drug may be useful in treating a disease and long-term animal testing has shown no unwarranted harm, the sponsor is allowed to proceed to Phase III.

In Phase III the drug is tested extensively. Again the effectiveness, desirable dosage, and safety are tested—this time on a large number of patients. In this phase the drug is used as it would be if prescribed by a physician. Several hundred or several thousand patients are involved in these tests. If the sponsor is satisfied that all has gone well up to this point, it applies to the FDA for approval to market the drug. This application, called a New Drug Application (NDA), may run into thousands of pages.

The FDA Bureau of Drugs reviews the NDA. The Bureau has six divisions: cardiopulmonary-renal, neuropharmaco-logical, metabolic-endocrine, anti-infective, oncology-radio-pharmaceutical, and surgical-dental. Each division is composed of physicians, pharmacists, chemists, and other professionals experienced in evaluating new drugs.

The Bureau of Drugs must determine whether the benefits of the drug when used properly outweigh the risks to the patient. If a drug is used to combat a deadly disease such as cancer, it is reasonable to allow it to be more of a risk to the patient than a drug that is an antacid, with no risk tolerated.

The amount of work involved is huge when several experts must read possibly several thousand pages of an NDA in order to make a decision on the safety and effectiveness of a drug. The result has been long delays in approving some drugs. Modern methods, such as computerized searches of literature on drugs, have helped, but the time needed for thorough investigation before approval is still great. This is another aspect of the risk-benefit equation: how short an investigation can be risked in order to obtain the possible benefits of a new drug.

Although the FDA makes every effort to assure the safety of drugs, the present procedure that leaves the testing in the hands of the sponsors has had some tragic results. In 1962 a firm filed a New Drug Application for a so-called anti-cholesterol drug, which was supposed to destroy cholesterol in the blood and thereby end the risk of hardening of the arteries. The manufacturer, in the Phase III testing, dispensed the drug widely. The result was that some of the test subjects suffered permanent loss of hair, cataracts, and total loss of sight. The FDA—by sheerest accident—found that the manufacturer's records had been falsified. This incident illustrates the risk involved in allowing the sponsor of a drug to do the testing. Yet it would be physically impossible for any government agency to take over such testing or even to closely supervise testing by sponsors.

## Mixing Medicines

Although the FDA requires that the manufacturer of a new drug prove its safety and effectiveness, the drug producer is not required by law to carry out tests that involve the use of the new drug along with other drugs. Such testing would be almost impossible, since there is no way of knowing what other medicines a patient might be taking. The only sources of information on drug interaction are the physicians and pharmacists who report harmful interactions to the FDA.

If you are taking one kind of medicine and wish to take an OTC medicine at the same time, read the label or the manufacturer's insert in the package carefully. It may tell you that you should not take the medicine along with certain other drugs. Even better, ask the pharmacist about mixing the drugs; he should be able to tell you whether doing so will be dangerous. If you are taking one or more $R_x$ drugs and want to take an OTC medicine, be sure to consult the physician who prescribed the $R_x$ medicines for you. A mistake in mixing drugs can cause them to become ineffective against the disease for which you are taking them, at best; at worst, it can kill you. The one rule to follow when thinking about mixing medicines is *consult your pharmacist or doctor first*.

## Food and Drug Interactions

If you are taking a drug, the food you eat could make it work faster or slower or even prevent it from working at all. Eating certain foods while taking certain drugs can be dangerous, and some drugs can affect the way your body uses food.

Would it occur to you not to swallow a tetracycline capsule with a glass of milk? Or to avoid aged cheese and Chianti wine if you are taking a certain medicine to combat depression. Or to eat more leafy green vegetables if you are on the Pill? Probably not. Yet the effects foods and drugs have on each other can determine whether medicines do their job and whether your body gets the nutrients it needs.

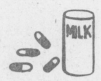

The extent of the interaction between foods and drugs depends on the drug dosage and on the patient's age, size, and medical condition. In general, however, the presence of food in the stomach and intestines can influence a drug's effectiveness by slowing down or speeding up the time it takes the medicine to go through the gastrointestinal tract to the part of the body where it is needed.

Foods contain natural and added chemicals that can react with certain drugs in ways that can make the drugs useless. Some reactions can be dangerous, and some can even cause death.

It is because of these interactions that your doctor tells you to take certain medicines before meals, with meals, or after meals.

There are many ways in which certain medicines can prevent the body from getting full benefit from the foods eaten. Usually the drug interacts with only a single kind of food. Fortunately, most Americans eat a sufficiently well-balanced diet so that a single medicine will not cause malnutrition.

More serious are certain specific reactions. For example, soybeans, rutabagas, brussels sprouts, cabbage, and kale contain substances that inhibit the production of the thyroid hormone, a condition that leads to goiter.

Alcohol does not mix well with a large number of medicines. A good rule of thumb is to avoid alcoholic beverages when taking any kind of OTC or R$_x$ medicine.

What can you do to prevent undesirable food-drug interactions?
• Read the label on an OTC drug to see when it should be taken and if it should not be taken with any particular foods.
• Follow your doctor's orders about when to take a drug and what foods or beverages to avoid while taking it.
• Ask your doctor how the drug he prescribes may interact with your favorite foods, especially if you eat large amounts of them. While taking a prescribed drug, be sure to tell your doctor about any unusual symptoms that follow eating particular foods.
• Eat a nutritionally well-balanced diet, so that any medicine you are taking will not be able to deplete the nutrients or vitamins you need.

## Painkillers: Their Uses and Abuses

Americans swallow 19 billion aspirin tablets a year, making aspirin the most widely used OTC drug. Aspirin and other painkillers, however easy they are to obtain, should not be taken lightly. A panel of experts cautioned against the use of any product containing aspirin by people who have an upset stomach — even if the aspirin is intended to relieve a headache that occurs at the same time as the stomach distress. Aspirin can cause bleeding of the stomach walls. For the same reason — the causing of stomach bleeding — the experts warned against the long-term use of aspirin or aspirin-containing products for the treatment of rheumatism or arthritis, except under the supervision of a doctor.

Although aspirin has the possible side effects noted above, it can be reasonably safe if used properly. Therefore aspirin was approved, along with four other aspirinlike drugs and one other drug, as safe and effective if taken as recommended on the package. The other drugs are calcium carbaspirin, choline salicylate, magnesium salicylate, sodium salicylate, and acetaminophen. Read the labels on these drugs. These analgesics (or painkillers) should be labeled "for temporary relief of occasional minor aches, pains, and headache," and should be used only for these purposes. The word "occasional" is important. If pain persists for more than a day or two, the use of painkillers should be discontinued and a doctor should be consulted.

Aspirin and the other salicylates interfere with blood-clotting and if taken in the last three months of pregnancy can prolong the pregnancy and cause bleeding before and after delivery. Chewable aspirin and aspirin-containing gum should not be taken for seven days after a tonsillectomy or oral surgery. Because aspirin and the other salicylates do cause bleeding of the stomach, they obviously should not be taken to relieve the pain of ulcers. Nor should they be taken by persons who are taking prescription drugs for thinning of the blood, diabetes, gout, or arthritis, except under the supervision of a physician.

Fortunately, salicylates have a built-in warning system. Overdosing causes a ringing in the ears. The panel of experts recommended that labels on these drugs caution consumers to stop taking the drugs if ringing in the ears occurs.

## Sleep Aids

Counting sheep is a time-worn remedy for sleeplessness, but it is not known to be very effective. Nowadays when sleep avoids you, you take a sleep-aid drug, many of which can be bought as OTC drugs.

A panel of experts reviewing sleep aids for the FDA found that some of the ingredients in the drugs do not do the job, some are dangerous, and others are safe but too low in dosage to be effective. The last named are antihistamines. If the sleep aid you have been using has not been working, look at the label to see if it contains antihistamines (such as propanolamine, phenylephrine, or pheniramine). If it does, discard it and ask your doctor for a sleep aid. If you have a sleep problem that lasts for a long time, you should not try to self-prescribe medicine. Rather consider it an illness and see your doctor.

Sleep aids that contain bromides are considered dangerous by the panel of experts. Large doses of bromides are necessary to produce sleep, and such doses can produce harmful concentrations of bromide. Side effects may include rash, dizziness, irritability, and mental disturbances. For a pregnant woman, the side effects include an increased danger that her child will be born mentally retarded or physically handicapped.

Scopolamine, which is found in some sleep aids, was labeled undesirable by the panel, which found that this drug can cause outbursts of uncontrolled behavior.

Three drugs — aspirin, salicylamide, and acetaminophen — that are found in some sleep aids, were said to have no sleep-inducing properties. Nor do passionflower extract and vitamin $B_1$ (thiamine), which are supposed to be good for the "nerves" that are supposed to be the cause of sleeplessness.

The panel on sleep aids also reviewed "wake-up" drugs, which are supposed to increase the mental alertness of persons who are lacking sleep. Only one drug — caffeine — was found to be effective, if taken in doses of 100 to 200 milligrams every three to four hours. A cup of strong tea or coffee has about 100 milligrams of caffeine.

## Laxatives: What Does "Regular" Mean?

Television commercials tell us that for good health and well-being we should all be "regular." We needn't be troubled with "irregularity," after-meal discomfort, biliousness, or headaches if we take the laxative being advertised.

A panel of experts reporting to the FDA said that "irregularity" as a reason for the use of laxatives is misleading because regularity of bowel movement is not essential to health or well-being. Studies show that having as few as three bowel movements a week can be regular and pose no threat to health.

Commercials and ads claim that laxatives made from certain plant products are best because they are "natural." The panel said, "Any statement that suggests a laxative is somehow 'natural' because of its source is misleading." It "implies that the product or ingredient is a 'natural way' to

induce laxation. It is not considered natural to take any laxative."

The panel divided laxatives into four broad categories:
• Bulk-forming laxative: promotes evacuation of the bowel by increasing bulk volume and water content of stools. Ingredients of this type of laxative found safe by the panel are dietary bran, cellulose derivatives, karaya, malt soup extract polycarbophil, and psyllium preparations. (Look at the package to see which ingredients a laxative contains.)
• Stimulant laxative: promotes bowel movement by one or more direct actions on the intestine. Safe ingredients are aloe, bisacodyl, cascara segrada, castor oil, danthron, dehydrocholic acid, phenolphthalein, and senna. Castor oil should be taken infrequently and then only as a one-time single dose.
• Hyperosmotic and saline laxatives: promote bowel movement by attracting water into the stool (hyperosmotic) and increasing the amount of water in the lower intestine (saline). Safe ingredients in hyperosmotic laxatives are glycerine and sorbitol; in saline laxatives, magnesium citrate (citrate of magnesia), magnesium hydroxide (milk of magnesia), magnesium sulfate, and phosphate preparations.
• Lubricant and stool softener laxatives: these lubricate the intestinal tract or penetrate and soften the stool. Safe ingredients are plain mineral oil and emulsified mineral oil (lubricants) and sulfosuccinate preparations (stool softener).

Some laxatives interact with certain medicines. If you are taking some kind of medicine regularly and want to take a laxative, consult your doctor on the effects of the laxative on the medicine.

The whole matter of taking laxatives over any period of time should be taken up with a doctor. First, laxatives can become habit-forming. Second, a doctor may be able to tell you what is the source of the irregularity, or constipation, that causes you to feel the need for continual use of a laxative; then this source may be eliminated.

Widespread use of tranquilizers to relieve tension and stress has led to a growing problem of dependency on legal drugs, especially among women. A person can become "hooked" on legal tranquilizers just as on narcotics. Women are much more likely than men to have tranquilizers prescribed for them, and surveys show that many women fail to recognize the danger in taking tranquilizers regularly.

The tranquilizer most frequently taken is Valium®, which is generally considered to be safe. No deaths have been attributed to Valium alone, but Valium in combination with other drugs — especially alcohol — can be deadly.

Other commonly used tranquilizers include Miltown® or Equanil®, Librium®, Librax®, Serax®, and Verstran®. Doctors write an estimated 90 million prescriptions annually for these and other chemicals that are intended to calm the nerves.

Job pressure has led businessmen to use tranquilizers as a way of helping them cope. Women are thought to feel the need for tranquilizers because of their changing social roles, feelings of worthlessness, boredom that comes from too much leisure, problems of child-rearing, or the "empty nest" syndrome that appears when the children are grown and leave home.

The FDA does not question the safety and effectiveness of most tranquilizers for short-term use. They do relieve minor tension and have medical uses in alcoholism, epilepsy, and severe muscle spasms. However, overuse can lead to dependency on these drugs. When this happens, the tranquilizer abuser is faced with new problems, usually much greater than the ones for which the drug was originally taken. Stopping the use of tranquilizers can result in true withdrawal symptoms similar to those associated with harder drugs such as barbiturates: delirium, trembling, psychoses, and exaggeration of reflexes.

Because use of tranquilizers can be easily abused, the Drug Enforcement Administration has placed a number of these drugs under the Controlled Substances Act. This means that a prescription for Miltown®, Valium®, Librium®, and other tranquilizers can be good for only six months and can be refilled only five times. Unfortunately, persons wanting tranquilizers visit several physicians, thereby obtaining more than one prescription.

If you believe that you have been taking tranquilizers for too long and are hooked on them, tell your doctor or visit

**47**

your local mental health center. There are ways to become "unhooked" that are painless and rewarding.

## Drugs and Pregnancy

Are you pregnant, or do you think you might be? If the answer is yes to either question, you should know that some drugs taken during pregnancy can harm the mother or her baby. We have become so used to "pill popping," taking medicines for every minor ache, pain, and other ailment, that we don't think about the amount of medicine we are taking. Thus, it is common for women to continue to "pop pills" when they become pregnant just as they did before.

A drug taken by an expectant mother enters her bloodstream and in most instances passes through her unborn child. It was formerly believed that the placenta served as a barrier to protect the child from the effects of drugs taken by the mother. It is now known, however, that most drugs pass through the placenta, enter the unborn child, and then pass back into the mother's bloodstream.

Some drugs are harmless to the unborn child, but others are very harmful. One of the most dramatic and tragic examples of the latter was the terrible consequence of taking the sedative thalidomide by pregnant women in the late 1950's and early 1960's. This supposedly safe sedative was sold without prescription in West Germany and England. Women who took thalidomide gave birth to infants with deformed limbs or no limbs at all.

The use of the hormones estrogen and progestin during the first three or four months of pregnancy can increase the risk of birth defects. Because estrogen and progestin are used in oral contraceptives, a woman who becomes pregnant or who thinks she may have become pregnant although taking oral contraceptives should stop using them immediately and consult her physician. Women who discontinue use of the Pill in the hope of becoming pregnant should wait at least three months before attempting to become pregnant, using some other method of contraception during the waiting period. A child conceived immediately after discontinuance of the Pill has a higher than normal risk of birth defects.

Antibiotics of the tetracycline type should be avoided during pregnancy because they have been shown to cause permanent discoloration of the child's teeth.

Minor tranquilizers such as Valium®, Librium®, Miltown®, and others containing meprobamate or benzodiazepine derivatives, when taken by a mother during early pregnancy, may increase the risk that the baby will be born with a cleft lip or palate.

Aspirin and other drugs containing salicylate should not be taken during the last three months of pregnancy except under a doctor's supervision. Salicylates may prolong pregnancy and labor and may cause excessive bleeding before and after delivery.

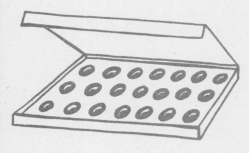

One of the most common causes of damage to the unborn child is the use of alcohol, which is actually a powerful drug. The more a pregnant woman drinks, the greater her risk of giving birth to an abnormal baby. Studies show that alcoholic women give birth to an increased number of premature, mentally retarded, or physically deformed infants; and these women have a higher than normal number of stillbirths.

Tars are not ordinarily considered to be drugs, but they are the sources of many drugs. Tar is ingested during smoking, and women who smoke heavily have an increased chance of having a baby of less than normal birth weight.

A pregnant woman, then, should be very careful of what drugs she takes. The only really safe way of finding out what drugs can and cannot be taken during pregnancy is to tell a doctor about all drugs being taken just before pregnancy and during very early pregnancy.

## Laetrile: The Fatal Cure

Cancer, as almost everyone knows, is an almost incurable disease except in its very early stages. There are drugs that can destroy or greatly slow the growth of cancers. The drug called Laetrile is *not* one of these drugs. This drug, which has recently been much in the news, was first tried several decades ago by a California physician and his son. Laetrile is made from apricot pits, which contain the poison cyanide. According to the makers of Laetrile, the cyanide can poison cancer cells while doing no harm to other cells of the body.

Laetrile has been carefully investigated by government and private laboratories. No proof of the makers' claim has been found. Several persons who have taken Laetrile in large doses have died of cyanide poisoning. Besides being useless as a cancer cure, Laetrile is very expensive. The drug is supposed to be taken every day. A three-dose vial of Laetrile may cost $50 to $100, thereby providng large profits for the sellers of this useless substance.

Far greater than the risk of being poisoned by Laetrile is

the certainty that untreated cancer will eventually kill the person suffering from it. Since Laetrile does nothing to destroy cancer cells, a person taking it is for all practical purposes going untreated. Except for the fact that rarely some cancers disappear (for an unknown reason), untreated cancer results in death. Taking a useless substance such as Laetrile is the same as letting a cancer go untreated; death will almost surely result.

It is understandable that persons who are in the terminal stages of cancer should be willing to try anything claimed to be a cure. Many such persons try Laetrile in a futile attempt to prolong their lives. These people actually lose little, although they gain nothing. The tragedy of Laetrile is that persons who could be cured of cancer in its early stages or who could have their lives prolonged for years by chemotherapy, surgery, or radiation therapy, take Laetrile and face certain death.

A 35-year-old mother of three children was diagnosed to have very early, treatable cancer of the uterus. Her doctor recommended surgery and radiation treatment. Instead, this woman went to Mexico and spent $3,000 on Laetrile treatments. When she realized that the Laetrile was worthless, she returned to her doctor for the treatment he had prescribed. But by that time, the cancer had spread to her pelvis and rectum. A month later she died.

## Drugs and You

Because of the extremely widespread use of drugs in the United States, the chances are that you are now taking one or more drugs, or that you use them occasionally. We hope this book has convinced you that the taking of drugs is a serious matter; that you should get the advice of a doctor before deciding to try to cure an illness by taking OTC drugs; that you should take both OTC and $R_x$ drugs only as recommended on the package or by your doctor; and that when buying drugs, you should consult a pharmacist and shop for the best buys.

Compiled by
DAVID W. DEE

# A Fitness Program for Adults

# Contents

WHAT IS FITNESS? .......................... 53

EXERCISE AND THE HEART ................... 54

EXERCISE AND AGING ...................... 54

EXERCISE AND WEIGHT CONTROL ........... 54

EVEN THE HANDICAPPED SHOULD EXERCISE .. 56

HOW LONG AND HOW OFTEN SHOULD YOU
    EXERCISE ................................. 56

MEDICAL ADVICE .......................... 57

ILLNESS OR INJURIES ...................... 58

WHAT THE EXERCISE PROGRAM CONSISTS OF .. 59
    Warm-Up Exercises ....................... 60
    Conditioning Exercises .................... 62

CIRCULATORY ACTIVITIES .................. 64
    Jogging Guidelines ........................ 64
        How to Jog ............................ 64
        What to Wear .......................... 65
        Where to Jog .......................... 65
        When to Jog ........................... 65

STARTER PROGRAMS ....................... 66

INTERMEDIATE PROGRAM ................... 67

ADVANCED TRAINING ...................... 71

# What Is Fitness?

Fitness means many things to many people. The physician may view fitness as the absence of disease. The body-builder may consider it well-developed muscles, while the young woman may think it's a curvaceous figure. The coach defines fitness as those factors related to success in sports, and the physical educator looks for strength, endurance, flexibility, speed, agility.

In more meaningful personal terms, fitness is a reflection of your ability to work with vigor and pleasure, without undue fatigue, with energy left for enjoying hobbies and recreational activities and for meeting emergencies. It relates to how you look and how you feel — and, because the body is not a compartment separate from the mind, it relates to how you feel mentally as well as physically.

Physical fitness is many-faceted. Basic to it are proper nutrition, adequate rest and relaxation, good health practices, and good medical and dental care.

But these are not enough. An essential element is physical activity — exercise for a body that needs it.

To look your best, to feel your best, and to be able to do your best, you must exercise regularly. That is man's nature, and modern technology can't change it.

When the activity required of you by your job and other duties falls below the level necessary to support good health, you must supplement it with planned activity. Your sense of well-being, your ability to perform and even your survival depend on it.

Regular, vigorous exercise increases muscle strength and endurance. It also improves the functioning of the lungs, heart, and blood vessels; promotes flexibility of the joints; releases mental and physical tensions; and aids in weight control or reduction.

More than half of all lower back pain is due to poor tone and flexibility of the back and abdominal muscles. In many cases, this problem could be prevented or corrected by proper exercise.

In short, exercise can make the difference. The options are mere existence or a full life. The choice is yours.

## Exercise and the Heart

An old-fashioned idea—that exercise may be bad for the heart—has been shown to be without scientific foundation. Not only that—it has been proven that appropriate exercise strengthens the heart.

A noted heart specialist recently commented: "The best insurance against heart disease is exercise—lots of it."

Backing up this conviction is a growing body of evidence. It includes findings of lower cholesterol values in active people, faster clearing of fats from the blood after meals, and sharply reduced heart-attack rates.

Additionally, studies indicate that, when a heart attack does occur, the physically active person is more likely to recover. One possible reason: there is evidence that exercise may promote development of supplementary blood vessels that can take over the burden of nourishing the heart muscle when a coronary artery is blocked in a heart attack.

## Exercise and Aging

There is strong authoritative support for the concept that regular exercise can help prevent degenerative disease and slow down the physical deterioration that accompanies aging.

The evidence is conclusive: people who consistently engage in proper physical activity have better job performance records, fewer degenerative diseases, and probably a longer life expectancy than the population at large. By delaying the aging process, proper exercise also prolongs your active years.

## Exercise and Weight Control

A common misconception is that exercise does not aid in weight control. This is not the case. Fat piles up in most people by only a few calories a day; an excess of only 100 calories a day can produce a 10-pound gain in a year—and the extra calories could be burned up by a 15- to 20-minute daily walk; obese people almost invariably tend to be much less active than those of normal weight; individual weight, moreover, is a factor in energy expenditure. If you are overweight, you burn up more calories in performing exercise than does a person of normal weight.

Weight control is maintained by keeping energy intake (food) and energy output (physical activity) in balance. This is true at all ages for both sexes. When the calories consumed in food equal those used to meet the body's needs, weight will remain about the same. When one eats more than this amount, one will put on fat unless physical activity is increased proportionately.

For years physicians have talked about the varying caloric needs of differing occupations and physical recreations. Yet in their attempts to lose excess fat, weight watchers have often concentrated on counting the calories in their diets and have neglected the role of exercise. For those who are fat, increasing physical activity can be just as important as decreasing food intake.

Weight depends not only on how many calories are taken in during the day, but also on how many are used up in physical activity. The fat person who merely cuts down his intake of food to lose weight will make slow progress, because the number of calories needed to maintain the body is much smaller than most people think.

In fact, lack of exercise has been cited as the most important cause of the "creeping" obesity found in modern mechanized societies. Few occupations now require vigorous physical activity. Although more time is available for recreation, many people fail to fill this gap by choosing leisure time activities that give them exercise. Even among those who do exercise, their activity is often neither vigorous nor sustained.

Recent studies indicate that lack of physical activity is more often the cause of overweight than is overeating. These studies have compared the food intake and activity patterns of obese persons with persons of normal weight. Several age levels — teen-agers, adults, and older persons —have been studied. In each instance, the findings showed that the obese people did not consume any more calories than their normal-weight age mates, but that they were very much less active. The person who has a trim figure and wants to keep it should exercise regularly and eat a balanced, nutritious diet that provides sufficient calories to make up for the energy expended. The thin person who wishes to gain weight should exercise regularly and increase the number of calories consumed until the desired weight is reached. The overweight person should decrease the food intake and step up the amount of physical activity. Since a large proportion of the U.S. population is overweight, the latter group is a matter of concern to those who are interested in the nation's fitness.

If you need to lose weight, do so under the direction of your physician. Don't lose more than two pounds per week without his knowledge and consent. Determine to reduce gradually and consistently. Determine to develop proper eating habits. A change in diet—perhaps a change as slight as taking a little less sugar or none in beverages—may be all that is necessary to bring your weight down and keep it down, especially if coupled with the essential exercise regimen.

## Even the Handicapped Should Exercise

Where there is impairment or illness, any and all exercise should be medically prescribed and regulated.

Today, physicians are using exercise as an aid in combatting many chronic problems, including arthritis, asthma, diabetes, and emphysema. A common type of low back pain has been traced to weakened back muscles, and exercise has been used both to produce relief and to help prevent recurrence.

## How Long and How Often Should You Exercise

The official position of the American Medical Association is that human beings must exercise regularly to become physically fit. Sufficient rest and sleep, an adequate diet, the absence of excesses, and physical activity are essential to maintaining physical capacity. The amount of exercise needed varies from one person to another, but the AMA recommends 30 to 60 minutes daily as a minimum.

No one can achieve satisfactory levels of strength, endurance, and flexibility by working out once a week. More frequent workouts are required to bring about significant changes, and both experience and scientific studies show that daily exercise produces the best results.

The way in which an exercise is done is just as important as how often it is done. For maximum benefit, physical activity must be vigorous enough to give a tonic effect. In other words, the person must work hard enough to breathe heavily and "break a sweat."

People who are unschooled in human physiology or

unfamiliar with the principles of exercise seldom work hard enough or long enough to improve circulatory and respiratory performance or to strengthen muscles. One reason for this is that many of our more popular and enjoyable participatory sports are not taxing enough for fitness purposes. They make a contribution but should be supplemented by an exercise regimen.

Popular games — tennis, handball, racketball, basketball — are fine for *maintaining* fitness. But no serious fitness enthusiast considers them adequate for training. Most tennis or handball players run to get in shape for competition. Games are not a substitute for real fitness activity. They don't allow you to maintain your heart rate in the training zone. They often include brief periods of extreme exertion. You should be fit before you compete in strenuous sports.

Dynamic good health is the objective of a physical fitness program. Performing exercises halfheartedly or working out briefly and sporadically cannot move you significantly closer to that goal. Hard work on a regular, sustained basis is the answer.

The level of fitness you can reach depends on your age, your body's built-in potential, and previous conditioning. It also depends on your state of mind. When you want to do something and believe you can, it is much easier to do than it would be otherwise.

When you begin your personal exercise program, you should not expect dramatic changes overnight. But, gradually over the next weeks and months, you will begin to notice a new spring in your step, a new ease in carrying out ordinary daily activities. You will find yourself with more energy left at the end of the working day and a new zest for recreation in the evening. Quite likely, you will be sleeping more soundly than you have for many years and waking more refreshed in the morning. In short, you will be on your way to a better and more complete life.

## Medical Advice

Before beginning any exercise program, it is advisable to have a medical checkup. If you have not had an examination in the past year, if you are past 30, if you are overweight, or if you have a history of high blood pressure or heart trouble, such an examination may help you to avoid serious consequences.

Chances are your physician will be able to give you an unconditional go-ahead. If not, he may be able to modify the exercises you plan so that they are suited to you.

There are few people who, for medical reasons, should not undertake any exercise program unless and until those reasons have been eliminated.

Only a qualified physician can say for sure if the exercise program outlined in the following pages is advisable for you. Show him this booklet and ask his advice.

## Illness or Injuries

If you develop an illness, ask your physician about the advisability of continuing to jog. Any persistent pain or soreness also should be reported.

**Blisters:** Blisters can be prevented by wearing good, properly fitted shoes. At the first hint of discomfort, cover the area with moleskin or a large bandage. If you do develop a blister, puncture the edge with a sterilized needle to drain the accumulated fluid, treat with an antiseptic, cover with gauze, circle with foam rubber, and go back to work. It's wise to keep the items needed for blister care at hand.

**Muscle soreness:** Soreness, usually due to exercise after long inactivity, may be caused by microscopic tears in the muscle or connective tissue, or to contractions of muscle fibers. It is almost impossible to avoid soreness when you first begin exercising. Minimize it by exercising modestly, at least at first, and by doing mild stretching exercises when soreness does occur. Massage and warmth also seem to minimize the discomfort of soreness.

**Muscle cramps:** Cramps are powerful involuntary muscle contractions. Immediate relief comes when the cramped muscle is stretched and massaged. However, that does not remove the underlying cause of the contraction. Salt and potassium are both involved in the chemistry of contraction and relaxation. Cold muscles seem to cramp more readily. It's always wise to warm up before vigorous effort and to replace salt and potassium lost through sweating in hot weather.

**Knee problems:** A knee injury suffered early in life can affect the ability to exercise. For example, a knee injured playing high school football may lead to signs of arthritis in the late 20's or early 30's. Such degenerative changes often restrict the ability to run, ski, or engage in other vigorous activities. Persons with knee problems should consult a physician for ways to relieve the limitations they impose. Knee problems also can result from improper foot strike, worn shoes, or improper foot support. Repair worn shoes, and if knee problems persist, see a podiatrist.

## What the Exercise Program Consists Of

There are three general categories — warm-up exercises, conditioning exercises, and circulatory activities.

The warm-up exercises stretch and limber the muscles and speed up the action of the heart and lungs, thus preparing the body for greater exertion and reducing the possibility of unnecessary strain.

The conditioning exercises are systematically planned to tone up abdominal, back, leg, arm, and other major muscles.

The circulatory activities produce contractions of large muscle groups for relatively longer periods than the conditioning exercises — to stimulate and strengthen the circulatory and respiratory systems.

Among the circulatory activities, you choose one each workout — alternate running and walking, skipping rope, and running in place. All are effective. You can choose running and walking on a pleasant day and one of the others for use indoors when the weather is bad. You can also switch about the variety.

The routines described in this booklet are equally beneficial for men and women.

Each exercise session should consist of warm-up, conditioning exercises, and circulatory activities.

If during the early stages of the program you become overly stiff or sore, and especially if you experience pain in the feet or knees, reduce or stop the walking-jogging part of the program until pain or soreness disappears.

Do not discontinue the warm-up or the conditioning exercises.

If pain or soreness persists for several weeks, check with your physician.

The following exercises are for both men and women (no matter which sex the illustrations show) and should be considered as a starter program for physical fitness.

### Standing Reach
*Starting position:* Stand erect, feet shoulder-width apart, arms extended over head.
*Action:* Stretch as high as possible, keeping heels on ground. Hold for 15 to 30 counts.

### Flexed-leg Back Stretch
Starting position: Stand erect, feet shoulder-width apart, arms at sides.
*Action:* Bend trunk forward and down, flexing knees. Stretch gently in attempt to touch fingers to toes or floor. Hold for 15 to 30 counts. Return to starting position.
Repeat 2 to 3 times.

### Knee Lift
*Starting position:* Stand erect, feet comfortably apart, arms at sides.
*Action:* Raise left knee as high as possible, grasping leg with hands and pulling knee against body while keeping back straight. Hold for a 5 count. Lower to starting position. Repeat with right knee.
Repeat 5 to 8 times with each leg.

### Double Knee Pull
*Starting position:* Lie on back, feet extended, hands at sides.
*Action:* Pull both legs to chest, lock arms around legs, pull buttocks slightly off ground. Hold for 20 to 40 counts. Return to starting position.
Repeat 7 to 10 times.

### Wing Stretch
*Starting position:* Stand erect, feet comfortably apart, elbows at shoulder height, fists clenched in front of chest.
*Action:* Thrust elbows backward vigorously without arching back. Return to starting position. Repeat 10 to 15 times.

### Quarter Knee Bend
*Starting position:* Stand erect, feet comfortably apart, hands on hips.
*Action:* Bend knees to 45°, keeping heels on floor. Return to starting position.
Repeat 15 to 20 times.

### Horizontal Arm Circles
*Starting position:* Stand erect, feet shoulder-width apart, arms extended sideways at shoulder height, palms up.
*Action:* Describe small circles backward with hands and arms. Reverse, turn palms down, and do small circles forward.
Repeat 12 to 15 times.

### Neck Circles
*Starting position:* Stand erect, feet shoulder-width apart, arms at sides.
*Action:* Gently roll head in full circle, first in one direction, then in the other.
Repeat 3 times in each direction.

### Body Bender
*Starting position:* Stand, feet shoulder-width apart, hands behind neck, fingers interlaced.
*Action:* Bend trunk sideward to left as far as possible, keeping hands behind neck. Return to starting position. Repeat to the right.
Repeat 6 times in each direction.

## CONDITIONING EXERCISES

### Knee Pushup (Beginner)

*Starting position:* Lie on floor, face down, legs together, knees bent with feet raised off floor, hands on floor under shoulders, palms down, fingers pointing forward.

*Action:* Push upper body off floor until arms are fully extended and body is in straight line from head to knees. Return to starting position. Repeat 5 to 10 times.

## PUSHUPS

When doing the following exercises it is important to keep the back straight. Start with the knee pushup and continue for several weeks until your stomach muscles are toned up enough to keep your back straight. Then try the intermediate. After mastering this, go on to the advanced.

### Pushup (Intermediate)

*Starting position:* Lie on floor, face down, legs together, feet on floor, hands on floor under shoulders, palms down, fingers pointing forward.

*Action:* Push body off floor by extending arms so that weight rests on hands and toes, keeping back straight. Lower the body until chest touches floor. Return to starting position. Repeat 10 to 20 times.

## CURLUPS

The following exercises are designed to strengthen the abdominal muscles. Select the one for you.

### Head and Shoulders Curl (Beginner)

*Starting position:* Lie on back, legs straight, hands tucked under small of back, palms down.

*Action:* Tighten abdominal muscles, lift head, and pull shoulders and elbows off floor. Hold this position for 5 counts. Return to starting position. Repeat 10 to 15 times.

### Situp, Arms Crossed (Intermediate)

*Starting position:* Lie on back, arms crossed on chest, hands grasping opposite shoulders, knees bent to right angle, feet flat on floor.

*Action:* Curl up to sitting position. Curl down to starting position. Repeat 10 to 15 times.

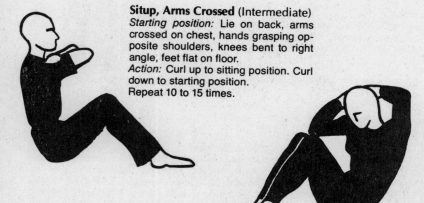

### Situp, Fingers Laced (Advanced)

*Starting position:* Lie on back, fingers laced behind neck, knees bent, feet flat on floor.

*Action:* Curl up, turn trunk to right, touch left elbow to right knee. Return to starting position. Curl up, turn trunk to left, touch right elbow to left knee. Curl down to starting position. Repeat 15 to 25 times.

### Sitting Single Leg Lift

*Starting position:* Sit erect, hands on side of chair seat for balance, legs extended at angle to floor.

*Action:* Raise left leg waist-high. Return to starting position. Repeat with right leg. Repeat 10 to 15 times.

### Back Leg Swing

*Starting position:* Stand erect behind chair, feet together, hands on chair for support.

*Action:* Lift one leg back and up as far as possible. Return to starting position. Repeat with other leg. Repeat 20 times.

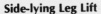

### Heel Raiser

*Starting position:* Stand erect, hands on hips, feet together.

*Action:* Raise body on toes. Return to starting position. Repeat 20 times.

### Side-lying Leg Lift

*Starting position:* Lie on right side, legs extended.

*Action:* Raise left leg as high as possible. Lower to starting position. Repeat on opposite side. Repeat 10 to 15 times.

### Giant Arm Circles

*Starting position:* Stand erect, feet shoulder-width apart, arms at sides.

*Action:* Bring arms upward and sideward, crossing overhead, completing a full arc in front of body. Do equal number in each direction. Repeat 10 times.

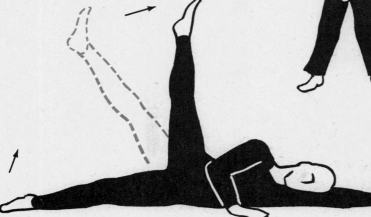

# Circulatory Activities

As we have mentioned, the circulatory activities can consist alternately of rope skipping, running in place, and walking-jogging-running.

**Rope:** Skip or jump rope continuously using any form for 30 seconds and then rest 60 seconds. Repeat 3 times.

**Run in place:** Raise each foot at least 4″ off floor and jog in place. Count 1 each time left foot touches floor. Do this for 1 to 3 minutes.

**Jogging:** As jogging has become increasingly popular, we shall treat it in more detail in the following pages, giving not only the starter program (developed by the President's Council on Physical Fitness and Sports) but also an intermediate jog-run program developed for the Forest Service of the U.S. Department of Agriculture. From the same source we provide some suggestions for advanced training.

## Jogging Guidelines

### HOW TO JOG

Run in an upright position, avoiding the tendency to lean. Keep back as straight as you can and still remain comfortable, and keep head up. Don't look at your feet.

Hold arms slightly away from body, with elbows bent so that forearms are approximately parallel to the ground. Occasionally shaking and relaxing the arms and shoulders will help reduce the tightness that sometimes develops while jogging. Periodically taking several deep breaths and blowing them out completely also will help you to relax.

It is best to land on the heel of the foot and rock forward so that you drive off the ball of the foot for your next step. If this proves difficult, try a more flat-footed style. Jogging only on the balls of the feet, as in sprinting, will produce severe leg soreness.

Keep steps short, letting foot strike the ground beneath the knee instead of reaching to the front. Length of stride should vary with your rate of speed.

Breathe deeply, with mouth open. Do not hold breath.

If for any reason you become unusually tired or uncomfortable, slow down, walk, or stop.

## WHAT TO WEAR

Select loose, comfortable clothes. Dress for warmth in the winter, for coolness in the summer. "Jogging suits" or "warmups" are not necessary, but they are extremely practical and comfortable, and they can help create a feeling of commitment to jogging.

Do not wear rubberized or plastic clothing. Increased sweating will not produce permanent weight loss, and such clothing can cause body temperature to rise to dangerous levels. It interferes with evaporation of sweat, which is the body's chief temperature control mechanism during exercise. If sweat cannot evaporate, heat stroke or heat exhaustion may result.

Properly fitting shoes with firm soles, good arch supports, and pliable tops are essential. Shoes made especially for distance running or walking are recommended. Ripple or crepe soles are excellent for running on hard surfaces. Beginners should avoid inexpensive, thin-soled sneakers. Wear clean, soft, heavy, well-fitting socks. Beginners may want to wear thin socks under the heavier pair.

## WHERE TO JOG

If possible, avoid hard surfaces such as concrete and asphalt for the first few weeks. Running tracks (located at most high schools), grass playing fields, parks, and golf courses are recommended. In inclement weather, jog in church, school, or YMCA gymnasiums; in protected areas around shopping centers; or in your garage or basement. Varying locations and routes will add interest to your program.

## WHEN TO JOG

The time of day is not important, although it is best not to jog during the first hour after eating, or during the middle of a hot, humid day. The important thing is to commit yourself to a regular schedule. Some believe that people who jog early in the morning tend to be more faithful than those who run in the evenings. Persons who jog with family members or friends also tend to adhere to their schedules better. However, companionship — not competition — should be your goal when jogging with someone else.

65

# Starter Programs

Take the *walk test* to determine your exercise level.

**Walk Test.** The object of this test is to determine how many minutes (up to 10) you can walk at a brisk pace, on a level surface, without undue difficulty or discomfort.

If you can't walk for 5 minutes, begin with phase I.

If you can walk more than 5 minutes but less than 10, begin with the third week of phase I.

If you can walk for the full *10 minutes* but are somewhat tired and sore as a result, start with phase II. If you can breeze through the full 10 minutes, you're ready for bigger things. Wait until the next day and take the 10-minute *walk-jog test*.

**Walk-Jog Test.** In this test you alternately walk 50 steps (left foot strikes ground 25 times) and jog 50 steps for a total of 10 minutes. Walk at the rate of 120 steps a minute (left foot strikes the ground at 1-second intervals). Jog at the rate of 144 steps a minute (left foot strikes ground 18 times every 15 seconds.)

If you can't complete the 10-minute test, begin at the third week of phase II. If you can complete the 10-minute test but are tired and winded as a result, start with the last week of phase II before moving to phase III. If you can perform the 10-minute walk-jog test without difficulty, start with phase III.

## Phase 1
### WALKING PROGRAM

| Week | Activity (every other day at first) |
|---|---|
| 1 | Walk at a brisk pace for 5 minutes, or for a shorter time if you become uncomfortably tired. Walk slowly or rest for 3 minutes. Again walk briskly for 5 minutes, or until you become uncomfortably tired. |
| 2 | Same as week 1, but increase pace as soon as you can walk 5 minutes without soreness or fatigue. |
| 3 | Walk at a brisk pace for 8 minutes, or for a shorter time if you become uncomfortably tired. Walk slowly or rest for 3 minutes. Again walk briskly for 8 minutes, or until you become uncomfortably tired. |
| 4 | Same as week 3, but increase pace as soon as you can walk 8 minutes without soreness or fatigue. |

When you've completed week 4 of phase 1, begin at week 1 of phase 2.

## Phase 2
### WALK-JOG PROGRAM

| Week | Activity (four times a week) |
|------|------------------------------|
| 1 | Walk at a brisk pace for 10 minutes, or for a shorter time if you become uncomfortably tired. Walk slowly or rest for 3 minutes. Again, walk briskly for 10 minutes, or until you become uncomfortably tired. |
| 2 | Walk at a brisk pace for 15 minutes, or for a shorter time if you become uncomfortably tired. Walk slowly for 3 minutes. |
| 3 | Jog 10 seconds (25 yards). Walk 1 minute (100 yards). Do 12 times. |
| 4 | Jog 20 seconds (50 yards). Walk 1 minute (100 yards). Do 12 times. |

When you've completed week 4 of phase 2, begin at week 1 of phase 3.

## Phase 3
### JOGGING PROGRAM

| Week | Activity (five times a week) |
|------|------------------------------|
| 1 | Jog 40 seconds (100 yards). Walk 1 minute (100 yards). Do 9 times. |
| 2 | Jog 1 minute (150 yards). Walk 1 minute (100 yards). Do 8 times. |
| 3 | Jog 2 minutes (300 yards). Walk 1 minute (100 yards). Do 6 times. |
| 4 | Jog 4 minutes (600 yards). Walk 1 minute (100 yards). Do 4 times. |
| 5 | Jog 6 minutes (900 yards). Walk 1 minute (100 yards). Do 3 times. |
| 6 | Jog 8 minutes (1,200 yards). Walk 2 minutes (200 yards). Do 2 times. |
| 7 | Jog 10 minutes (1,500 yards). Walk 2 minutes (200 yards). Do 2 times. |
| 8 | Jog 12 minutes (1,760 yards). Walk 2 minutes (200 yards). Do 2 times. |

# Intermediate Program (jog-run)

If you've followed the starter program or are already reasonably active, you're ready for the intermediate program. You're able to jog 1 mile slowly without undue fatigue, rest 2 minutes, and do it again. Your sessions consume about 250 calories.

You're ready to increase both the intensity and the duration of your runs. You'll begin jogging 1 mile in 12 minutes, and when you finish this program you may be able to complete 3 or more miles at a pace approaching 8 minutes a mile. Each week's program includes three phases — the basic workout, longer runs (overdistance), and shorter runs (underdistance). If a week's program seems too easy, move ahead; if it seems too hard, move back a week or two. Remember to make a warm-up and a cool-down part of every exercise session.

**Week 1**

**Basic Workout** (Monday, Thursday)

1 mile in 11 minutes; active recovery (walk). Run twice.

**Underdistance** (Tuesday, Friday)

¼ to ½ mile slowly.

½ mile in 5 minutes 30 seconds. Run twice (recover between repeats).

¼ mile in 2 minutes 45 seconds. Run 4 times (recover between repeats).

Jog ¼ to ½ mile slowly.

**Overdistance** (Wednesday, Saturday or Sunday)

2 miles slowly. (Use the talk test: Jog at a pace that allows you to converse.)

**Week 2**

**Basic Workout** (Monday, Thursday)

1 mile in 10 minutes 30 seconds; active recovery. Run twice.

**Underdistance** (Tuesday, Friday)

¼ to ½ mile slowly.

½ mile in 5 minutes.

¼ mile in 2 minutes 30 seconds. Run 2 times (recover between repeats).

¼ mile in 2 minutes 45 seconds. Run 2 times (recover between repeats).

220 yards in 1 minute 20 seconds. Run 4 times (recover between repeats).

¼ to ½ mile slowly.

**Overdistance** (Wednesday, Saturday or Sunday)

2¼ miles slowly.

**Week 3**

**Basic Workout** (Monday, Thursday)

1 mile in 10 minutes, active recovery. Run twice.

**Underdistance** (Tuesday, Friday)

¼ to ½ mile slowly.

½ mile in 4 minutes 45 seconds.

¼ mile in 2 minutes 30 seconds. Run 4 times (recover between repeats).

220 yards in 1 minute 10 seconds. Run 4 times (recover between repeats).

100 yards in 30 seconds. Run 4 times (recover between repeats).

¼ to ½ mile slowly.

**Overdistance** (Wednesday, Saturday or Sunday)

2½ miles slowly.

**Week 4**

**Basic Workout** (Monday, Thursday)

1 mile in 9 minutes 30 seconds; active recovery. Run twice.

**Underdistance** (Tuesday, Friday)

¼ to ½ mile slowly.

½ mile in 4 minutes 45 seconds. Run twice (recover between repeats).

¼ mile in 2 minutes 20 seconds. Run 4 times (recover between repeats).

220 yards in 1 minute. Run 4 times (recover between repeats).

¼ to ½ mile slowly.

**Overdistance** (Wednesday, Saturday or Sunday)

2¾ miles slowly.

**Week 5**

**Basic Workout** (Monday, Thursday)

1 mile in 9 minutes; active recovery. Run twice.

**Underdistance** (Tuesday, Friday)

¼ to ½ mile slowly.

½ mile in 4 minutes 30 seconds.

¼ mile in 2 minutes 20 seconds. Run 4 times (recover between repeats).

220 yards in 60 seconds. Run 4 times (recover between repeats).

100 yards in 27 seconds. Run 4 times (recover between repeats)

¼ to ½ mile slowly.

**Overdistance** (Wednesday, Saturday or Sunday)

3 miles slowly.

**Week 6**

**Basic Workout** (Monday, Thursday)

1½ miles in 13 minutes 30 seconds; active recovery. Run twice.

**Underdistance** (Tuesday, Friday)

¼ to ½ mile slowly.

½ mile in 4 minutes 30 seconds. Run twice (recover between repeats).

¼ mile in 2 minutes 10 seconds. Run 4 times (recover between repeats).

220 yards in 60 seconds. Run 4 times (recover between repeats).

100 yards in 25 seconds. Run twice (recover between repeats).

¼ to ½ mile slowly.

**Overdistance** (Wednesday, Saturday or Sunday)

3 miles slowly; *increase pace* last ¼ mile.

**Week 7**

**Basic Workout** (Monday, Thursday)

1½ miles in 13 minutes; active recovery. Run twice.

**Underdistance** (Tuesday, Friday)

¼ to ½ mile slowly.

½ mile in 4 minutes 15 seconds. Run twice (recover between repeats).

¼ mile in 2 minutes. Run 4 times (recover between repeats).

220 yards in 55 seconds. Run 4 times (recover between repeats)

¼ to ½ mile slowly.

**Overdistance** (Wednesday, Saturday or Sunday)

3½ miles slowly; always increase pace near finish.

•

## Week 8

**Basic Workout** (Monday, Thursday)

1 mile in 8 minutes; active recovery; run 1 mile in 8 minutes 30 seconds; active recovery; repeat (total of 3 miles).

**Underdistance** (Tuesday, Friday)

¼ to ½ mile slowly.

½ mile in 4 minutes. Run twice (recover between repeats).

¼ mile in 1 minute 50 seconds. Run 4 times (recover between repeats).

220 yards in 55 seconds. Run 4 times (recover between repeats).

100 yards in 23 seconds. Run 4 times (recover between repeats).

¼ to ½ mile slowly.

**Overdistance** (Wednesday, Saturday or Sunday)

3¾ miles slowly.

## Week 9

**Basic Workout** (Monday, Thursday)

1 mile in 8 minutes. Run 3 times (recover between repeats).

**Underdistance** (Tuesday, Friday)

¼ to ½ mile slowly.

½ mile in 3 minutes 30 seconds.

¼ mile in 1 minute 45 seconds. Run 4 times (recover between repeats).

220 yards in 50 seconds. Run 4 times (recover between repeats).

100 yards in 20 seconds. Run 4 times (recover between repeats).

50 yards in 10 seconds. Run 4 times (recover between repeats).

¼ to ½ mile slowly.

**Overdistance** (Wednesday, Saturday or Sunday)

4 miles slowly.

•

## Week 10

**Basic Workout** (Monday, Thursday)

1½ miles in 12 minutes. Run twice (recover between repeats).

**Underdistance** (Tuesday, Friday)

¼ to ½ mile slowly.

½ mile in 3 minutes 45 seconds. Run 3 times (recover between repeats).

¼ mile in 1 minute 50 seconds. Run 6 times (recover between repeats).

220 yards in 45 seconds. Run twice (recover between repeats).

¼ to ½ mile slowly.

**Overdistance** (Wednesday, Saturday or Sunday)

4 miles; increase pace last ½ mile.

●

**Week 11**

**Basic Workout** (Monday, Thursday)

1 mile in 7 minutes 30 seconds. Run 3 times (recover between repeats).

**Underdistance** (Tuesday, Friday)

¼ to ½ mile slowly.

½ mile in 3 minutes 50 seconds. Run 4 times (recover between repeats).

¼ mile in 1 minute 45 seconds. Run 4 times. Recover between repeats.

220 yards in 45 seconds. Run 2 times (recover between repeats).

¼ to ½ mile slowly.

**Overdistance** (Wednesday, Saturday or Sunday)

*Over* 4 miles slowly (more than 400 calories per workout).

●

**Week 12**

**Basic Workout**

1½ miles in 11 minutes 40 seconds.

You have now achieved the fitness standard that allows you to proceed to the advanced training programs.

# Advanced Training

This section is for the well-trained runner. Some suggestions are provided for advanced training, but keep in mind that there is no single way to train. If you enjoy underdistance training, by all means use it. If you find that you prefer overdistance, you'll like the suggestions offered here.

Long, slow distance running seems to be the ideal way to train. It combines the features of overdistance and underdistance with a minimum of discomfort. Simply pick up the pace as you approach the end of a long run, and you'll receive an optimal training stimulus. Moreover, since the speed work is limited to a short span near the end of the run, discomfort is brief.

Consider the following suggestions:

Always warm up before your run.

Use the high fitness heart rate training zone.

Vary the location and distance of the run day by day (long-short; fast-slow; hilly-flat; hard-easy).

Set distance goals:

Phase 1: 20 miles a week

Phase 2: 25 miles a week (ready for 3- to 5-mile road races)

Phase 3: 30 miles a week
Phase 4: 35 miles a week (ready for 5- to 7-mile road
races)
Phase 5: 40 miles a week
Phase 6: 45 miles a week (ready for 7- to 10-mile road
races)
Phase 7: More than 50 miles a week (consider longer
races such as the marathon — 26.2 miles)

Don't be a slave to your goals, and don't increase weekly mileage unless you enjoy it.

Run 6 days a week if you enjoy it; otherwise, try an alternate-day schedule with longer runs.

Try one long run (not over one-third of weekly distance) on Saturday or Sunday.

Try two shorter runs if the long ones seem difficult: 5 + 5 instead of 10.

Keep records if you like — you'll be surprised! Record date, distance, comments. Note resting pulse, body weight. At least annually, check your performance over a measured distance to observe progress (use a local road race or the 1½-mile-run test). Check your fitness score on the step test several times a year.

Don't train with a stopwatch. Wear a wristwatch so you'll know how long you've run.

Increase speed as you approach the finish of a run.

Always cool down after a run.

Compiled by
DAVID W. DEE

# First
# Aid

# Contents

**WHAT IS FIRST AID?** ......................... 75

**THE FIRST AID KIT** ......................... 75

**LIFESAVING MEASURES** ...................... 76
  **Impaired Breathing** ..................... 76
    Artificial Respiration for Adults
    Mouth-to-Mouth (-Nose) Technique ........ 77
    Back Pressure Arm Lift Method ............ 78
    Artificial Respiration for Children and Infants 79
  **Choking** ........................., ............ 79
  **Cardiac Arrest** ........................... 80
  **Severe Bleeding** ......................... 81
  **Internal Bleeding** ....................... 83
  **Shock** ................................... 83

**FIRST AID FOR SPECIFIC INJURIES** ............. 84
  **Burns** ................................... 84
    Heat Burns
      First-degree Burns ..................... 84
      Second-degree Burns ................... 84
      Third-degree Burns .................... 85
    Chemical Burns ...................... 85
  **Frostbite** ............................... 85
  **Fractures** ............................... 86
  **Open Wounds** ........................... 87
  **Eye Injuries** ............................. 89
  **Nosebleed** .............................. 90
  **Poisoning** .............................. 90
    Food Poisoning ...................... 90
    Acid, Alkali, and Petroleum Poisoning ....... 91
    Inhaled Poison ....................... 91
  **Insect Bites** ............................. 91
  **Animal Bites** ............................ 92
  **Snakebite** .............................. 92

**DRESSINGS AND BANDAGES** .................. 93
  **Principles of Bandaging** .................. 94

## What Is First Aid?

First aid is emergency treatment for illness or injury while waiting for medical help. At one time or another almost everyone is called upon to render first aid. Unless he or she has taken a course on the subject, there is usually confusion and doubt as to what should be done.

Statistics show that in most cases it is better for the person untrained in first aid to do too little than too much. This is particularly true in urban and suburban areas where medical help can easily be obtained. If it is not possible to reach a doctor, police or firemen are better equipped to give first aid than are the uninitiated.

It is advisable for at least one member of the family to take a First Aid course, and it is a necessity for each household to have a good emergency medical manual and a first-aid kit. Consult your local Red Cross for First Aid instructions, and ask your physician to advise you which of the many medical manuals to buy.

This booklet is designed to be used *only* as a quick reference during an emergency. Therefore it contains *only* the basic-life support techniques. Always keep in mind that first aid does *not* replace the doctor but merely attempts to keep the victim alive and in the best condition possible until medical aid arrives.

Telephone operators usually know how to obtain help in the quickest way. Dial O and tell the operator that it's an emergency. Be sure the operator has your right address. But to be prepared, one should have a list of emergency telephone numbers handy.

## The First Aid Kit

You can buy a pre-assembled commercial kit, or you can put together your own kit. You should have also one for your car. If you go hiking or camping, special snakebite kits are available. A basic kit should contain:*

First-aid manual • Small box of absorbent cotton • Box of adhesive strip bandages, assorted sizes (such as Band-Aids or Curads) • Rolls of adhesive tape, ½", 1", 2" wide • Rolls of gauze bandage, 1", 2", 3" wide • Box of cotton-tipped swabs

*Not included are boric acid, Mercurochrome, tincture of iodine, or pain or discomfort relievers containing either bromides or phenacetin (available over the counter) because some physicians consider them either useless or toxic or both.

• Large triangular bandages • Small boxes of gauze pads, 3x3-inch, 2x4-inch • Sterile eye pads • Wood arm splint • Sturdy cloth 2″ wide and 20″ long for tourniquet • Wood tongue depressors • Tweezers • Bandage scissors (sharp scissors with rounded ends) • Paper cups • Measuring cup • Measuring spoons • Thermometer • Small bottle of 70% alcohol (to be used as a disinfectant) • Ammonia inhalant (in case of fainting) • Tube of antibiotic ointment • Tube of antibiotic eye ointment • Box of salt tablets (in case of heat exhaustion) • Calamine lotion • Hydrogen peroxide • Petroleum jelly • Oil of cloves (in case of minor toothache) • Safety pins • Sharp needles (must be sterilized before removing splinters).

## Lifesaving Measures

There are four basic life-threatening conditions in which correct and immediate first-aid procedures are in the true sense a question of life and death.

They are: *impaired breathing, heart failure, severe bleeding,* and *shock.* Seconds count in the recognition and correction of these conditions. Emergency treatment should be given in this order, as necessary: 1. Clear the air passage. 2. Restore breathing and heartbeat. 3. Stop bleeding. 4. Administer treatment for shock.

Do not move an injured person until you have a clear idea of the injury and have applied first aid, unless the victim is exposed to further danger at the accident site. If the injury is serious, if it occurred in an area where the victim can remain safely, and if medical aid is readily obtainable, it is sometimes best not even to attempt to move the person, but to employ such emergency care as is possible at the site until more highly qualified emergency personnel arrive.

### Impaired Breathing

*The causes* of impaired breathing could be: (a) suffocation; (b) electrical shock; (c) gas poisoning; (d) drowning; (e) heart failure.

*The symptoms* are easily recognizable: The chest or abdomen does not rise and fall; air cannot be felt exiting from the nose or mouth.

*Actions to take:* If a patient stops breathing you must assist him immediately. The situation will dictate the method to be used. The respiratory failure can be caused by blockage of

Clear the upper airway of the victim.

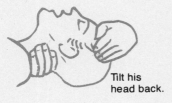
Tilt his head back.

Breathe forcefully into the victim's mouth.

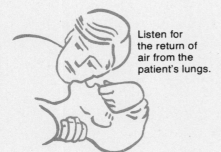
Listen for the return of air from the patient's lungs.

the air passages by foreign matter such as water (drowning), mud, food particles, etc. In an unconscious patient in the supine position (lying on the back), the tongue may drop back and block the throat. The cardiovascular system may fail to circulate red blood cells, which can be caused by heart failure. Regardless of the cause, however, immediate steps must be taken to clear the airway. When the airway is cleared, if spontaneous breathing does not resume, artificial respiration must be applied immediately. There are two methods of artificial respiration; mouth-to-mouth or mouth-to-nose resuscitation and a manual method. The manual method is not recommended except when the rescuer is unable to perform mouth-to-mouth or mouth-to-nose resuscitation; for example, when massive facial injuries absolutely prevent it. In cases of heart failure, mouth-to-mouth resuscitation in combination with cardiac compressions should be administered. However, the cardiac compressions should be executed only by a person with special training in this method.

### ARTIFICIAL RESPIRATION FOR ADULTS
**Mouth-to-Mouth (-Nose) Technique**

1. Place the patient on his back. If it is necessary to roll the victim over, try to roll him over as a single unit, keeping the back and neck straight to avoid aggravation of any spinal injury.
2. Loosen all tight clothing.
3. Clear the upper airway by running your fingers behind his lower teeth and over the back of his tongue. Remove dentures or foreign material.
4. Turn his head face up. Tilt the head back so that the neck is stretched and the chin is up.
5. Adjust the lower jaw so that it juts out. This positioning moves the base of the tongue away from the back of the throat, thus clearing or enlarging the air passage to the lungs.
6. Seal the airway opening (either the nose or the mouth) that is not being used. The seal must be secure to keep air from leaking during inflation. Pinch the nostrils shut with your free fingers (if you use mouth-to-mouth resuscitation) or seal the mouth by placing two fingers lengthwise over the patient's lips (if you use mouth-to-nose resuscitation).
7. Take a deep breath. Open your mouth wide and make an airtight seal around the patient's mouth or nose by placing

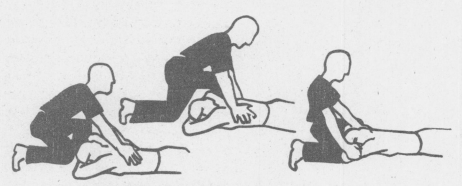

Kneel at the victim's head, place your hands on the victim's back (left).
Rock forward until your arms are vertical (center).
Rock back grasping the victim's elbows (right).

your mouth over his mouth or nose. Breathe into the victim's mouth or nose until his chest rises.

8. Breathe into the patient a total of four times as quickly as possible. If you feel or hear no air exchange, retilt his head and try again. If you still feel no air exchange, again sweep the mouth of foreign objects and breathe again into the victim. If you still have no air exchange, turn the victim on his side and slap him on the back between the shoulder blades. This should free anything blocking the throat. Again sweep his mouth to remove foreign matter. (If none of the above steps clear the air passage, repeat the blows to the back and retilt the head.)

9. Repeat breathing. Remove mouth each time to allow air to escape. If the exhalation is noisy, elevate his jaw further.

10. This procedure should be repeated twelve times per minute. Use deep breaths. As the victim begins to breathe, maintain head tilt.

### Back Pressure Arm Lift Method

If it is impossible because of severe facial injuries to administer mouth-to-mouth or mouth-to-nose resuscitation try the following:

1. Place the victim face down, after first having cleared his mouth. Bend his elbows and place his hands one upon the other at eye level under his head. Turn the victim's head to one side, making sure the chin juts out.

2. Kneel at the victim's head. Place your hand on his back so that palms lie just below an imaginary line between his armpits.

3. Rock forward until your arms are vertical and the weight of your body exerts steady pressure on your hands.
4. Rock back, grasping victim's elbows, and draw victim's arms up toward you until you feel resistance at the shoulders.
5. Lower victim's arms to the ground.

Repeat about twelve times per minute (every 5 seconds). Keep checking to see if the mouth is clear, the airway is open, and the heart is beating. *Note:* In both methods of artificial respiration, continue your efforts until the victim breathes normally or a doctor pronounces him dead, or a more qualified person takes charge, or you are physically unable to continue. If the patient must be moved, continue artificial ventilation.

### ARTIFICIAL RESPIRATION FOR CHILDREN AND INFANTS
The method is similar with slight modifications.
1. Clear mouth with finger.
2. Place child on his back.
3. Lift jaw so it juts out as with adults.
4. Place your mouth over both mouth and nose of the child to make an airtight seal.
5. Gently blow puffs of air, about twenty per minute.

Otherwise the procedure is the same with one exception: instead of the slaps between the shoulder blades to remove foreign matter, hold the infant by the ankles upside down and give several sharp pats between the shoulder blades to free the air passage.

How to help
a choking victim.

## Choking

*The cause:* In most cases food particles or bones caught in the windpipe instead of going into the esophagus.
*The symptoms:* The victim gasps for breath or has violent fits of coughing, quickly turns pale then blue, and cannot talk.
*Actions to take:* If the victim is still able to cough, don't interfere. It is quite possible that he will cough up the foreign object. If any of the other symptoms occur, open the victim's mouth and grasp the foreign object with your index and middle finger, trying to remove it.

If you can't reach the obstruction with your fingers, use the following method:
1. Stand behind the choking victim, with your arms around

him, thumb side of your fist against his stomach, just above the navel and below the ribcage.

2. Grasp your fist with your other hand and make four quick upward thrusts. This will force air out of the lungs and may expel the obstruction. Repeat this procedure if necessary.

### Cardiac Arrest

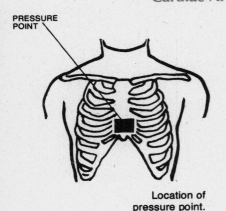

PRESSURE POINT

Location of pressure point.

Apply cardiac compression only if you are trained in CPR.

*The causes:* Insufficient oxygen supply to the heart or the brain, blockage of blood vessels of the heart, heart disease, embolism (foreign particles in the bloodstream), or overdose of certain drugs. Respiratory arrest is the most common cause of cardiac arrest. The heart stops within minutes after breathing ceases.

*The symptoms:* No breathing, no pulse, unconsciousness, dilated pupils of the eyes, limp body, and flaccid skin.

*Actions to take:*

1. Roll the victim on his back.
2. Loosen all tight clothing.
3. Check the airway and remove any obstruction.
4. Hyperextend the neck and lift the lower jaw for mouth-to-mouth artificial respiration.
5. Give the patient five quick puffs of air by mouth-to-mouth.
*6. Place the heel of your hand on the lower half of the breastbone and press down until the breastbone is depressed about 2 inches. Repeat the compression about 15 times, about once per second. (To determine the pressure point for cardiac compressions, locate the bony tip of the breastbone with your ring finger and place two fingers just above that point.)
7. Return to mouth-to-mouth artificial respiration and give the victim two respirations.
8. Repeat this 15–2 cycle until help arrives or the patient is pronounced dead.
9. If help is available, one person should give the cardiac compressions and the other should give mouth-to-mouth artificial respiration. The ratio with two operators should be five compressions to one artificial respiration. The compressions should not be interrupted, even for

---

*Cardiac compressions should be attempted only if the first aider is well trained in cardiopulmonary resuscitation (CPR).

respirations. When respiration is being applied, the compressions must be stopped only momentarily.

10. The cardiac compressions should equal about 60 per minute, the respirations about 12 per minute.

### Severe Bleeding

Acute hemorrhage is a rapid loss of blood from the blood vessels. In the event of an acute severe hemorrhage (loss of at least 2 pints of blood) an emergency is present. If the bleeding is not stopped, the patient will die.

1. Arterial bleeding

*The symptoms:* Spurting blood, bright red in color.

The blood leaves the heart through the arteries under pressure. If an artery is opened, blood will spurt out forcefully. With each beat of the heart there will be a corresponding spurt of blood. The larger the artery, the more rapid the blood loss.

2. Venous bleeding

*The symptoms:* Continuous flow of blood, dark red in color.

Blood flowing through the veins is under less pressure than in the arteries. However, a break in a vein will allow blood to flow out of it. The rate of blood loss depends upon the size of the opened vein.

3. Capillary bleeding

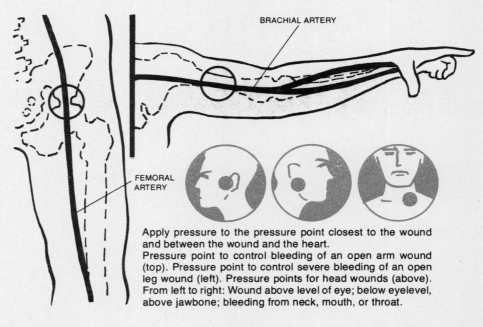

Apply pressure to the pressure point closest to the wound and between the wound and the heart.
Pressure point to control bleeding of an open arm wound (top). Pressure point to control severe bleeding of an open leg wound (left). Pressure points for head wounds (above). From left to right: Wound above level of eye; below eyelevel, above jawbone; bleeding from neck, mouth, or throat.

*The symptoms:* Blood oozing from a wound.

The blood loss is usually not serious, as the bleeding is limited.

*Actions to take:* Control of hemorrhage is primarily mechanical and consists of closing off the opened blood vessel.

1. Direct pressure: Cover the wound with the cleanest cloth immediately available or with your bare hand, and apply direct pressure on the wound. Most bleeding can be stopped this way.

2. Digital pressure (in case of arterial bleeding and if direct pressure does not do the trick). Apply your fingers to the appropriate pressure point — a point where the main artery supplying blood to the wound is located (see diagram). The three pressure points in the head and neck should be used only as a last resort if there is a skull fracture and direct pressure cannot be used. If direct pressure can be used, it will stop bleeding on the head in about 95 percent of injuries.

The pressure-point method is not recommended if pressure must be maintained for a long period of time, but it may be useful temporarily until a pressure dressing can be applied.

Use a tourniquet only as a last resort.

3. Elevation: If bleeding from a wound is only venous or capillary, elevation of the wound above the heart may slow the flow of blood. However, elevation is of no value in control of arterial bleeding, and it may aggravate fractures.

4. Tourniquet: Applying a tourniquet to an arm or a leg should be done only as a last resort when all other methods fail. A tourniquet is applied between the wound and the point at which the limb is attached to the body, as close to the wound as possible but never over a wound or fracture. Make sure it is applied tightly enough to stop bleeding completely.

Although the tourniquet will stop the bleeding by compressing all the vessels, it is potentially dangerous, because it deprives the uninjured tissues of blood.

Patients who have tourniquets applied should be clearly identified with a "T" on the forehead. Once applied, a tourniquet should never be loosened or removed except under the supervision of a doctor.

In the case of an improvised tourniquet, the material should be wrapped twice around the extremity and half-knotted. Place a stick or something similar on the half-knot and tie a full knot. Twist the stick to tighten the tourniquet only until the bleeding stops — no more. Secure the stick or level in place with the loose ends of the tourniquet, another strip of cloth, or other improvised material.

*Note:* A tourniquet can be improvised from a strap, belt, handkerchiefs, necktie, cravat bandage, etc. Never use wire, cord, or anything that will cut into the flesh.

### INTERNAL BLEEDING
*The symptoms:* Cold and clammy skin, weak and rapid pulse, eyes dull and pupils enlarged, nausea and vomiting, pain in the affected area, especially the abdomen and chest.
*Actions to be taken:*
1. Treat victim for shock (see below).
2. Anticipate that victim may vomit; therefore give nothing by mouth.
3. Keep the patient still to allow maximum flow of blood to vital organs and prevent further internal damage.
4. Get the patient to professional medical help as quickly and safely as possible.

## Shock

*The causes:* Shock is a complex subject, but basically the causes may be: Loss of blood, breathing impairment, heart failure, or burns. The most common cause is hemorrhage, when blood escapes from the vascular system and consequently does not reach the tissues.

Shock can kill; treat as soon as possible, and continue until medical aid is available.
*The symptoms:* Shallow breathing, rapid and weak pulse,

nausea, collapse, vomiting, shivering, pale and moist skin, mental confusion, drooping eyelids.

*Actions to take:*

1. Establish and maintain an open airway.
2. Stop the bleeding and insure that the patient is breathing adequately.
3. Place the patient on his back with his head down (by elevating the feet with a pillow or blankets) to improve the flow of blood to the brain. Exceptions: head and chest injuries, heart attack, stroke, sunstroke. If there is no spine injury, the victim may be more comfortable and breathe better in a semireclining position. If in doubt, keep the victim flat.
4. Make sure the patient is comfortable and reassure him. This can help to prevent worsening of the shock.
5. Maintain normal body temperature. Place blankets under and over the victim.
6. Give nothing by mouth, especially stimulants or alcoholic beverages.
7. Always treat for shock in cases of serious injuries, and watch for it in minor ones.

# First Aid for Specific Injuries

## Burns

Burns are damage to tissue caused by exposure to excessive heat, strong chemicals, or electricity. They are classified by cause, degree, and extent. All classifications should be considered in the treatment and disposition of a burn patient.

### HEAT BURNS

#### First-degree Burns

*The symptoms:* Reddened skin.

*Actions to take:*

1. Immerse quickly in cold water or apply ice until pain stops.
2. Apply a dry dressing if necessary.

#### *Second-degree Burns

*The symptoms:* Reddened skin, blisters.

*Actions to take:*

1. Cut away loose clothing.

2. Apply freshly laundered cloth that has been wrung out in ice water.

3. If limb is involved, immerse in cold water (not ice water) for relief of pain.

4. Apply dry, sterile gauze or clean cloth as protective bandage.

5. Do *not* break blisters or remove tissue; do *not* apply ointment, commercial preparations, grease, or other home remedies.

**\*Third-degree Burns**

*The symptoms:* Skin destroyed, tissues damaged, charring.

*Actions to take:*

1. Cut away loose clothing (do *not* remove clothing adhering to skin).

2. Cover burns with thick sterile dressing or fresh household linen.

3. If hands are involved keep them above the level of the victim's heart. Keep burned feet or legs elevated.

4. Treat for shock.

5. Arrange transportation to the hospital as quickly as possible.

**\*CHEMICAL BURNS**

*The causes:* Harsh chemicals or corrosive poisons spilled on the skin.

*Actions to take:*

1. Remove victim's clothing, because chemical may be retained by it.

2. Remove all chemicals by flooding the affected area with water for at least 20 minutes.

3. Apply a dressing and get medical aid.

## Frostbite

*The cause:* Constriction of vessels by extreme cold prevents circulation of blood in the involved area and the tissue freezes.

*The symptoms:* The skin at first is red, then pale or waxy white. The injured part has no feeling while it is frozen.

---

\*If medical help is not available within an hour and the victim is conscious and not vomiting, give him a weak solution of salt and soda: 1 level teaspoon of salt and ½ level teaspoon of baking soda to 1 quart of water. The water should be lukewarm. Allow the victim to sip a half glass slowly over a period of 15 minutes.

*Actions to take:*
1. Remove all wet or tight clothing from the frostbitten area.
2. Warm the area. The best method of warming is to place the area in a warm-water bath (102°–105°F) and make sure the water remains warm. Never thaw the area if the victim has to go back out into the cold, which may cause the affected area to be refrozen.
3. Cover the frostbitten area with a loose, dry dressing.
4. Once the area is thawed, have the victim gently exercise it.

*Do not* rub, chafe, or manipulate frostbitten parts. *Do not* use hot water bottles or a heat lamp. *Do not* place the victim near a hot stove. *Do not* allow the victim to walk if the feet are affected. *Do not* allow the victim to smoke, because the nicotine in tobacco may further constrict the blood vessels.

## Fractures

Fractures, or broken bones, are the result of a strong blow or stress against the body causing one or more bones to crack or break completely. Fractures are either closed (no break in the skin) or open (skin broken). Open fractures are generally more serious, because of the danger of infection.
*The symptoms:* Pain at the fracture site, great difficulty in moving the part of the body beyond the fracture, swelling and tenderness of the fracture, possible deformity of the limb, discoloration of the skin, exposed bone and bleeding (in case of broken fracture). Ultimately, X rays will be needed to establish the diagnosis and extent of the fracture.
*Actions to take:*
1. Stop external bleeding.
2. Treat for shock, as almost every fracture is accompanied by significant internal bleeding with the danger of developing hemorrhagic shock.
3. Administer analgesic against pain.
4. Splint the broken part.
*Splinting:*
A. Splints should be long enough to support joints above and below the fracture.
B. Splints should be rigid enough to support the fracture.
C. Improvised splints should be well enough padded to insure even contact and pressure between the limb and the splint and to protect all bony prominences. (An improvised splint may be made of any rigid material that is readily

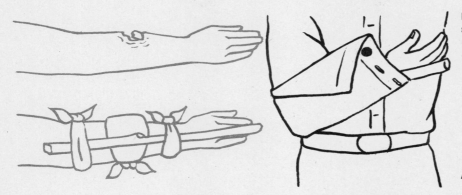

Dressing and using an improvised splint for an open fracture (left top and bottom). If available, a more rigid material for the splint and more ties are preferable.

A jacket is used as improvised sling.

available, as a padded board, a rolled blanket, tools, newspapers, or magazines.)

When you apply a splint, handle the patient as gently as possible. This work should be done in pairs, one person to immobilize the limb and one to apply the splint:

1. Apply slight traction to the affected limb.

2. A second person (if available) should place the padded splint under, above, or beside the limb.

3. Tie the limb and the splint together with bandaging material so the two are held firmly together. Leave fingers or toes exposed, if they are not involved, so that the circulation can be checked constantly.

*Note:* Do *not* attempt to reduce or set the broken bone. In general, splint the fractured limb as you find it, checking the pulse beyond the fracture before and after splinting. If the pulse disappears after the splint is applied, it is too tight and must be loosened.

## Open Wounds

There are five types of wounds.

• 1. Abrasions: The outer layers of the protective skin are damaged, as when the skin is scraped against a hard surface. Limited bleeding.

If there is nothing available to splint a broken leg, tie the injured leg to the uninjured one with padding between the legs.

Cover the wound with the cleanest cloth available and apply direct pressure.

• 2. Incisions: Tissue is cut by a knife or other sharp object. Bleeding may be heavy.

• 3. Lacerations: Tissue is cut, and the wound displays a jagged, irregular, or blunt tearing. Heavy bleeding is possible, and chance of later infection is present.

• 4. Punctures: Skin layers and tissue are pierced by pointed objects such as nails, pins, splinters, glass fragments. Little bleeding.

• 5. Avulsions: These wounds occur when tissue is forcibly separated or torn from a victim's body; for instance, a torn ear. Heavy rapid bleeding is usually observed.

*Actions to take:*

1. Stop the bleeding (as previously described).

2. Cover with the cleanest cloth available, preferably a sterile dressing.

3. Provide shock care when wound is bleeding severely.

4. Obtain medical attention.

5. Wash with soap and water wounds that involve surface area with little bleeding.

6. If a puncture wound is caused by wood splinters or glass fragments, they often remain in the skin tissue or tissues just beneath the surface. Such objects usually only irritate the victim, but if they are not removed, they can cause infection. Therefore, sterilize tweezers over a flame or in boiling water, and pull out the foreign matter.

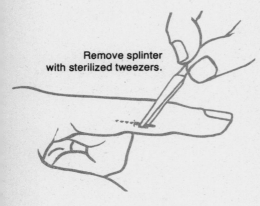

Remove splinter with sterilized tweezers.

If the objects are imbedded just beneath the skin, sterilize the tip of a needle in a flame or in rubbing alcohol, scratch the top layer of the skin, and lift the object out with the top of the needle. If the object is more deeply imbedded, it should be removed by a physician.

*Note:* If a wound is caused by being impaled by an object, do *not* remove the imbedded object. Cut clothing away from injury site. Stabilize the object with a bulky dressing. If available, put a paper cup over the imbedded object to prevent movement, and apply a bandage. If a large object is imbedded, cut off only enough to permit transportation of victim.

## Eye Injuries

*The cause:* Foreign object blown or rubbed into the eye.
*The symptoms:* Redness of eye, burning sensation, pain, headache, tearing.
*Actions to take:*
1. Try to flush out the foreign object with clean water (if available, use an eye cup).
2. If you don't succeed, pull down the lower lid to determine whether or not the object lies on the inner surface of the lid.
3. If so, lift it gently with the corner of a clean handkerchief, a paper tissue, or sterile gauze.
4. If the object is not on the lower lid, check whether it is lodged beneath the upper lid. While the victim looks down, gently grasp the lashes of the upper lid. Pull the upper lid forward and down over the lower lid. The object may be dislodged by the tears.

Roll up upper eyelid over matchstick (left) and remove foreign object with corner of clean handkerchief (right).

5. If this does not help, depress the victim's upper lid with a matchstick placed horizontally on the cartilage and roll the lid by pulling upward on the lashes against the matchstick. If you see the foreign object, remove it with a clean handkerchief or sterile gauze.
6. Flush the eye again with clean water.
7. If the object is still there, you have to suspect that it is imbedded in the eyeball. Cover the eye with a dry protective dressing and consult a doctor.
*Note:* In all phases, prevent the victim from rubbing the eye.

## Nosebleed

*The cause:* Injury of the nose, including fracture, or disease such as high blood pressure. Very often nosebleeds occur after a cold, exposure to high altitudes, or strenuous activity.

Disregarding fracture and disease as causes, nosebleeds are generally more annoying than dangerous, and they usually stop spontaneously. If, however, nosebleeds occur often within a short period, see a doctor.

*Actions to take:*

1. Keep the victim quiet.
2. Place him with head bent slightly forward in a sitting position.
3. Apply pressure with your thumb and index finger directly at the site of the bleeding if bleeding occurs from both nostrils, or press the bleeding nostril with your index finger toward the middle.
4. Apply cold compresses to victim's nose and face.
5. If bleeding is not stopped by the preceding measures, insert a small, clean pad of gauze into one or both nostrils. Part of the gauze should extend outside the nostril, so that the pad can be removed later without blowing the nose and reinjuring it. Do not use cotton instead of gauze. If bleeding cannot be stopped, call a physician.

## Poisoning

*Note:* It is important in all cases of poisoning, which might have many more causes than we mention, that you call a physician immediately. If you suspect that drugs are the cause, call your poison center to find out the antidote for the poison. Get the patient to a hospital at once, and take with you the bottle that may have contained the poisonous drug. Only if you cannot get the patient to a hospital or a doctor immediately should you start first aid.

### FOOD POISONING

When a person complains of stomach pain, nausea, vomiting, or diarrhea after eating or drinking some questionable substance, you should suspect poisoning. Do not wait for more symptoms to develop. Additional symptoms may include dizziness, drowsiness, slurred speech, lack of coordination, cold clammy skin, thirst, convulsions.

*Actions to take:*

1. Encourage the patient to drink plenty of water. Filling the stomach with water dilutes the poison.
2. Instruct the patient to stick his finger behind his tongue to trigger the gag reflex. If he is unable to do this, you can do it for him to induce vomiting.
3. When he starts to vomit, make sure his head is between his legs.
4. This process may be repeated once or twice, depending on how much foreign material is flushed out of the stomach. If the contents of the stomach comes out as a clear liquid it is proof that it is free of foreign material.
5. Treat for shock.

*Note:* This treatment is a first-aid measure if you don't know exactly what poisonous substance the patient has swallowed, and if it was not acid, alkali, or petroleum poisoning.

### ACID, ALKALI, AND PETROLEUM POISONING

*The symptoms of acid and alkali poisoning:* Burns around the mouth, lips, and tongue; burning sensation in the mouth, throat, and stomach; bloody diarrhea.

*The symptoms of petroleum poisoning:* Burning irritation; coughing; coma.

*Actions to take:*

1. If the patient is conscious, make him drink as much milk as he can tolerate.
2. Loosen tight clothing.
3. Treat for shock.

*Note:* Do not induce vomiting.

### INHALED POISON

*The cause:* Auto exhaust, chemical fumes, industrial gases.

*The symptoms:* Irritated nose, throat, eyes; coughing; shortness of breath, dizziness, unconsciousness.

*Actions to take:*

1. Remove person from the source of the poison.
2. Loosen tight clothing.
3. Treat for shock.

## Insect Bites

*The symptoms:* Local irritation and pain, moderate swelling and redness, itching and/or burning.

*Actions to take:*

1. If stinger is left in the wound, withdraw it with tweezers.
2. Apply paste of baking soda and water.
3. Immediate application of ice or ice water to the bite or sting relieves pain.
4. Insect bites may be merely a nuisance, but they may be serious for persons who are allergic to them. Severe reaction may follow. Use a constricting bandage (if the sting is on an extremity) and ice. Get medical help immediately.

## Animal Bites

*Actions to take:*

1. Wash animal bites with soap and water. If possible, use running water.
2. Cover with a sterile gauze pad.
3. If the bite goes through the skin, see a doctor, as a tetanus shot might be necessary.

*Note:* Try to find out what animal made the wound. Bites by dogs, skunks, cats, bats, and other animals can cause rabies. If the animal is not found and examined for rabies, the patient must undergo rabies treatment, as rabies is a killer. Even bites from healthy animals can cause serious infections. That is why a doctor should be consulted if a bite is bleeding.

## Snakebite

Snakebite is unusual, even in snake-infested areas. Generally, a snake will avoid a human unless it is forced to defend itself. If you encounter a snake at close range, do not make any sudden moves. Back away slowly. A snake can strike accurately for a distance equal to about one-half of its length. Both poisonous and nonpoisonous snakes will bite if provoked.

*The symptoms of poisonous snakebites:* Puncture marks, severe burning, pain and spreading swelling, discoloration, early signs and symptoms of shock, headache, dizziness, blurred vision, respiratory distress.

*Actions to take:*

1. Immobilize the victim immediately, with the injured part lower than the rest of the body. Any activity will stimulate the spread of the poison.
2. Remove rings, watches, and bracelets.

3. Apply a constricting band above the swelling caused by the bite. It should be tight, but not tight enough to stop arterial circulation.

4. If medical help is more than one-half hour away, make an incision, no more than ⅛ inch deep nor more than ½ inch long, lengthwise through fang marks. Press around cut to make it bleed.

5. Apply suction to the wound with the device found in a snakebite kit. If no kit is available, use your mouth (if you have no open sores in your mouth or on your lips) and spit out the blood. Cutting and suction are of no value unless done immediately. Do not cut if bite is near a major blood vessel.

6. If there are no serious signs or symptoms, treat the symptoms that are present but still call for medical help.

## Dressings and Bandages

A *dressing* is a pad that is applied directly over a wound. A prepared dressing is usually made of gauze, but it can be made of any absorbent material. The main purpose of a dressing is to control hemorrhage and protect the wound against further contamination. Almost all external bleeding can be controlled with a correctly applied dressing.

A *bandage* is a piece of material used to cover a dressing, apply additional pressure, or immobilize a part of the body. Bandages may be made of gauze, muslin, or elastic cotton.

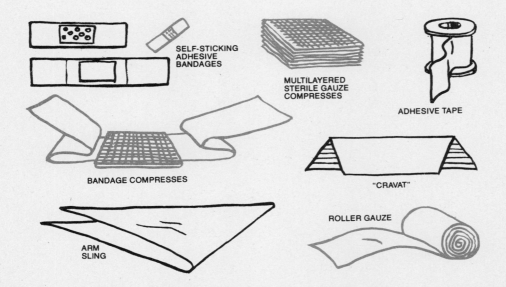

SELF-STICKING ADHESIVE BANDAGES

MULTILAYERED STERILE GAUZE COMPRESSES

ADHESIVE TAPE

BANDAGE COMPRESSES

"CRAVAT"

ARM SLING

ROLLER GAUZE

They may be rolled or folded. Elastic bandages are used to reinforce dressings in the control of hemorrhage and to support ankles, knees, wrists, and elbows in case of strain or sprain. Triangular muslin bandages are sometimes used for support but are used mostly as tourniquets. Folded triangular bandages (cravats) are useful in applying improvised splints.

## Principles of Bandaging

1. Never tie a tight bandage around the neck; it may cause strangulation.
2. A bandage should be tight enough to prevent slipping, but not so tight as to cut off circulation.
3. Loosen bandages immediately if victim complains of numbness or a tingling sensation.
4. Leave fingers and toes exposed, if not injured, to watch for swelling or changes of color and feel for coldness, which signal interference with circulation.
5. Once a dressing is in place do not remove it. If blood saturates the dressing, put another on top of it.

Written by
MARTIN SHARP

# The
# Food
# You Eat

# Contents

"TELL ME WHAT YOU EAT, AND I WILL TELL YOU WHAT YOU ARE" .................................... 97

NUTRIENTS– WHAT THEY DO AND WHERE THEY ARE FOUND ................................ 98
  Carbohydrates ........................... 98
  Fats ..................................... 99
  Proteins ................................. 100
  Vitamins ................................. 101
    Vitamin A ............................ 102
    Vitamin D ............................ 102
    Vitamin C, or Ascorbic Acid ........... 102
    The B Vitamins ...................... 103
    Vitamin K ............................ 103
    Vitamin E ............................ 104
  The RDA ................................. 104
  Cholesterol .............................. 104
  Minerals ................................. 104
  Water ................................... 106

A HEALTHFUL DIET ........................... 106
  A Guide to Good Eating .................. 106

A DAILY FOOD GUIDE ........................ 107

HOW TO USE THE DAILY FOOD GUIDE ....... 109

TIPS ON MEAL PLANNING .................... 110

THE BONUS OF BREAKFAST .................. 110

BUYING FOOD ............................... 111

FOOD LABELS ............................... 112
  Nutritional Information .................. 113
  What "Imitation" Means ................. 113
  Common or Usual Name ................. 113
  Grades .................................. 114
  Food Fads ............................... 114
  Food Additives .......................... 114

FOOD SAFETY ............................... 115
  Fruits and Vegetables ................... 115
  Meat, Poultry, Fish ..................... 116
  Cured and Smoked Meats, Dried Foods ....... 116

SPOILAGE ................................... 116

## "Tell Me What You Eat, and I Will Tell You What You Are"

Nutrition is one of the most important factors in the achievement of good health. Good health does not only mean being free of disease; it also means having a sense of vitality and well-being. Nutrition is important for your physical fitness and your mental alertness. Eating the proper foods will help you to feel better, think better, work better.

"Tell me what you eat, and I will tell you what you are." This is a quotation from Anthelme Brillat-Savarin, a Frenchman known for his witty sayings on the art of dining. His aphorism is true in more ways than one, because one of the main jobs of food is to supply enough energy to support the many functions of the body. Food energy is measured in calories.

Your body is continually replacing many of its parts. The outer layer of the skin is shed and renewed; your nails grow during your entire life; hairs grow, fall out, and new ones grow; all the red blood cells are replaced within weeks, and so is the entire lining of the digestive tract. The food you eat is responsible for your growth from infancy to adulthood and the constant renewal of your body.

If you eat the right foods or **nutrients** in the proper quantities, you will have a very good chance of fighting off diseases and staying healthy.

# Nutrients— What They Do and Where They Are Found

Nutrients are divided by food scientists into six classes: carbohydrates, fats, proteins, vitamins, minerals, and water.

It is interesting to know that, if a complete chemical analysis were made of a person whose proper weight, for example, was 150 pounds, 90 pounds would be water; 30 pounds, fat; almost 30 pounds protein, carbohydrate, and the major minerals of the bones (calcium and phosphorus); and a fraction of a pound vitamins and other minerals.

Most foods contain not only the nutrients mentioned, but also materials that cannot be broken down by the body but are needed for bulk, and some minerals that are of no nutritional value. Let's examine the various nutrients:

## Carbohydrates

The necessity for carbohydrates in the diet is often under-estimated by people who are weight-conscious in the belief that they are too fattening. This, however, is only partially true. The main job of carbohydrates in the diet is to provide energy for the work of the body. They also aid in the manufacture of some of the B vitamins, and they form parts of many compounds in the body.

Carbohydrate is the name of a group of organic substances that are made up of carbon, hydrogen, and oxygen. The name itself indicates the combination: Carbo (carbon), hydrate (water, which is a combination of hydrogen and oxygen).

Plants that contain chlorophyll (the substance that gives them their green color) are the main source of carbohydrates. These plants use energy from the sun to combine carbon dioxide from the air and water from the soil to manufacture carbohydrates. Because carbohydrates are a main source for life, no living creature can exist without eating plants. Even animals that eat only meat get their carbohydrate supply by eating the flesh of animals that live on plants.

Foods supply carbohydrates in three main forms: starches, sugars, and cellulose (fiber). Starches and sugars are the main

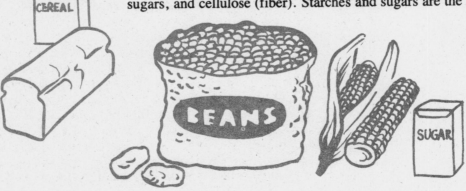

sources of energy for human beings. Cellulose is among the food materials that cannot be digested; it provides bulk in the diet.

Glucose, commonly called blood sugar, is the form in which starches and sugars are mainly used by body cells to furnish energy for body processes, activity, and growth.

Carbohydrates are economical to produce; growing plants is cheaper than raising animals for food. In the United States and Canada carbohydrates provide 40 to 50 percent of the total food energy. The entire population of the world obtains 70 percent of its energy from carbohydrates, because most peoples cannot afford foods containing large amounts of the other nutrients, proteins and fats.

Good sources of carbohydrates are grains (such as corn, oats, wheat, and rice), products made from grain (such as macaroni, spaghetti, noodles, grits, breads, and breakfast cereals), and potatoes, sweet potatoes, dried beans, and peas.

Carbohydrates can also be obtained from other vegetables and from fruits. In vegetables, the carbohydrates are mainly in the form of starches; in fruits, they are chiefly sugars. Cane and beet sugars, jellies, jams, candy and other sweets, honey, molasses, and syrups are concentrated sources of sugar in our diets.

Sucrose, which is common table sugar, is produced mostly from sugar cane and sugar beets. Table sugar, or refined sugar, is an unusual food in that it is pure carbohydrate. It is a source of calories (measures of heat energy) only; that is, it contains no vitamins, minerals, or any other food substances. For this reason, sugar is sometimes called "empty calories."

## Fats

The main sources of fat in foods are butter, margarine, lard, meat fat, animal and vegetable oils, cream, most cheeses, and nuts. There are other foods that have smaller amounts of fat.

Although the main nutritional task of carbohydrates is to provide energy for the body, fats are even more concentrated sources of energy. Weight for weight, fats give twice as much energy — calories — as either carbohydrates or proteins.

There are saturated and unsaturated fats, and the difference between them is important. Large amounts of saturated fats can eventually produce very serious diseases such as high blood pressure and consequent heart attacks.

Fats are composed mainly of fatty acids. Each fatty acid is made up of carbon atoms joined like links in a chain. The carbon chains vary in length, with most edible fats containing 4 to 20 carbon atoms. Each carbon atom has hydrogen atoms attached to it as charms might be attached to the links of a bracelet. When each carbon atom in the chain has attached to it as many hydrogen atoms as it can hold (usually two), the fatty acid is said to be saturated. When a hydrogen atom is missing from two neighboring carbon atoms, a double bond forms between them, and the fatty acid is said

**99**

to be unsaturated. A fatty acid that contains more than one such double bond is called polyunsaturated.

Probably the most important polyunsaturated fatty acid is linoleic acid. The body cannot manufacture this acid, so it must be obtained from food. A lack of this fatty acid causes the skin to become reddened and irritated and abnormalities of the liver to develop, especially in very young children. Linoleic acid is found in valuable amounts in many plant oils, such as corn, cottonseed, soybean, sesame, safflower, and wheat-germ oils. (The difference between a fat and an oil is that an oil is liquid at ordinary temperatures and fat is solid.) Margarine, salad dressings, mayonnaise, and cooking fats are usually made from one of these oils. Walnuts are high in linoleic acid, but other kinds of nuts are not. Poultry fat and fish fat and oil have more linoleic acid than do other animal fats, which rank fairly low as sources of this acid.

The body changes some fats into compounds called lipids. These can, over a period of years, form fatty deposits on the insides of arteries, causing the condition called hardening of the arteries, which may lead to high blood pressure and possible heart attack. Food scientists believe that polyunsaturated fats are less likely to be turned into lipids and therefore may help to prevent heart attack and high blood pressure.

Another important function of fats in the diet is to carry the fat-soluble vitamins A, D, E, and K.

In cooking, fats add flavor and variety to many foods. Fats also make foods and meals satisfying, because they are digested slowly and delay a feeling of hunger before the next meal.

## Proteins

All life requires protein. It is the basic substance of every cell in the body, the chief tissue builder. Proteins are the body builders and maintainers: they help in the development of muscles, and they create a feeling of well-being and fitness. In addition, proteins help to make hemoglobin (the blood protein that carries oxygen to the cells and carries carbon dioxide away from the cells). Proteins make the parts of cells that control the genetic code and therefore all hereditary characteristics in body cells; build the thousands of enzymes, the substances that control the speed of chemical reactions within the body; and make hormones, such as insulin and thyroxin, which regulate chemical processes and growth in the body. Proteins also form antibodies that can prevent diseases caused by foreign proteins (such as bacteria) that enter the body.

Proteins supply energy when the diet does not provide enough carbohydrates and fats.

The chief sources of protein are meat, poultry, fish, milk, eggs, cheese, beans, peas, and nuts.

Breads, cereals, vegetables, and fruits contain relatively smaller amounts of protein.

Proteins are made up of smaller units called amino acids. When foods containing proteins are digested, the proteins are broken down into the amino acids. These are then rearranged to make enzymes, hormones, and other special proteins.

The proteins in foods are usually made up of 18 or more amino acids. The body can make its own supply of more than half of the needed amino acids, but the rest, called essential amino acids, must come ready-made from food.

The amino acid makeup of a food protein determines its nutritive value. Proteins that supply the essential amino acids in about the same proportions as needed by the body are the proteins that are highest in nutritional value. Foods that provide good amounts of these top-ranking proteins are the foods that best meet the body's needs. Generally, these are foods of animal origin—meat, poultry, fish, eggs, and milk.

Proteins from cereal grains, vegetables, and fruits do not provide as broad an assortment of amino acids as do animal proteins, but legumes, especially soybeans, peanuts, and chickpeas, provide proteins almost as good as those from animal tissues.

Combining a small amount of animal protein—eggs, milk, cheese—with cereal, and meat or fish with vegetables will help to provide sufficient protein at a lower cost. Examples of tasty combinations are milk and cereal, macaroni and cheese, beans and peas with corn, beans with rice, and peanut butter with wheat (in bread).

Children urgently need protein for normal growth, and every person needs protein throughout life for maintenance and repair of body tissues.

## Vitamins

Vitamins are substances that occur in small amounts in a wide variety of foods and are needed for good health. They take part in the release of energy from foods, promote normal growth of many kinds of tissues, and are essential for the proper functioning of nerves and muscles.

More than a dozen vitamins that are needed for good health have been identified. Ordinarily, you can get all the vitamins you need by

**101**

eating a well-balanced diet of everyday foods, such as those suggested in the Daily Food Guide given later in this book.

Following is a summary of the most important vitamins, including some of their functions, and a list of foods that are dependable sources.

### VITAMIN A

Vitamin A is needed for normal bone growth, and it helps the eyes adjust to dim light. It also promotes healthy, infection-resistant skin and mucous membranes.

Vitamin A is found only in foods of animal origin. Liver is a good source; so are eggs, butter, margarine, whole milk, and cheese made from whole milk.

Dark-green and deep-yellow vegetables and deep-yellow fruits contain a substance called carotene that the body can convert into vitamin A.

### VITAMIN D

Vitamin D is important in building strong bones and teeth, because it enables the body to use calcium and phosphorus supplied by food.

Not many foods contain vitamin D naturally. Cod liver oil is a good source but is not likely to be part of a daily diet. Smaller amounts are found in eggs, butter, and liver; and somewhat larger amounts are found in sardines, salmon, tuna, and herring. Since vitamin D is not found in most foods and since it is so important for normal growth of children, synthetic vitamin D is added to almost all the milk sold in the United States and Canada.

Vitamin D is also produced in the human body by the direct action of sunlight on the skin.

### VITAMIN C, OR ASCORBIC ACID

Vitamin C helps to form and maintain "cementing materials" that hold body cells together and strengthen the walls of blood vessels. Because of this property, it assists in normal tooth and bone formation and aids in healing wounds.

Citrus fruits—oranges, lemons, grapefruits, and their juices, and fresh strawberries are excellent sources of ascorbic acid. Less important, but still good, sources are tomatoes and tomato juice, broccoli, brussels sprouts, cabbage, cantaloupe, cauliflower, and green peppers. Other sources are some dark-green leafy vegetables —such as collards, kale, mustard greens, spinach, and turnip greens — and watermelon. White and sweet potatoes cooked in their skins provide vitamin C.

When a person is under stress, the body utilizes larger-than-normal amounts of vitamin C. A person in this situation should make sure that he or she gets an extra amount of it.

This vitamin is soluble in water; therefore, foods containing it should not be overcooked, causing all the vitamin C to be dissolved in the cooking water.

### THE B VITAMINS

There are a number of B vitamins — thiamin, riboflavin, niacin, pyridoxine, folic acid, cobalamin, and possibly others.

Three of these, thiamin, riboflavin, and niacin, play a central role in the release of energy from food. They also help in maintaining normal appetite, good digestion, healthy skin, and good nerve functioning. Meats are the leading source of the B vitamins, and whole grain bread and enriched white bread and cereals supply small but important amounts. A few foods are outstanding sources: lean pork for thiamin, milk for riboflavin, and organ meats for all three.

A deficiency of thiamin causes the disease known as beriberi, which is practically unknown in the U.S. and Canada. Too little riboflavin causes sore lips, tongue, and mouth and a rough, scaly skin. A deficiency of niacin causes pellagra, the symptoms of which

are inflamed skin, diarrhea, and mental confusion progressing to delirium; untreated, it can be fatal.

Obtaining enough niacin is not a problem if sufficient protein is included in the daily diet, because an essential amino acid — tryptophan — present in protein can be converted into niacin by the body.

Other B vitamins — pyridoxine (B6), folic acid, and cobalamin (B12) — help to prevent anemia (the loss of red blood cells) and to build proteins. Vitamin B6 and folic acid are widely distributed in foods. The largest amounts of folic acid are found in organ meats and dark-green leafy vegetables. Good sources of vitamin B6 include most meats, whole-grain cereals, beans, potatoes, and dark-green leafy vegetables. Vitamin B12 is found only in foods of animal origin — liver, kidney, muscle meats, fish, eggs, oysters, and milk.

### VITAMIN K

Vitamin K is important for its role in the clotting of blood and the proper functioning of the liver. Egg yolks, organ meats, and green leafy vegetables are sources of this vitamin. Some Vitamin K is produced by bacteria that live in the intestinal tract.

## VITAMIN E

Vitamin E is known as an antioxidant; it prevents an unwanted chemical reaction — oxidation — from destroying certain nutrients such as polyunsaturated fats. It is stored in muscles and fat deposits and is found in wheat germ, leafy vegetables, legumes, whole grains, liver, milk, butter, and eggs.

## The RDA

Food scientists have worked out the amounts of vitamins the body should have each day. This amount is called the **recommended daily allowance,** or **RDA**. If for some reason you cannot eat enough of the foods that provide the needed vitamins, you can supplement them by taking vitamin capsules. For people below the age of 60, such capsules and a reasonably good diet will provide the RDA for all vitamins. Capsules that provide larger doses are not recommended; the body destroys or excretes most vitamins in amounts larger than it can use or store; therefore, buying large-dose capsules is a waste of money. Also, overdoses of some vitamins, such as A and D, can cause serious bodily harm.

For persons over 60 the RDA increases, but the amount of vitamins they should take must be established by consulting a doctor, not by arbitrarily increasing the dose.

## Cholesterol

Cholesterol is a fatlike substance made in the body and found in every cell. It is a normal constituent of blood and tissues. A certain amount of cholesterol is necessary for good health, but large amounts are suspected of causing fatty deposits to form on the insides of arteries and, like lipids, causing hardening of the arteries. There is still no certainty about how much cholesterol is necessary and how much is too much. Many factors influence the amount of cholesterol found in blood; one of these is the foods we eat.

Cholesterol is found in foods of animal origin. It is not found in fruits, vegetables, cereal grains, legumes, nuts, or vegetable oils. The greatest amounts of cholesterol are found in organ meats — brain, liver, kidney, heart, sweetbreads, and gizzard. Egg yolk, too, is high in cholesterol.

## Minerals

Minerals make up another important food group. They influence a large number of bodily functions and give strength and rigidity to certain body tissues.

• Calcium is the most abundant mineral in the body. Combined with phosphorus, it causes bones and teeth to be hard. Ninety-nine percent of the calcium in the body is found in bones and teeth.

The rest of the calcium is important for the proper functioning of the heart and other muscles as well as the nerves. Calcium also is a factor in the coagulation of blood during bleeding.

Milk and milk products are the main source of calcium. It is also present in certain dark-green leafy vegetables (collards, kale, mustard greens, turnip greens).

• Iodine. Iodine deficiency results in the disease called goiter, a swelling of the thyroid gland. Iodine is found in seafood — fish, clams, oysters, and mussels — and in seaweed. People who live near the seacoast usually get enough iodine because their diet includes seafood. People living inland will get enough iodine if it is a constituent of the soil. Where the soil does not contain iodine, people are at risk of developing goiter. The absence of iodine in the environment can be made up for by eating canned or frozen seafood and using iodized salt, which is ordinary table salt with a little potassium iodide added.

• Iron is needed by the body in relatively small amounts, but these amounts are vital. Iron combines with protein to make hemoglobin, the red substance of blood that carries oxygen from the lungs to body cells and removes the waste product carbon dioxide from the cells. By carrying oxygen to each cell, iron makes it possible for the cells to obtain energy from food.

Only a few foods contain much iron. Liver is a particularly good source (but remember that liver is high in cholesterol). So are heart and kidney, but again these are high in cholesterol. Other sources of iron are lean meats, shellfish, dry beans, dry peas, dark-green vegetables, oats, dried fruit, egg yolk (high in cholesterol), and molasses. Whole-grain breads and cereals contain smaller amounts of iron, but because they are eaten frequently they can be an important source.

Research shows that the diets of young children, preteen- and teenage girls, and women of childbearing age are most likely to have iron deficiencies. It is therefore recommended that they eat enough foods containing this mineral.

• Two other vitally important minerals are phosphorus and magnesium. Like calcium, the body needs them for bones and teeth; they also aid in converting foods into energy.

Good amounts of magnesium are found in nuts, whole-grain products, dry beans, dry peas, and dark-green vegetables.

If your diet contains foods that provide enough protein and calcium, you probably will get enough phosphorus as well.

• There are about 10 other essential minerals, only very small amounts of which are needed for good health. If your diet is balanced between carbohydrates, fats, and proteins you will get sufficient amounts of these minerals.

Fluorine, which is one of the 10 essential minerals not specifically discussed here, and which helps to protect teeth from decay, may be an exception to the above statement, as you will not get it automatically in a balanced diet. During the years when teeth are being formed, drinking water should contain a proper amount of fluorine in the form of natural or added fluoride, which will make teeth more resistant to decay.

## Water

Water is essential for life. It ranks next to oxygen in importance. The body's need for water exceeds even its need for food. You can live for days, even weeks, without food, but only for two or three days without water.

About one-half to two-thirds of the body is made up of water. It is the solvent for everything we digest, and it holds nutrients in solution and carries them through the bloodstream. Water is an important part of every cell structure, and it carries away the body's waste products.

Water also regulates body temperature by evaporating through the skin as perspiration.

A healthy body needs a regular and generous intake of water to perform all these tasks. It is provided largely by the fluids we drink, whether water itself or other liquids such as coffee, tea, juices, milk, or soft drinks. Many foods also contain water: celery and lettuce are good examples.

Although water supplies neither energy nor vitamins, it does contain minerals, for instance fluorine, which are helpful for the body.

# A Healthful Diet

Now that you understand a little of the what, why, and how of nutrients, let's apply this information to daily eating patterns.

Keep in mind that everyone needs the same nutrients throughout life, but in different amounts. Proportionately greater amounts are needed for the growth of the body than just for its upkeep. Boys and girls need proportionately more energy and nutrients than do men and women. Large people need more than small people. Active persons need more food energy than inactive ones.

Foods vary in the amounts of nutrients they contain. No single food provides all the necessary nutrients. That is why you need a variety of foods each day.

A diet that provides all the nutrients in the amounts needed is called a balanced diet.

## A Guide to Good Eating

Nutrition scientists have translated knowledge of the nutritional needs of the average family into an easy-to-use form: the Daily Food Guide. The Guide is divided into four categories according to the similarity in nutrient content of the foods in each. The categories are: the **milk group,** the **meat group,** the **fruit and vegetable group,** and the **bread and cereal group.** Each of the broad groups makes a special contribution toward a nourishing balanced diet.

## A Daily Food Guide

**Meat Group:** Beef • Lamb • Pork • Variety meats such as liver, heart, kidney. Poultry and eggs • Fish and shellfish. **As Alternates:** Dry beans • Dry peas • Lentils • Nuts • Peanuts • Peanut butter.

**Amounts Recommended:** Choose 2 or more servings every day.

**Count as a serving:** 2 to 3 ounces of lean cooked meat, poultry, or fish (all without bone) • one egg • ½ cup cooked dry beans, dry peas, or lentils • 2 tablespoons peanut butter may replace ½ serving of meat.

**Vegetable Group:** All vegetables and fruits. This guide emphasizes those that are valuable as sources of vitamin C and vitamin A.

**Good Sources of Vitamin C:** Grapefruit or grapefruit juice • Orange or orange juice • Cantaloupe • Guave • Mango • Papaya • Raw strawberries • Broccoli • Brussels sprouts • Green pepper • Sweet red pepper.

**Fair Sources of Vitamin C:** Honeydew melon • Lemon • Tangerine or tangerine juice • Watermelon • Asparagus • Cabbage • Collards • Garden cress • Kale • Kohlrabi • Mustard greens • Potatoes and sweet potatoes cooked in the jacket • Spinach • Tomatoes or tomato juice • Turnip greens.

**Sources of Vitamin A:** Dark-green and deep-yellow vegetables and a few fruits: Apricots • Broccoli • Cantaloupe • Carrots • Chard • Collards • Cress • Kale • Mango • Persimmon • Pumpkin • Spinach • Sweet potatoes • Turnip greens • Other dark-green leaves • Winter squash.

**Amounts Recommended:** Choose 4 or more servings every day, including: 1 serving of a good source of vitamin C or 2 servings of a fair source • 1 serving, at least every other day, of a good source of vitamin A (if the food chosen for vitamin C is also a good source of vitamin A, the additional serving of a vitamin A food may be

omitted) • The remaining 1 to 3 servings may be of any vegetable or fruit, including those that are valuable for vitamin C and for vitamin A. **Count as 1 serving:** ½ cup of vegetable or fruit • 1 medium: apple • banana • orange • potato • half a medium grapefruit • half a medium cantaloupe • juice of 1 lemon.

**Milk Group:** Milk (fluid whole, evaporated, skim, dry, buttermilk) • Cheese (cottage, cream, Cheddar-type, natural, or process) • Ice cream.

**Amounts Recommended:** Some milk every day for everyone. Recommended amounts are given in terms of 8-ounce cups of whole fluid milk: Children under 9: 2 to 3 cups • Children 9 to 12: 3 cups or more • Teenagers: 4 cups or more • Adults: 2 cups or more • Pregnant women: 3 cups or more • Nursing mothers: 4 cups or more.

Part or all of the milk may be fluid skim milk, buttermilk, evaporated milk, or dry milk.

Cheese and ice cream may replace part of the milk. The replacement is figured on the basis of calcium content. Common portions of cheese and of ice cream and their equivalents in calcium are: 1-inch cube Cheddar-type cheese = ½ cup milk • ½ cup cottage cheese = ⅓ cup milk • 2 tablespoons cream cheese = 1 tablespoon milk • ½ cup ice cream or ice milk = ⅓ cup milk.

**Bread-Cereal Group:** All breads and cereals that are whole grain, enriched, or restored (check labels to be sure). Specifically, this group includes: Breads • Cooked cereals • Ready-to-eat cereals • Cornmeal • Crackers • Flour • Grits • Macaroni and spaghetti • Noodles • Rice • Rolled oats • Quick breads and other baked goods if made with whole-grain or enriched flour • Bulgur and parboiled rice and wheat.

**Amounts Recommended:** Choose 4 servings or more daily. If no cereals are chosen, have an extra serving of breads or baked goods, which will make at least 5 servings from this group daily. **Count as 1 serving:** 1 slice bread • 1 ounce ready-to-eat cereal • ½ to ¾ cup: cooked cereal • cornmeal • grits • macaroni • noodles • rice • spaghetti.

**Other Foods:** To round out meals and meet energy needs, everyone will use some foods not specified in the four groups. Such foods

include: Unenriched, refined bread, cereals, flours • Sugars • Butter
• Margarine • Other fats. These often are ingredients in a recipe or
are added to other foods during preparation or at the table. Try to
include some vegetable oil among the fats used.

## How to Use the Daily Food Guide

Homemakers who follow the Guide will find it flexible enough to
use in choosing foods for the entire family.

Food choices within the groups are wide enough to allow for a
variety of everyday foods. Meals can be planned to include family
favorites, foods in season, and foods to fit the family budget.

The size of the servings can be suited to the needs of family
members—small servings for children and for those wanting to lose
weight; extra larger servings (or seconds) for very active adults,
teenagers, those wanting to gain weight, and pregnant and nursing
women, who also need more food.

Foods from the Daily Food Guide can easily fit into the family's
pattern of eating. Enough milk is suggested for children to have
some at each meal, and for adults at two meals. Milk can be served
as a beverage, used in cooking, or poured over cereals or fruit.
Some of the milk allowance may be used in the form of cheese and
ice cream.

A meat or alternate is usually a part of noon and evening meals
and may be included in breakfast as well. This more than takes care
of the minimum servings suggested from the meat group.

A fruit or juice at breakfast is customary in many families. The
additional three or more servings of fruits and vegetables suggested
can be divided between the other two meals.

A serving of bread or cereal readily fits into each meal. Cereal
includes items such as macaroni, spaghetti, noodles, and rice. Some
meals may contain both bread and cereal.

Foods from each group often appear in each meal, but this is not
essential. The important thing is that the suggested number of
servings from each food group be included sometime during the day.

Many people need and want more food than the minimum
servings suggested from the four food groups. To round out meals
and satisfy appetites, you can include additional foods from the four
groups as well as other foods not listed in the groups.

Meal planning from the Food Guide is more easily said than
done. The problem is that many foods we buy are not single foods,
and since in some cases we can add nutrients, we cannot identify
which food group they fall into. This does not mean that you cannot

**109**

use the basic four food groups to guide yourself in selecting a good diet, but there are two types of foods that make it difficult. The first are conventional foods that are combinations of several groups. Pizza is a good example. The base of a pizza pie is a cereal product. This is then covered with tomato paste and has cheese, a dairy product, on top; some pizzas also contain meat. The quality of the cheese and meat determines whether it is really a good source of the nutrients expected from those products. But you won't find pizza in any food group in the Guide, so you must try to estimate how much cereal, cheese, and meat are contained in such a complex food.

The second type of foods that make the use of food groupings difficult are the reconstituted foods. For example, soybeans fall into the cereal group, but food processors reconstitute soybeans so that they look like meat. Then they fortify the product so that it provides all the nutrients not only of meat but also of the dairy group. If the consumer puts the soybean product in the cereal group, she or he will miss the fact that soybeans are a good source of protein as well as calcium and vitamin A that are normally found in the dairy group and part of the vegetable group.

Despite these difficulties in identifying the food group for some foods, the complex and reconstituted foods can be good sources of nutrition. Whatever errors you make in judging how much of the basic food groups a certain food contains, you will not do yourself or your family any harm—unless you make these hard-to-judge foods a main part of most of your meals.

## Tips on Meal Planning

Keep these points in mind when you plan meals:
• Include a variety of foods each day and from day to day. Introduce a new food from time to time.
• Vary flavors and textures. Contrast strong flavor with mild, sweet with sour. Combine crisp textures with smooth.
• Try to have some meat, poultry, fish, eggs, milk, or cheese at each meal.
• Make a collection of nutritious recipes that you or your family enjoy and serve them often.
• Brighten food with color—a slice of red tomato, a sprig of dark greens, or other garnish.
• Combine different sizes and shapes of food in a meal when possible.

## The Bonus of Breakfast

Food starts to work for you early in the day when you eat breakfast. It is a research fact that people who eat a good breakfast are more alert and productive in the morning and more resistant to fatigue through the day than those who skip breakfast.

After the fast of the night, the body needs to be replenished with food to get the energy and other materials—proteins, minerals, and vitamins—required to keep it working efficiently. With today's convenience foods, breakfasts can be prepared in a matter of minutes.

## Buying Food

After knowing what you want your family to eat by having consulted the Daily Food Guide, you should shop for that food wisely.

• For economy, select the less expensive foods from each of the four food groups.

• Check special sales in food store advertisements.

• Look at each food critically:
Is it costly compared to other foods that might be served?
Will the family eat and enjoy it?
Is there time to prepare it?

• Learn to estimate accurately the amount of food needed to feed your family. No eating pleasure or nourishment comes from food that is bought and then thrown out.

• Use unit pricing to find the brand and container size of food that costs the least per unit—pound, ounce, or pint. Even if it is a better buy, select a food only if it can be stored properly and conveniently and used without waste.

• Avoid foods that are packed as individual servings. The extra packaging boosts the price. Examples are individual bags of potato chips, ready-to-eat cereals, raisins, and tea.

• Check the date on a perishable food. Be sure you can use all of the food before it spoils.

• Use meat, poultry, and fish sparingly—usually no more than a moderately large serving for each person daily. Use some egg, cheese, dry beans, dry peas, or peanut butter, too. These foods provide protein and most other nutrients that meat, poultry, and fish supply.

• When buying meat, consider the amount of lean meat in the cut, as well as the price per pound. A relatively high-priced cut of meat with little or no waste provides more meat for your money than a low-priced cut with a great deal of bone, gristle, or fat. Chicken and turkey are usually bargains when compared to other meats. One way to find the best buy is to compare the cost of packages of meat, poultry, and fish that will provide enough for a family meal. It may help control costs to set a top limit on the amount to spend for the main meal of the day, or to set an average amount to spend, allowing for some medium- and some low-cost items throughout the week.

• Use nonfat dry milk, which is less expensive than fluid milk, in cooking and as a beverage at least part of the time. Buy fresh milk in a food or dairy store in half- or one-gallon containers. Milk in smaller containers, and milk home-delivered or from special service stores usually costs more.

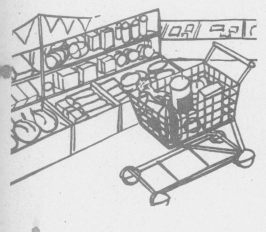

• When buying vegetables and fruit, take advantage of seasonal abundance. Foods in season are at their peak in quality and often are lower in cost. However, you must judge whether its cost fits into your budget.

• Try low-priced brands. They may be similar in quality to the more expensive ones.

• Use whole-grain and enriched flour, bread, or cereal in some form at every meal to get your money's worth in nutrients. Enriched bread and flour are important for the iron and certain B vitamins that they contribute. In addition to the many nutrients cereals supply, whole grains, especially bran, provide fiber, which is necessary for the normal functioning of the intestinal tract.

• For economy, use cereals prepared at home rather than instant or ready-to-eat ones; for example, whole-grain, rather than precooked, rice. When buying ready-to-eat cereals, select those that are not sugar-coated and those in family-size boxes.

• Consider the cost and the quality of the finished product in deciding whether to buy convenience foods. Some convenience foods are both easy to prepare and inexpensive. Among these are many canned and frozen vegetables, fruits, and juices; instant dehydrated potatoes; canned and dried soups; nonfat dry milk; prepared mixes for making biscuits and cakes; and some ready-to-eat or "quick" cereals.

After groceries are brought home, check them critically. Are your choices economical compared to other choices that might have been made? Did you buy some foods that were not on the list? If so, can these impulse purchases be justified as important for meeting food needs, being real bargains, or providing a worthwhile taste treat?

## Food Labels

No matter how shrewd a shopper a person may be, she or he cannot tell what the ingredients of most prepared foods are. For this reason, the federal government requires that food processors provide on the label information as to the contents of their products. Some of this information is required by the Food and Drug Administration; some is included voluntarily by the processor.

Certain information must be on all food labels:

• The name of the product.

• The net weight or net contents in ounces, pints, or quarts. On canned food, the net weight includes the liquid in which the product is packed, such as water in canned vegetables or syrup in canned fruit.

• The name and place of business of the manufacturer, packer, or distributor.

• The ingredient present in the largest amount, by weight, followed in descending order of weight by the other ingredients.

• Any additives used in the product, with the exception of the names of artificial color and flavor where it is sufficient, but necessary, to mention the fact that artificial color or flavor has been used.

The Food and Drug Administration (FDA) has set "standards of identity" for certain foods such as butter, cheese, catsup, mayonnaise, and ice cream. These foods must contain certain ingredients, and the manufacturer is not required to list them on the label.

## Nutritional Information

Under FDA regulations, any food to which a nutrient has been added, or any food for which a nutritional claim has been made, must have the nutritional content of its ingredients listed on the label. Many manufacturers give this information on their products voluntarily.

Nutrition labels tell you how many calories and how much protein, carbohydrate, and fat are in a serving of the product, as well as the U.S. Recommended Daily Allowance (RDA) of protein and seven important vitamins and minerals that the product might contain. The listing of 12 of the vitamins and minerals and of cholesterol, fatty acid, and sodium content is optional.

## What "Imitation" Means

Some foods are labeled as imitations of other foods. Under FDA regulations, the word "imitation" must be used on the label when the product is not as nutritious as the product it resembles and for which it is a substitute. If a product is similar to an existing one and is just as nutritious, a new name can be given to it instead of calling it "imitation." For example, eggless products that are as nutritious as eggs have been given names such as Eggbeaters and Scramblers.

## Common or Usual Name

To prevent deception if a product is packaged or looks like another more nourishing or expensive product, the FDA has ruled that such foods must have a "common or usual" name that gives the consumer accurate information about what is in the package or container. For example, a beverage that looks like orange juice but contains very little orange juice must use a name such as "diluted orange juice drink" or simply "orange drink." It must also state how much of the characterizing ingredient it contains; for example, "orange drink, contains 10 percent orange juice."

Another special labeling requirement concerns packaged food designated as "main dishes" or "dinners" which do not contain the main ingredient or component of a recipe (for example, a product called "chicken casserole" that does not contain chicken). On such foods the label must mention:
• The common name of each ingredient in descending order by weight, for example, "noodles and tomato sauce."
• Identification of the food to be prepared from the package, for example, gravy "for preparation of chicken casserole."

- A statement of ingredients that must be added to complete the recipe, for example, "You must add chicken to complete the recipe."

## Grades

Some food products carry a grade on the label, such as "U.S. Grade A." Grades are set by the U.S. Department of Agriculture, based on the quality levels inherent in a product: its taste, texture, and appearance. U.S. Department of Agriculture grades are *not* based on nutritional content. Milk products in most states carry a "Grade A" label based on FDA recommended sanitary standards for the processing of milk, and also certain amounts of vitamins A and D when these vitamins are added to the milk.

## Food Fads

There are many foods and food supplements on the market that promise the consumer improvement in health, longer life, the cure of certain diseases, or greater vitality, as well as a host of other health and psychological benefits. These foods and food supplements often are labeled by their makers as "natural" or "organic."

In the first place, a consumer who buys such foods is at the mercy of the seller. For example, an "organic" food or a "natural" food is one that is grown without the use of chemical fertilizers or pesticides. To monitor the growing of any crop from seed to harvest would be very difficult, time-consuming, and prohibitively expensive. So the storekeeper must depend on the honesty of the distributor, who in turn must depend on the honesty of the grower— and the customer depends on the honesty of all three. Even if all three are honest, the consumer, who pays a much higher price for organically grown foods, gains nothing nutritionally. Many tests have found no difference between organically and chemically fertilized foods.

The same lack of benefits applies to "natural" versus synthetic food supplements. Research has shown that there are no benefits in natural nutrients that are not also in synthetic ones, which are usually cheaper. Synthetic vitamin C, for example, is cheaper than vitamin C from rose hips.

## Food Additives

Synthetic materials or extracts from plants and minerals are added to many food items by the manufacturer or processor for one or another reason. These materials are called food additives. Food manufacturers contend that consumers expect food to keep well and be nutritious and consistent in taste and appearance. They also contend that consumers expect the food to be processed and ready-to-eat and to be abundantly available at the lowest possible price, all year round, regardless of where the consumer may live. Nevertheless, many concerned persons would prefer to do without the literally thousands of additives food technologists have produced during the years.

The law requires that most additives, such as dough softeners and anti-spoilage agents, be mentioned on food labels.

Besides the agents put intentionally into food by the manufacturer or processor, incidental or indirect additives get into the food during the processing or from the package material.

The Food and Drug Administration has set standards to regulate additives. There are those that are called GRAS substances; the acronym stands for "*G*enerally *R*ecognized *A*s *S*afe." These are additives that have been used for many decades and are recognized as safe by food experts. Then there are "prior sanctioned substances," which were permitted as food additives before 1958, when an important amendment to the Food, Drug, and Cosmetic Act was passed by Congress. These have "squatter's rights" but can be banned if they are shown not to be safe. Color additives used for coloring foods must be given provisional or final approval by the FDA. Last are pesticides used to kill insects, worms, and rodents during growing and storage of food crops, which may enter crops through the roots or leaves or may remain on leaves and skins as a residue. There are strict federal regulations for the use of pesticides. However, the various government agencies are hard pressed to keep up with the testing of the many new ones appearing continually on the market.

The whole matter of pesticides and food additives is a very controversial one, especially with the increasing cancer research and the finding that many additives are cancer-causing agents in test animals.

## Food Safety

You have shopped wisely for nutritious and economical foods. You have avoided as many food additives as you can. You still have one more thing to do in order to insure the health of yourself and your family: store the food safely.

### Fruits and Vegetables

Fresh fruits and vegetables should be thoroughly washed to remove any pesticide residues and waste-matter droppings from insects, worms, and rodents. After washing, inspect the food carefully to see that there are no rotten, ill-smelling, or moldy spots. If you find any areas that look or smell bad, immediately throw out the affected food unless you can cut out the bad spots. Be sure to cut deeply and widely around them. Don't skimp on this! This safety precaution applies to all kinds of food, but especially to fruits and vegetables.

Fresh fruits should be ripe when stored in the refrigerator. Some unripe fruits may be left at room temperature—preferably in a cool room between 60° and 70°F—to ripen.

Sweet corn keeps best if refrigerated uncovered but still in the husks; use it promptly. Removing tops from carrots, beets, and radishes reduces wilting. Storing potatoes in a cool, dark place prevents greening of the skin and retards sprouting. (Green-skinned and sprouting potatoes contain small amounts of powerful poisons that can make you very sick. Peeling and thoroughly boiling these potatoes will make them edible again.)

### Meat, Poultry, Fish

All meat should be promptly refrigerated. So should poultry and fish, immediately upon being brought home from the store. Eggs, too, should be put into the refrigerator immediately, stored large end up.

Butter and margarine should be kept in the refrigerator, as should open containers of lard and other cooking fats, and also cooking and salad oils.

## Cured and Smoked Meats, Dried Foods

Ham, frankfurters, bacon, and sausage should be stored in their original containers in the refrigerator. When the containers have been opened, use whole hams within one week, half hams and slices within 3 to 5 days; bacon, franks, and smoked sausages within a week.

Dried foods may ordinarily be kept at room temperature. In hot, humid weather, however, these foods should be refrigerated.

## Spoilage

Spoilage, or rotting, is due to the growth of bacteria, molds, or other organisms on food. These organisms cannot grow well—or at all—in cold temperatures. That is why foods are refrigerated or frozen. Broiling, frying, roasting, or baking kill these organisms. However, the cooking processes must be thorough. Simply warming food will not kill harmful organisms; it may make them grow faster. Eating raw or undercooked animal products is risky to your health.

There is one type of bacteria that deserves special mention: *Clostridium botulinum,* which produces a deadly poison. The illness that comes from eating this bacterium is botulism, or ptomaine poisoning.

The cause of botulism is mainly canned food. Contamination with these deadly bacteria results from inadequate sterilization techniques in the preparation of the food. A sign of inadequate sterilization is the presence of gas in the can. Therefore, *never* buy a can of food that is even slightly swollen at the top or bottom.

Another tip: Cook pork products thoroughly, as heat will kill disease-bearing trichina, a parasitic worm that sometimes occurs in pork.

• • •

If you plan menus according to their nutritional values, shop wisely, and keep food safe, you and your family can live healthy lives.

**116**

Compiled by
CULINARY ARTS INSTITUTE STAFF

# Food and Cooking Tips

# Contents

**EQUIPPING YOUR KITCHEN** .................. **119**

**MEASUREMENTS AND EQUIVALENTS** ......... **121**

**SPECIFIC EQUIVALENTS** .................... **121**

**SOME APPROXIMATE SUBSTITUTIONS** ........ **122**

**COOKING TEMPERATURES** .................. **122**

**METRIC EQUIVALENTS FOR U.S COOKING MEASURES** ............................ **122**

**A HANDY METRIC CONVERSION TABLE** ....... **123**

**WHAT YOU SHOULD KNOW ABOUT:** ........ **123**
    Chocolate ................................. **123**
    Fats and Oils ............................. **123**
    Flour ..................................... **124**
    Milk and Milk Products ................... **125**
    Sugars and Syrups ....................... **126**

**DEFINITIONS** ............................. **127**

**HELPFUL HINTS FOR THE COOK** ............ **131**
    Beverages ................................ **131**
    Bread .................................... **131**
    Cakes, Cookies, and Pies ................. **132**
    Eggs and Cheeses ........................ **132**
    Fish ..................................... **133**
    Shellfish ................................. **134**
    Meats .................................... **134**
    Poultry .................................. **135**
    Fruits .................................... **136**
    Vegetables ............................... **137**
    Soups .................................... **138**
    Preserving ............................... **138**

## Equipping Your Kitchen

Your choice of equipment often depends upon the amount of cupboard and other storage space available. With a minimum of space one must choose essential items wisely, making sure that a bulky item such as a large saucepot or skillet can serve more than one purpose. The following list should help in making a wise choice of equipment.

### For Food Preparation:

- Set of measuring spoons: ¼ teaspoon, ½ teaspoon, 1 teaspoon, 1 tablespoon
- Set (or nest) of measuring cups: ¼ cup, ⅓ cup, ½ cup, 1 cup
- Glass measuring cups for liquids: 1 cup, 2 cups (1 pint), 4 cups (1 quart)
- Mixing bowls: 1 pint, 1 quart, 3 quarts
- Knives: butcher knife, serrated bread knife, slicing knife (with long, thin blade), chopping knife (French), paring knives, grapefruit knife
- Forks: long-handled fork, two-tined fork, two or three small forks, blending fork
- Spoons: three wooden spoons of various sizes and lengths, slotted metal spoon, slotted wooden spoon, two metal tablespoons, three metal teaspoons
- Spatulas: small, medium
- Rubber scrapers: two plate and bowl scrapers (wide), one bottle and jar scraper (narrow)
- Beater: hand rotary type
- Strainers: small, medium
- Colander
- Cookie cutters: assorted sizes and shapes
- Juicer or reamer
- Vegetable parer
- Vegetable brush (stiff)
- Kitchen shears

- Apple corer
- Graters: small hand grater, set of larger graters for fine and coarse grating and shredding
- Cutting board
- Wire cooling racks: two or three
- Pancake turner
- Pastry blender
- Rolling pin (stockinette cover)

- Pastry brush
- Pastry canvas
- Flour sifter
- Flour shaker
- Salt and pepper shakers
- Can opener (wall-type or electric)
- Funnels
- Ladle
- Tongs

## For Baking and Top-of-Range Cooking:

- Custard cups: six (6 ounce)
- Muffin (or cupcake) pans: two sets of six (one set 1¾ x 1 inch, one set 2½ x 1¼ inch)
- Casseroles with covers: 1½, 2, and 3 quarts
- Individual casseroles or ramekins: six
- Pie pans: 8 inch, 9 inch
- Cake pan (square): 8 inch, 9 inch
- Cake pans (round): two or three 8 or 9 inch
- Cake pan (tubed): 9 or 10 inch
- Baking pan: 11 x 7 x 1½ inch
- Loaf pan: 9 x 5 x 3 inch

- Open roasting pan: 13 x 9 x 2 inch
- Double boiler: 1½ quarts
- Saucepans with tight fitting covers: 1, 2, and 3 quarts
- Dutch oven: 3 quarts
- Coffee maker: 4 or 6 cups
- Teakettle
- Teapot: 6 cups
- Toaster
- Skillets with tight fitting covers: two (one small 6 or 8 inch, one large deep 10 inch)
- Molds: two or three, including a ring mold

## Miscellaneous Items (Handy to Have):

- Corkscrew and bottle opener
- Knife sharpener
- Tea ball
- Thermometers: meat, candy, deep frying, portable oven thermometer (if oven is unreliable)
- Sink strainer
- Steam cooker
- Ice cream scoop
- Juice can opener
- Biscuit and bun warmer
- Jars with screw-top covers (for storing foods in refrigerator and on cupboard shelves)
- Canister set
- Hot pads, tiles, or stands (for hot dishes)

- Food mill
- Garlic press
- Meat grinder
- Timer
- Wooden chopping bowl and chopper
- Potato masher or ricer
- Melon ball cutter
- Pot holders
- Garbage can
- Freezer storage containers and moisture-vaporproof bags
- Refrigerator storage dishes with covers
- Aluminum foil
- Paper baking cups
- Waxed paper
- Paper towels

## Nice-to-Have Appliances:

- Coffee maker
- Waffle baker
- Blender

- Electric mixer (table-type or portable)
- Electric skillet

## MEASUREMENTS AND EQUIVALENTS

Dash, speck or few grains . . . . . . . . . . . . . . .less than ⅛ teaspoon
60 drops . . . . . . . . . . . . . . . . . . . . . . . . . . . . . . . . . . . .1 teaspoon
3 teaspoons (½ fluid ounce) . . . . . . . . . . . . . . . . . . . . .1 tablespoon
⅛ cup (1 fluid ounce) . . . . . . . . . . . . . . . . . . . . . . . . . .2 tablespoons
¼ cup (2 fluid ounces) . . . . . . . . . . . . . . . . . . . . . . . . .4 tablespoons
⅓ cup . . . . . . . . . . . . . . . . . . . . . . . .5 tablespoons plus 1 teaspoon
½ cup (4 fluid ounces) . . . . . . . . . . . . . . . . . . . . . . . . .8 tablespoons
⅔ cup . . . . . . . . . . . . . . . . . . .10 tablespoons plus 2 teaspoons
¾ cup (6 fluid ounces) . . . . . . . . . . . . . . . . . . . . . . . .12 tablespoons
1 cup (8 fluid ounces) . . . . . . . . . . . . . . . . . . . . . . . .16 tablespoons
2 cups (16 fluid ounces) . . . . . . . . . . . . . . . . . . . . . . . . . . . .1 pint
4 cups (32 fluid ounces) . . . . . . . . . . . . . . . . . . . . . . . . . . .1 quart
2 pints . . . . . . . . . . . . . . . . . . . . . . . . . . . . . . . . . . . . . . . .1 quart
2 quarts . . . . . . . . . . . . . . . . . . . . . . . . . . . . . . . . . . . .½ gallon
4 quarts (liquid) . . . . . . . . . . . . . . . . . . . . . . . . . . . . . . . .1 gallon
8 quarts (dry) . . . . . . . . . . . . . . . . . . . . . . . . . . . . . . . . . .1 peck
4 pecks . . . . . . . . . . . . . . . . . . . . . . . . . . . . . . . . . . . .1 bushel
16 ounces (dry measure) . . . . . . . . . . . . . . . . . . . . . . . . .1 pound

## SPECIFIC EQUIVALENTS

Bread:
    1 to 2 slices (soft) . . . . . . . . . . . . . . . . . . . . . . . . .1 cup crumbs
    1 pound loaf . . . . . . . . . . . . . . . . . . . . .10 cups small bread cubes

Butter or margarine:
    1 ounce . . . . . . . . . . . . . . . . . . . . . . . . . . . . . . . .2 tablespoons
    1 stick (4 ounces) . . . . . . . . . . . . . . . . . . . . . . . . . . . . . . .½ cup

Chocolate, unsweetened:
    1 ounce . . . . . . . . . . . . . . . . . . . . . . . . . . . . . . . . . . .1 square

Cream, heavy (40%):
    1 cup . . . . . . . . . . . . . . . . . . . . . . . . . . . . . . . . .2 cups whipped

Eggs:
    4-6 whole . . . . . . . . . . . . . . . . . . . . . . . . . . . . . . . . . . .1 cup
    8-10 whites . . . . . . . . . . . . . . . . . . . . . . . . . . . . . . . . . . .1 cup
    10-14 yolks . . . . . . . . . . . . . . . . . . . . . . . . . . . . . . . . . . .1 cup

Marshmallows:
    16 large . . . . . . . . . . . . . . . . . . . . . . . . . . . . . . . . . . .4 ounces

Sugar:
    granulated, 2¼ cups . . . . . . . . . . . . . . . . . . . . . . . . . . .1 pound
    superfine, 2⅓ cups . . . . . . . . . . . . . . . . . . . . . . . . . . . .1 pound
    brown, about 2¼ cups firmly packed . . . . . . . . . . . . . . . .1 pound
    granulated brown, about 3⅛ cups . . . . . . . . . . . . . . . . . .1 pound
    confectioners', 3½ cups . . . . . . . . . . . . . . . . . . . . . . . .1 pound

Syrup:
    corn, about 1½ cups . . . . . . . . . . . . . . . . . . . . . . . . . . .1 pound
    maple, about 1½ cups . . . . . . . . . . . . . . . . . . . . . . . . . .1 pound

# SOME APPROXIMATE SUBSTITUTIONS

**Baking powder:** In place of 1 teaspoon baking powder use ¼ teaspoon baking soda plus 1 teaspoon cream of tartar.

**Butter:** In place of 1 cup butter use ⅞ to 1 cup vegetable shortening or lard plus ½ teaspoon salt.

**Chocolate:** In place of 1 square use 3–4 tablespoons cocoa plus 1 tablespoon shortening.

**Cornstarch:** In place of 1 tablespoon cornstarch use 2 tablespoons all-purpose flour.

**Cream, light (20%):** In place of 1 cup light cream use ⅞ cup milk plus 3 tablespoons butter.

**Cream, heavy (40%):** In place of 1 cup heavy cream use ¾ cup milk plus ⅓ cup butter.

**Flour, cake:** In place of 1 cup sifted flour use ⅞ cup all-purpose flour (⅞ cup–1 cup minus 2 tablespoons).

**Garlic:** In place of 1 clove garlic use ¼ teaspoon garlic powder.

**Marshmallows:** In place of 10 miniature marshmallows use 1 large marshmallow.

**Onion:** In place of 1 cup chopped onions use 1 tablespoon instant minced onion or 1 teaspoon onion powder.

### COOKING TEMPERATURES

| Heat | Fahrenheit | Celsius |
|---|---|---|
| Very slow | 250–275 | 121–135 |
| Slow | 300–325 | 149–163 |
| Moderate | 350–375 | 177–191 |
| Hot | 400–425 | 204–218 |
| Very Hot | 450–475 | 232–246 |
| Broil | 500–525 | 260–274 |

### METRIC EQUIVALENTS FOR U.S. COOKING MEASURES

| U.S. Measure | | Metric Equivalent | U.S. Measure | | Metric Equivalent |
|---|---|---|---|---|---|
| ¼ teaspoon | = | 1.25 milliliters | 1 ounce | = | 28 grams |
| ½ teaspoon | = | 2.5 milliliters | 2 ounces | = | 56 grams |
| 1 teaspoon | = | 5 milliliters | 4 ounces | = | 113 grams |
| 2 teaspoons | = | 10 milliliters | 8 ounces | = | 226 grams |
| 3 teaspoons | = | 15 milliliters | 16 ounces | = | 452 grams |
| 1 tablespoon | = | 15 milliliters | ¼ pound | = | .11 kilogram |
| 2 tablespoons | = | 30 milliliters | ½ pound | = | .23 kilogram |
| 1 fluid ounce | = | 30 milliliters | ¾ pound | = | .34 kilogram |
| 2 fluid ounces | = | 59 milliliters | 1 pound | = | .45 kilogram |
| 4 fluid ounces | = | 118 milliliters | 2 pounds | = | .90 kilogram |
| 8 fluid ounces | = | 236 milliliters | 4 pounds | = | 1.81 kilograms |
| 16 fluid ounces | = | 472 milliliters | 6 pounds | = | 2.72 kilograms |
| 1 cup | = | .24 liter | 8 pounds | = | 3.62 kilograms |
| 2 cups | = | .47 liter | 10 pounds | = | 4.54 kilograms |

## A HANDY METRIC CONVERSION TABLE

| To Change | Into | Multiply By | To Change | Into | Multiply By |
|---|---|---|---|---|---|
| ounces | grams | 28 | grams | ounces | .035 |
| pounds | kilograms | .45 | kilograms | pounds | 2.2 |
| teaspoons | milliliters | 5 | milliliters | teaspoons | .2 |
| tablespoons | milliliters | 15 | milliliters | tablespoons | .067 |
| fluid ounces | milliliters | 30 | milliliters | fluid ounces | .033 |
| cups | liters | .24 | liters | cups | 4.2 |
| pints | liters | .47 | liters | pints | 2.1 |
| quarts | liters | .95 | liters | quarts | 1.06 |
| gallons | liters | 3.8 | liters | gallons | .26 |

## What You Should Know About:

### Chocolate

The term chocolate refers to **unsweetened chocolate. Sweet chocolate** is chocolate with sugar added. It may also contain cocoa butter and flavorings. It is used for dipping candies and other confections.

**Semisweet chocolate** is small pieces or 1-ounce squares formed from slightly sweetened chocolate and used for candymaking or baked products, or eaten as a confection. (Also available in the form of bars.)

**Cocoa** is a powdered chocolate product from which some of the cocoa butter has been removed. The fat content varies from 10% to 22%. **Breakfast cocoa** is a high-fat cocoa which contains at least 22% cocoa fat.

**Dutch process cocoa** can be either "cocoa" or "breakfast cocoa" which is processed with one or more alkaline materials as permitted under government regulations.

**Instant cocoa** is a mixture of cocoa, sugar, and an emulsifier. It can be prepared for use by dissolving in hot liquid with no cooking necessary.

### Fats and Oils

**Butter** is fat from sour or sweet cream gathered in a mass, sometimes salted and colored. It contains not less than 80% by weight of milk fat. **Unsalted butter** is butter made from sweet cream. Also called sweet butter. **Whipped butter** is butter into which air has been whipped.

**Cooking or salad oils** include: corn oil, refined from the dried, crushed corn germ; cottonseed oil, refined from the crushed seed of the cotton plant; peanut oil, the oil extracted from peanuts, a by-product of peanut butter; safflower oil, the oil extracted from the seed of the safflower plant, used for cooking purposes and also used commercially for the manufacture of safflower margarine.

**Cracklings** are the residue from rendered fat of meat.

**Hard fats** are coconut or palm oils in solid form used mostly in candymaking.

**Lard** is fat rendered from the fatty tissues of the hog.

**Margarine** is made by the emulsification of various oils with cultured milk and further processing to produce a consistency similar to that of butter; contains 80% fat; usually colored; may or may not have salt added. Soft-type and whipped margarine are also available.

**Olive oil** is oil from the flesh of ripe olives. Virgin olive oil is that which is first extracted and is better in flavor and appearance than the oil produced by the second or third pressing. Use olive oil when specified in a recipe.

**Poultry fat** is a cooking fat made commercially by rendering the leaf fat removed from the body cavities of chickens and turkeys and sometimes from the fat that is skimmed from vats of poultry being cooked for canning.

**Shortening** is a general term used for cooking fats. May be meat fats or vegetable oils. Or, may be a blend of animal fats; or a blend of vegetable oils; or a blend of animal and vegetable.

**Suet** is the clear, white fat of beef and mutton.

## Flour

The term flour when used in recipes with no other qualifications as to special purpose or preparation (bread, cake, self-rising flour) usually refers to all-purpose or general-purpose flour.

**Bread flour** is milled from blends of spring and winter hard wheats or from either type alone. It has a fairly high protein content and is slightly granular to the touch. It may be bleached or unbleached and is milled mostly for commercial bakers.

**All-purpose flour** is a blend of hard or soft wheat flours which are lower in protein content than bread flour, but higher than cake flour. It can usually be used with good results for most home-baked products. Blends are prepared to satisfy the demands of different areas. In the South, for instance, a softer blend is available to make satisfactory quick breads, while in the North a harder blend is marketed for use in making yeast breads and rolls.

**Instant-blending flour** is an all-purpose flour which some associate with the term "instantized" to indicate that the flour dissolves readily in liquids without forming lumps.

**Self-rising flour** is flour to which leavening agents and salt have been added in proper proportions for home-baking. The leavening agent most often used, with soda, is calcium phosphate.

**Whole-wheat flour** (also graham flour) is flour milled so that the natural constituents of the wheat kernel remain unaltered.

**Pastry flour** is made of either hard or soft wheats, but usually the latter. It is fairly low in protein and finely milled though not as fine as cake flour. It is used chiefly by bakers and biscuit manufacturers.

**Cake flour** is milled from soft wheats. The protein content is low and the granulation so fine that the flour feels soft and satiny.

## Milk and Milk Products

**Fresh fluid milk** contains not less than 3.25% milk fat and not less than 8.25% milk solids other than fat. **Vitamin D milk** is whole or skim milk in which the vitamin D content has been increased.

**Homogenized milk** is fresh milk in which the size of the fat globules is reduced so that the cream does not rise to the top.

**Evaporated milk** is sterilized homogenized milk containing about 60% less water than whole milk. When diluted with an equal amount of water, it is used as fresh whole milk. It is also used, undiluted, as cream.

**Sweetened condensed milk** is milk from which about half the water has been removed. It contains a large amount of added sugar which acts as a preservative.

**Skim milk** is milk from which most of the fat has been removed thereby reducing its vitamin A content. Some skim milks are fortified by adding a water-soluble vitamin A and D concentrate.

**Buttermilk** as sold in retail markets is usually a cultured (fermented) product made of fresh skim milk. (It is also the by-product from churning cream into butter.) The bacterial culture used converts the milk sugar into lactic acid. Cultured buttermilk may also be made from fresh fluid whole milk, concentrated fluid milk, or reconstituted nonfat dry milk.

**Dry milk (whole) and dry milk (nonfat)** are made from fresh whole milk and skim milk respectively. After most of the water has been removed from them they are dried until a fine-textured powder results. The process has no appreciable effect on the nutritive value and when mixed with water these products have the original composition of pasteurized milk.

**Yogurt** is a cultured product (with a consistency resembling custard) usually made from fresh partially skimmed milk enriched with added milk solids other than fats. Fermentation is accomplished by a mixed bacterial culture.

**Half and half** is a mixture of milk and cream, usually 10% to 12% fat. **Light cream,** sometimes referred to as table or coffee cream contains 18% to 20% fat. **Heavy (or whipping) cream** contains between 30% and 36% fat.

**Dairy sour cream** is a cultured product sold commercially and made by adding bacterial cultures to pasteurized and homogenized cream.

## Sugars and Syrups

**Granulated sugar** is a highly refined white sugar composed of almost pure sucrose which is found in large quantities in sugar cane and sugar beets.

**Superfine granulated sugar** is a specially screened, uniformly fine-grained sugar used in cakes and in mixing drinks.

**Confectioners' (powdered) sugar** is granulated sugar crushed and screened to desired fineness. A small amount of cornstarch is added to prevent caking. Confectioners' sugar is used in frostings and icings and for dusting doughnuts, pastries, etc.

**Brown sugar** is unrefined cane sugar which varies in color from very light to very dark. It contains various amounts of molasses, some non-sugars (ash) naturally present in molasses, and moisture.

**Granulated brown sugar** is a specially processed brown sugar which does not harden and can be poured from the package. To substitute for regular brown sugar, see manufacturer's equivalents table.

**Maple sugar** is a solid product obtained by evaporating maple sap or maple syrup to the point where crystallization occurs.

**Molasses** is the liquor remaining after the crystallization of raw sugar from the concentrated sap of the sugar cane. Sometimes a second and third crystallization is made, resulting in two grades of molasses known as "light" and "dark" molasses. When a large proportion of the sugar has been removed, the resulting product has a strong flavor and is called "black strap." It is used for fermentation purposes.

**Sorghum (or sorgo)** is a syrup somewhat resembling molasses produced from a cane-like grass. It has a mild flavor appealing to many people especially in the Southwest where the grass is grown.

**Corn syrup** is a product resulting from the partial hydrolysis of cornstarch with coloring and flavoring usually added to the syrup. Light and dark corn syrups are marketed. Many table syrups contain some corn syrup combined with such sweeteners as sorghum, cane syrup, or honey and butterscotch or vanilla for flavoring.

**Honey** is defined as "the nectar and saccharine exudations of plants gathered, modified, and stored by the honey bee." Honey must contain not more than 25% water. The flavor and color of honey depends upon the source of the nectar. Orange blossoms, clover, buckwheat, and basswood are common sources.

**Maple syrup** comes from the sap of the maple tree collected in early spring and concentrated to the desired consistency. Pure maple syrup contains not over 35% water.

**Sugar syrup** is a solution of sugar and water used to sweeten beverages.

**Sugar substitutes** are non-caloric sweetening agents.

## Definitions

**Bake:** To cook in a container (covered or uncovered) in an oven or oven-type appliance. Usually called roasting when applied to meats.

**Barbecue:** To roast or broil on a rack over hot coals or on a revolving spit in front of or over heat source.

**Baste:** To spoon liquid (or use baster) over cooking food to add moisture and flavor.

**Beat:** To make a mixture smooth by introducing air with a brisk motion that lifts the mixture over and over, or with a rotary motion as with a hand rotary beater or electric mixer.

**Blanch:** To preheat or precook in boiling water or steam. This process is used to inactivate enzymes and shrink food for canning, freezing, and drying. The blanching process is also used to aid in the removal of skins from nuts.

**Blend:** To mix two or more ingredients so that each loses its identity.

**Boil:** To cook in liquid in which bubbles rise continually and break on the surface. Boiling temperature of water at sea level is 212°F.

**Braise:** To cook slowly in a covered utensil in a small amount of liquid or in steam. (Meat may or may not be browned in small amount of fat before braising.)

**Bread:** To coat with bread crumbs alone or to coat with bread crumbs, then with diluted slightly beaten egg or evaporated milk, and again with crumbs.

**Broil:** To cook by direct heat.

**Candy:** To cook fruit (also citrus fruit peel and ginger) in a heavy syrup until plump and transparent, then drain and dry. Candied product is also known as crystallized fruit, peel, or ginger. Term also applied to vegetables cooked in a syrup or sugar and fat mixture (*i.e.*, candied sweet potatoes or carrots). Candy is synonymous with glaze (*i.e.*, glazed or candied cherries).

**Caramelize:** To heat dry sugar or foods containing sugar until a brown color and characteristic flavor develop.

**Chop:** To cut into pieces with a knife or other sharp tool. (Also see *Mince, below*.)

**Coddle:** To cook slowly just below the boiling point (as applied to eggs and fruit).

**Combine:** To mix ingredients.

**Cream:** To mix one or more foods together until soft and creamy. Usually applied to shortening and sugar.

**Cube:** See *Dice, below.*

**Cut in:** To distribute solid fat in dry ingredients by chopping with pastry blender or knives until finely divided.

**Devil:** To mix with hot seasoning as pepper, mustard.

**Dice:** To cut into small cubes.

**Dissolve:** To cause a liquid and a dry substance to pass into solution.

**Dredge:** To coat or sprinkle with flour or other fine substance.

**Flake fish** (freshly cooked or canned): Gently separating the fish into flakes, using a fork. Remove the bony tissue from crab meat while flaking it. (Bones of salmon are edible and need not be removed.

**Fold:** To combine by using two motions, one which cuts vertically through the mixture (using a flexible metal or rubber spatula or wire whisk) and the other which turns the mixture over by sliding the implement across the bottom of the mixing bowl.

**Fricassee:** To cook by braising (usually applied to poultry, rabbit, and veal).

**Fry:** To cook in fat; called **sauté** or **panfry** when cooking with a small amount of fat; called **deep-fat frying** when cooking in a deep layer of fat.

**Glacé:** To coat with a thin sugar syrup cooked to the crack stage. When used for pies and certain types of bread the mixture may contain a thickening, but it is not cooked to such a concentrated form as for a glacé; or it may be uncooked.

**Grate:** To reduce to small particles by rubbing on anything rough and indented. Use a rotary-type grater with hand-operated crank for grating chocolate and nuts, following manufacturer's directions. Grated chocolate and nuts should be fine and light.

**Grill:** To broil on open grill or griddle.

**Grind:** To reduce food to particles by cutting, crushing (electric blender may be used), or by forcing through a food chopper.

**Knead:** To manipulate with a pressing motion plus folding and stretching.

**Lard:** To insert matchlike strips of fat, called lardoons, into gashes in side of uncooked lean meat by means of a larding needle or skewer; or to place on top of meat.

**Marinate:** To allow food to stand in liquid (usually a seasoned oil and acid mixture) to impart additional flavor.

**Mask:** To cover completely; usually applied to the use of mayonnaise or other thick sauce but may refer to forcemeat or jelly.

**Mince:** To cut or chop into small, fine pieces.

**Mix:** To combine ingredients in any way that effects a distribution.

**Panbroil:** To cook uncovered on a hot surface, usually in a skillet.

**Parboil:** To boil uncooked food until partially cooked. The cooking is usually completed by another method.

**Parch:** To brown by means of dry heat. Applied to grains.

**Pare:** To cut off the outside covering. Applied to potatoes, apples, etc.

**Pasteurize:** To preserve food by heating to a temperature (140° to 180°F) which will destroy certain microorganisms and arrest fermentation. Applied to milk and fruit juices.

**Peel:** To strip off the outer covering. Applied to oranges, grapefruit, etc.

**Poach:** To cook in a hot liquid using precautions to retain shape. The temperature used varies with the food.

**Purée:** To force through a fine sieve or food mill or to blend in an electric blender until a smooth thick mixture is obtained.

**Reconstitute:** To restore concentrated foods to their normal state, usually by adding water. Applied to such foods as nonfat dry milk or frozen fruit juices.

**Reduce liquid:** To continue cooking the liquid until the amount is sufficiently decreased, thus concentrating flavor and sometimes thickening the original liquid. Simmer when wine is used; boil rapidly for other liquids.

**Render:** To remove fat from connective tissue over low heat.

**Rice:** To force food through ricer, sieve, or food mill.

**Roast:** To cook by dry heat, usually in an oven.

**Scald milk:** To heat in top of a double boiler over simmering water or in a heavy saucepan over direct heat just until a thin film appears. The term scald is also used when simmering certain foods in boiling water for a few seconds.

**Scallop:** To bake food, usually with sauce or other liquid. The top may be covered with crumbs. The food and sauce may be mixed in the baking dish or arranged in alternate layers with or without crumbs.

**Score:** To make cuts in the surface of meat before roasting, usually making a diamond pattern (example roast ham).

**Sear:** To brown meat quickly with intense heat.

**Shirr:** To break eggs into a dish with cream or crumbs and bake in oven.

**Sieve:** To force through a sieve.

**Simmer:** To cook in a liquid just below boiling point; bubbles form slowly and break below surface.

**Skewer:** To pierce or fasten with skewers—as a piece of meat.

**Steam:** To cook in steam with or without pressure. The steam may be applied directly to food (*i.e.,* pressure cooker).

**Steep:** To allow a substance to stand in liquid below the boiling point for the purpose of extracting flavor, color, or other qualities.

**Sterilize:** To destroy microorganisms. For culinary purposes this is usually done at a high temperature with steam, dry heat, or by boiling in a liquid.

**Stew:** To cook slowly in a small amount of liquid.

**Stir:** To mix food ingredients with a circular motion in order to blend them.

**Truss:** To fasten the cavity of stuffed poultry or meat with skewers and/or cord.

**Whip:** To beat rapidly to produce expansion due to incorporation of air as applied to eggs, gelatin mixtures, and cream.

# Helpful Hints for the Cook

## Beverages

• To frost glasses rub the edge of each glass with cut surface of lemon, lime, or orange. Or brush rim with citrus juice. Dip the rim of each glass in fine granulated or confectioners' sugar. Place glasses in refrigerator to chill. Carefully pour beverage into glasses without touching frosted edges.

• To make decorative ice cubes fill ice cube tray one third full with water. Place in freezing compartment of refrigerator; remove ice cube tray when water is partially frozen. Place well-drained maraschino cherry, mint sprig, pineapple chunk, orange wedge, berry, or small piece of fruit, and a mint leaf in each cube section. Fill tray with water and freeze.

• To make stronger flavored iced coffee pour coffee over coffee ice cubes. Using ½ measuring cup water per standard measure of coffee, prepare drip coffee or any variation. Pour coffee into ice cube tray and place in freezing compartment of refrigerator. Fill tall glasses to brim with ice cubes. Pour the hot coffee over the ice. Serve with granulated or confectioners' sugar, sugar syrup, cream, or whipped cream sprinkled with ground cinnamon.

## Bread

• To butter bread for thin sandwiches, spread end of loaf with softened butter, then cut off a slice as thin as possible. Repeat buttering and slicing.

• To freshen rolls, place them in a heavy paper bag. Twist top of bag and place in a 400°F oven 10 to 15 minutes. (Or wrap securely in aluminum foil.)

• Store bread in a cool dry place. If a loaf is not consumed in several days, keep it fresh by placing in a moisture-vaporproof bag and storing it in the refrigerator. If you bake or purchase more than one loaf at a time, keep one loaf in the refrigerator and wrap the other loaf in freezer wrap and place it in the freezer. If loaf has been sliced before freezing, remove only the number of slices required for a single meal and thaw at room temperature. Baked rolls and biscuits are stored in a similar manner.

## Cakes, Cookies, and Pies

• Use fluted paper baking cups when preparing cupcakes. They save greasing of pans and eliminate sticking. They also make pan washing easy.

• When baking an upside-down cake, line cake pan with aluminum foil, folding foil over the edges of pan. After cake is baked, let cool on rack about 5 minutes. Then place serving plate on top of cake, turn cake upside down and remove the pan. Carefully lift off the foil. Cake comes out of pan easily and pan is easy to clean.

• To store cookies, cool thoroughly before placing in cookie jar, canister, or casserole having a cover. Do not store crisp cookies with other types. If they have softened during storage, place them in a 300°F oven for a few minutes to restore crispness.

• To soften cookies, store for several days with a piece of apple or orange.

• To pack cookies for mailing, wrap (separately if possible) in moisture-vaporproof material in sturdy container lined with extra wrapping material. Use crumbled waxed paper, popcorn, or shredded packing material to fill extra space.

• To prevent juice from cooking out of pies into the oven, place a strip of dampened cloth or pastry tape around the edge of the pie or place a tiny funnel or 4-inch stick of uncooked macaroni in the center of the pie.

• To avoid shrinkage of a pastry crust, roll out the pastry, place in a pie pan without stretching, and set aside about 5 minutes before fluting the edge. Or place a second pie pan on the pastry before baking. Remove the second pan after about 10 minutes of baking to allow the pastry shell to brown on the inside.

## Eggs and Cheeses

• Whether the color of the egg shell is brown or white makes no difference in the quality or food value of the egg, though in some localities it does influence price. Eggs with brown shells sometimes have yolks of deeper yellow color than those with white shells.

• As soon as possible after purchasing, store eggs in the refrigerator in their own egg container to keep them upright, or store on the egg shelf of the refrigerator door, small ends down. Remove only as many eggs as needed at one time.

• To divide a raw egg, beat well before measuring with a tablespoon.

• To hard-cook egg yolks, use only unbroken yolks and slip

them gently into simmering water. Keep below boiling point until yolks are firm. Remove with a slotted spon.
• To slice hard-cooked eggs without breaking the yolk, dip knife into water before slicing.
• When adding whole eggs or egg yolks to a sauce, always stir a little of the hot sauce into the slightly beaten eggs; immediately blend into the remaining hot sauce. Cook 3 to 5 minutes, stirring to keep the mixture cooking evenly.
• For the fullest enjoyment of most cheeses, remove them from the refrigerator at least 1 hour before serving; the interior of Camembert and Brie should be almost runny. Serve Neufchâtel, cottage, and cream cheeses chilled.

## Fish

• Fresh fish are best prepared as soon as possible after being caught. When fresh, they have red gills, bright eyes, and bright-colored scales adhering tightly. The flesh is firm and elastic, and practically free from odor. Fresh fish should be packed in ice until purchased; at home, wrap in foil or moisture-vaporproof material and store in the refrigerator.
• Frozen fish is available the year around in market forms such as steaks, fillets, and sticks. It should be solidly frozen and *never refrozen after thawing*.
• Salted fish are prepared either by "dry-salting" or by pickling in a brine. Firm, coarse-fleshed fish such as cod, hake, and haddock are dry-salted by packing in dry salt after cleaning. Fat and oily fish are "salted" in brine, then are frequently smoked. Finnan Haddie is prepared in this way.
• Smoked fish is a delicacy: salmon, whitefish, and haddock are popular varieties. It is usually eaten without further cooking.
• Canned fish is easy to store and convenient to serve. Sardines, tuna, cod, salmon, mackerel, and kippered herring are some of the varieties.
• To make poached fish firm and white, add a little lemon juice to the cooking liquid.
• To remove fish odors from utensils, add 2 tablespoons baking soda to the dishwashing water.
• To store fresh fish, wrap the whole fish or fillets or steaks in moisture-vaporproof material or in waxed paper. Use fish the same day as purchased, if possible. Place in freezer if fish is not to be used in one or two days.

## Shellfish

• Live shellfish are those which should be alive when purchased, such as crabs, lobsters, clams, and oysters (except when purchasing cooked lobsters and crabs in the shell).

• Shucked shellfish are those which have been removed from their shells.

• Frozen shellfish available are shrimp, crab, lobster, lobster tails, scallops, and oysters.

• When clams are purchased, the shells should be tightly closed or should close at a touch. They may be opened with a knife or be steamed open.

• If serving boiled lobster whole and cold, rub shell parts with salad oil to improve color. If saving shell parts for Thermidor, brush them with oil.

• Oysters in the shell are sold by the dozen. They must be alive with shells tightly closed; when dead, the shells open automatically and shellfish are no longer edible.

• To open oyster shells wash them thoroughly and rinse in cold water but do not soak. Insert a strong thin knife between shells near the thick end and run it around back of shell until muscle holding shells is cut. Discard flat shell, save liquor from oysters, and remove any small pieces of shell from oysters. Serve oysters on the deep half of the shell.

• Fresh shrimp with heads removed are sold by the pound either fresh or frozen. Shrimp are graded according to the number per pound—jumbo (under 25); large (25 to 30); medium (30 to 42); and small (42 and over). *Cooked shrimp* with shells removed are also sold by the pound; the meat is pink. *Canned shrimp* are available in several sizes of cans and may be used in place of cooked shrimp.

## Meats

• All meats processed by packers must pass Federal inspection and be stamped with the Federal inspection stamp. The quality grading is also done by stamping the meat. The purple ink used for both inspection and grading stamps is a harmless vegetable dye which need not be cut away before cooking.

• 1 pound boneless meat (boned meats, ground meats, flank steaks, liver, heart, kidneys, sausages, brains, sweetbreads, and most canned meats) makes 4 servings.

• 1 pound meat with a small amount of bone (round steak, pot roasts, ham slices, rib roasts) makes 3 servings.

• 1 pound meat with a large amount of bone or fat (most

steaks, poultry, shoulder cuts, short ribs, neck, chops, breasts, plate, brisket) makes 2 servings.

• Purchase ground beef that has been *freshly* ground, either regular (contains not more than 25% fat) or lean (contains not more than 12% fat). Or buy a cut of beef such as chuck, round, flank, plate, brisket, shank, or neck meat and have it ground. If the cut is quite lean, have 2 ounces of suet per pound of beef ground with the cut. A coarse grind helps to insure extra-juicy patties.

• Purchase pork that has been *freshly* ground or have pork shoulder meat ground.

• Purchase lamb that has been *freshly* ground or have lamb shoulder meat ground.

• Store ground meat uncovered or lightly covered in refrigerator. Partial drying on the surface of meat increases its keeping quality. Use within two days of purchase.

• Store frozen ground meat in the freezing compartment of the refrigerator or in a freezer, wrapped in freezer wrapping material.

• Always cook pork until well done.

• To keep bacon from curling while broiling or panfrying, snip edges with shears before cooking.

• To make a flavorful gravy from pot roast drippings, add canned consommé (instead of water) to the meat during cooking.

## Poultry

• When grading and inspection labels are not present, the consumer may be guided by some of the standards used in official grading. Young birds have smooth, soft, thin skin, little fat, and flexible-tipped breastbones; as the bird ages, the skin coarsens, more fat is deposited along the backbone, and the breastbone becomes more rigid. Grade A quality requires that a bird be well-formed and full-fleshed, with no defects, tears, or bruises in the skin, clean and free from pinfeathers.

• To store fresh poulty or ice-chilled ready-to-cook chicken or

turkey, remove from store wrappings. Remove neck and giblets. Wrap bird (whole or cut in pieces) loosely in waxed paper or transparent, moisture-vaporproof material, ends open to let in air. Place in a shallow pan and store in the coldest part of the refrigerator. Use within 48 hours. If poultry is to be frozen, wrap securely in freezer wrap and place immediately in freezer.

• Quick-frozen poultry must be kept frozen until ready to use and once thawed must not be refrozen. In thawing frozen poultry before cooking, follow directions on the label, if available. Or use one of the following methods: *Refrigerator thawing* — Keep in original wrapping and place on a tray in refrigerator from 1 to 3 days. A 4-pound chicken or turkey requires about 1 day while a 20- to 24-pound turkey may take as long as 3 to 3½ days. *Cold-water thawing* — Place bird in its original wrapper in a large pan or in the sink; cover completely with very cold water. Change water frequently so that it will remain cold. An 8- to 12-pound requires 3 to 6 hours; 12- to 20-pound bird 6 to 8 hours; 20- to 24-pound bird 10 to 12 hours. Once it is thawed, refrigerate poultry if not cooking immediately. *Room-temperature thawing* — This method is less satisfactory than other methods. If time permits, refrigerator thawing is the most satisfactory method.

• Cooked poultry, gravy, and stuffing should not be left at room temperature for longer than it takes to finish the meal. Never store bird with stuffing; remove stuffing and store it covered in refrigerator; cover gravy and refrigerate. If only one side of a roast bird has been carved, wrap remainder of bird in waxed paper, aluminum foil, or moisture-vapor-proof material; store in refrigerator. If more than one half of the meat has been used, remove the remaining meat from the bones and wrap tightly before storing. Cooked pieces should be tightly wrapped and refrigerated. Do not keep cooked poultry, however carefully stored, for more than a few days. If keeping leftover turkey or other poultry for more than several days, immediately remove meat from bones, wrap meat in moisture-vapor-proof material, and store in freezer.

### Fruits

• To obtain maximum juice from lemons and limes, firmly roll the fruit on a hard surface before squeezing.
• To extract juice from a lemon when only a small amount is needed, puncture fruit with a fork and gently squeeze out desired amount of juice.

• To keep juice in fruit which has been cut, cover exposed part with waxed paper and place fruit, cut side down, on a dish, or fit cut side with a transparent bowl cover.
• To remove pits from cherries, insert a new pen point into penholder, pointed end in, and remove pits with the rounded end of pen point.
• To keep cut fruits from discoloring sprinkle lemon or pineapple juice over them.
• Wash berries before hulling to retain juice.

## Vegetables

• To freshen fresh asparagus, stand the stalks upright in icy cold water.
• To remove the skins from carrots easily, cover them with boiling water and let stand for a few minutes until the skin loosens.
• To keep cauliflower white while cooking, use half milk and half water; cook, uncovered, until just tender.
• To make celery curls, cut stalks (about 3 inches long) lengthwise into thin strips to within 1 inch of end. Place in cold water until strips begin to curl.
• To make celery very crisp, let stand in icy cold water to which 1 teaspoon sugar per quart of water has been added.

• To garnish lettuce leaves sprinkle some paprika on waxed paper and dip edges of leaves into it.
• To keep onions from affecting eyes, peel them under running water.

• To prevent odor while cooking onions and cabbage, add 1 tablespoon lemon juice or a wedge of lemon to the cooking water.
• Store less perishable vegetables, such as cabbage, potatoes, dry onions, winter squash, and rutabagas, in a cool, dry, well-ventilated place without beforehand washing. Keep onions separate from other vegetables. Store potatoes in a dark place and not directly on the floor.
• Wash vegetables, such as radishes, lettuce, and other leaf vegetables before storing; drain thoroughly and gently pat dry with a soft clean towel or absorbent paper. Rinse head lettuce under running water, drain, and shake off excess water thoroughly. For long storage do not remove core until lettuce is used. Place vegetables in refrigerator in vegetable drawers or plastic bags, or wrap tightly in waxed paper or

moisture-vaporproof material to prevent vegetables from wilting unless refrigerator maintains a high humidity. Do not soak vegetables for any length of time when washing them. If they are wilted, put them in icy water for only a few minutes. Shake off all moisture left from washing, drain thoroughly amd gently pat dry.

• Store peas and lima beans in the pod to keep fresh. Pods may be washed before storage; quickly rinse peas and lima beans after shelling.

## Soups

• To avoid curdling of cream of tomato suup, thicken the sieved tomatoes before adding (hot) to the cold milk, stirring constantly.

• The electric blender is the modern way to quick-and-easy blending of everything and anything into savory soups. Remember, when using it, to pour the liquid into container first, usually ½ to 1 cup, then gradually add the other ingredients.

• Cool soups to lukewarm before storing in covered container in the refrigerator; keep several days only. Store in freezer for longer periods.

## Preserving

• To remove odors from jars and bottles, pour a solution of water and dry mustard into them and let stand several hours. Or use a dilute chlorine solution and rinse jars in hot water.

• When covering jelly with melted paraffin, pour a thin layer over top; place a strong piece of string on paraffin with end over edge of glass. Pour another layer of paraffin over string. Set aside until paraffin is firm. When jelly is to be used, lift off the paraffin layer by using the string.

• To open glass jars containing fruit easily, set them upside down in hot water for a few minutes.

Written by
CULINARY ARTS INSTITUTE STAFF

# How To Entertain

# Contents

**ENTERTAINING IS EASY!** . . . . . . . . . . . . . . . . . . . . . 141
   **Brunch and Morning Coffee** . . . . . . . . . . . . . . . 142
   **Luncheons** . . . . . . . . . . . . . . . . . . . . . . . . . . . . 143
   **Teas** . . . . . . . . . . . . . . . . . . . . . . . . . . . . . . . . 144
      **The Informal Tea** . . . . . . . . . . . . . . . . . . 144
      **The Formal Tea** . . . . . . . . . . . . . . . . . . . 146
   **Dinners** . . . . . . . . . . . . . . . . . . . . . . . . . . . . . 147
      **The Semiformal Dinner** . . . . . . . . . . . . . 147
      **The Informal Dinner** . . . . . . . . . . . . . . . 148
      **Table Setting** . . . . . . . . . . . . . . . . . . . . . 148
      **Seating of Guests** . . . . . . . . . . . . . . . . . 149
      **Serving Procedure** . . . . . . . . . . . . . . . . 150
      **Some Factors in a Successful Dinner** . . . . . . 151
      **The Cocktail Hour** . . . . . . . . . . . . . . . . 151
   **Buffets** . . . . . . . . . . . . . . . . . . . . . . . . . . . . . 152
      **The Cocktail Party** . . . . . . . . . . . . . . . . 155
      **Smörgåsbord** . . . . . . . . . . . . . . . . . . . . 155
   **Dessert Parties** . . . . . . . . . . . . . . . . . . . . . . 157

**SERVING WINE WITH YOUR MEAL** . . . . . . . . . . . 157
   **Wine-serving Tips** . . . . . . . . . . . . . . . . . . . . 158
   **Wine Glasses** . . . . . . . . . . . . . . . . . . . . . . . 160

## Entertaining
## Is Easy!

The secret of successful entertaining is to enjoy your own parties. Entertaining should be as much fun for the hostess as it is for the guests. If you plan carefully, adapting your plans to the special conditions of your home, everything is bound to run along smoothly with everyone having a wonderful time, including you.

Some people seem to be born with a knack for entertaining. Good food appears at their parties as if by magic, the guests are relaxed and conversation flourishes. You may be sure, however, that none of this just "happens." The food appears because someone has prepared it; the guests are relaxed because their hostess feels no strain; conversation flows because their hostess is on hand to help it along instead of coping with a crisis in the kitchen. And all of this means that she has planned carefully. She has planned a menu that requires a minimum of attention after the guests arrive, planned and arranged the flowers and other accessories, and set out all the little appurtenances of comfort. She probably

**141**

has planned her guest list, too, inviting only persons who will be congenial. And if she is the completely thoughtful hostess, her menu has been planned with due regard for the food likes and dislikes of her guests.

In planning a company menu it is wise to follow the same principles that guide all menu-making. Avoid repetition of foods in the same meal—if fish is the appetizer do not use it for the main dish. Maintain a balance between firm and soft foods. Do not serve too many starches (rice, potatoes, and bread at the same meal are not good planning) or too much of any other single food stuff. Avoid too many strong flavors— flavors should harmonize or contrast but not compete. Plan meals with an eye to the over-all arrangement, varying the foods in color, texture and flavor. Include something sweet and something tart, something hot and something cold in every meal. Delight guests with an occasional surprise, but try out the new recipe on the family first.

It is a good idea to make notes in a diary about what you served to whom and at which party to avoid serving the same menu to the same guests when you invite them again.

## Brunch & Morning Coffee

Brunch, a delightful meal combining both breakfast and lunch, may be served any time before one o'clock in the afternoon. When served early, brunch usually means simple breakfast foods. Served later, the menu may be an expanded and more elaborate breakfast, possibly served buffet style. Or it may more closely resemble a luncheon except for soup and salad which seldom are included in a brunch menu. If dessert is served it is a light fruit in season and/or cookies.

A mid-morning social gathering often called simply "morning coffee" is sometimes used by hostesses as an easy, informal, and friendly means of entertaining a few friends. It is almost certain to be a feminine affair with the menfolks safely out of the house. It is a gracious way to entertain an out-of-town friend when time is limited.

Most informal of all is the impromptu coffee (the *kaffeeklatsch*) to which neighbors drift in and are welcomed by plenty of hot coffee accompanied by coffee cake, sweet rolls, or doughnuts. No specific service is required; a bright sunny kitchen is usually a pleasant place for a gathering of a few neighbors or good friends.

When guests have been invited for a real morning coffee "party," usually about 10 or 11 o'clock, more elaborate preparations are in order.

Coffee, coffee breads, and one or more trays of bite-size relishes of contrasting color and flavor (sweet and sour, bland and savory), may all be arranged on a prettily spread buffet table in living or dining room. The hostess herself will want to pour the coffee for her guests—a hospitable as well as a practical gesture; but a stack of plates on the table, with napkins and teaspoons arranged beside them, will permit each guest to serve herself to whatever she wants of the other foods provided. The "main course" will be bread and a good plan is to allow one big, beautiful coffee cake of the good-without-butter kind, already cut for the convenience of the guests, when the party is small; when the group is larger, a selection of delicious sweet rolls should be added.

The relish tray may hold tangy cheese bits, crisp radish roses or celery curls, ripe or green olives, along with fruits such as small clusters of grapes, whole strawberries washed but with hulls intact for finger eating, pineapple chunks, melon balls, or hulled berries impaled on picks. An attractive fresh fruit relish bowl can be made by cutting into halves and scooping out a chilled honeydew melon or a fresh pineapple with its spiny crown intact, and heaping with balls or chunks cut from the fruit bowl itself and other fruits, all on wooden picks.

## Luncheons

All parties are fun, but luncheons are in a class by themselves. They are usually given by women and for women, and so the light and even "fancy" touches which are special fun for the hostess are quite appropriate.

Whether you invite one guest or a dozen, you will summon all the artistry at your command to make the setting of your party beautiful and appropriate. Almost any kind of cloth, table mat, or runner is suitable if it harmonizes with the dishes and other accessories, the flowers, and to some extent with the season.

Table decorations, as at any meal, should be kept low, pretty but unobtrusive. Flowers are always appropriate, and so are attractive arrangements of fruits, foliage, handsome vegetables, vines, shells, quaint or beautiful figurines, and low-growing plants. Since luncheons are mid-day affairs, candles are not suitable. Flatware and crystal are placed as for a dinner party.

Luncheon for a group may be introduced by cocktails and appetizers in the living room. The luncheon menu itself may include two to four courses, the wise hostess planning it

according to what she can handle easily and gracefully. The main dish is often a creamed mixture served in croustades, patty shells, or over split baking powder biscuits. It may be accompanied by salad or not. Particularly if salad is omitted, a nice touch is to garnish the plates with spiced fruit such as spiced crab apples or peaches, watermelon pickles or the like, or with crisp bread-and-butter pickles or preserved kumquats. The dessert should be keyed to the rest of the meal: If the main dish is a rich creamed mixture, serve a light dessert—fruit or a fruit mold or sherbet; if a salad bowl is the main course, an elaborate dessert is in order.

The manner of service depends upon your home, your facilities and your guests. Keep it simple and informal, and be your most gracious self.

### Teas

A pleasant and flexible way of entertaining friends or acquaintances is the afternoon tea. There is not very much difference between a formal and informal tea, except the difference involved in serving a larger or a smaller number of guests. The usual hour for tea is between four and five, but it may be extended if many of the guests are career women, and may start earlier if a large number is expected.

#### THE INFORMAL TEA

Invitations to informal teas are usually extended in person, by telephone, or by an informal note, with the time stated. The number invited may vary from five or six to a large number, depending upon the occasion. If a hostess has asked a few friends to drop in for tea, she may serve it in the living room. The tea service should be arranged on an uncovered tray and placed on a low table, spread with a cloth which may barely cover the table or may hang as much as eighteen inches over the sides.

If the hostess has a silver tea service with an alcohol lamp, the tray will contain a kettle of water kept boiling over the flame (which should be lighted only after the tray is safely placed on the table), an empty tea pot, creamer, sugar bowl, a plate of lemon slices with a lemon fork, a tea caddy, and an empty bowl for tea leaves and for dregs poured from the guests' cups before refilling. In this case the hostess makes the tea in the presence of the guests and serves it with or without additional hot water, according to preference, and with or without cream, sugar, or lemon. If the hostess prefers, or if she does not have a tea service with a means of keeping water boiling, the tea may be brewed and strained in the kitchen into a heated tea pot, and boiling water poured into a second heated pot to dilute the strong tea as guests request. In this case water should be kept boiling on the range so the supply may be frequently replenished and always hot.

Cups and saucers with teaspoons laid on the saucers to the right of the cups may be placed on the tea tray if it will hold them all, or some may be on the table beside it. Tea plates (7 to 8 inches in diameter), in a stack, and 12-inch tea napkins are also on the table near the tray. If possible little tables or some other convenient surface should be provided near the chair of each guest to hold plate, cup, and saucer. Many hostesses omit saucers entirely, in which case tea cup and food are both placed on the tea plate.

The food provided may consist only of strips of cinnamon toast, finger sandwiches spread with whipped butter, cucumber or watercress sandwiches, or tiny hot biscuits with jam. Small crisp cookies or thinly sliced fruit cake, mints, and salted nuts may be served too. Only at small intimate teas will hot crumpets or buttered toasted English muffins be offered in the fashion of a hearty English tea. The serving of these, or of jam, requires spreaders. At formal teas or for a larger group, serve only finger foods.

For a large group, or even in a small group if the hostess knows that some guests prefer it, coffee may be offered as well as tea; and in warm weather there may be some who will like the strong, hot tea or coffee poured over cracked ice in tall glasses. On very hot days a bowl of fruit punch with plenty of ice may replace the tea service altogether.

If the group, even at an informal tea, is quite large, the hostess may ask one close friend to pour the tea for her, another to pour the coffee, and perhaps a third to assist by keeping the serving plates replenished with food, so that she herself may be free to greet her guests. Constant replenishing of the serving plates is necessary to keep the arrangement of the tea table attractive.

### THE FORMAL TEA

These large teas are seldom given except for a special occasion—perhaps to introduce a visiting celebrity, or for a club meeting or other official event. Invitations (on a correspondence card or on the hostess' visiting card, with "To meet _____" across the top and the date and hour in a lower corner) are issued about two weeks before the event.

A long table is used for a formal tea, with flowers and tall, white, formal candles (which if present should be lighted, but should not be present unless needed). The cloth, of formal damask or lace, usually hangs over the table edge from one-quarter to one-half yard. The tea tray, arranged just as for an informal tea, will be at one end of the table. At the other end will be a coffee or chocolate service, or on a warm day, a bowl of ice fruit punch. Only finger foods should be served. Cucumber and watercress sandwiches are traditional at a formal tea, as are little cakes such as petits fours, thinly sliced fruitcake, mints, and salted nuts.

Tea cups and saucers with teaspoons laid on the saucer at the right of the cup are usually arranged near each beverage service; additional plates for sandwiches and cakes may be stacked (not more than six or eight high) on the table with napkins. The foods and the cups, saucers, plates, and napkins should be replenished as they are used.

Two intimate friends of the hostess, preferably ladies who are acquainted with most of the guests, should be asked to pour the beverages. They may be replaced by two others at the end of an hour, if the tea is large. Their assistance, and that of a third person to replenish the serving plates and remove the guests' cups and plates as they are emptied, will permit the hostess, together with the guest of honor, to receive her guests.

## Dinners

"Company" dinners are classified according to their formality. Most of the dinners an average hostess will give are informal and the rest are semiformal. The formal dinner is characterized by written or engraved invitations in the third person (also answered in the same manner), by full-evening dress, by a menu written in French (sometimes accompanied by an English translation), and consisting of no fewer than seven courses, but often as many as twelve with six or more wines. Preparation and serving of a seven course formal dinner consisting of appetizer, soup, fish, meat with vegetables, salad, dessert, and fruit (also nuts), followed by coffee or liqueurs in the drawing room, demands skilled help provided by a trained service staff. The style of service used is known as *Russian* or *Continental,* with host and hostess taking no part in it. The average family would find little occasion to use this formal style of service.

For the family with no outside kitchen help the *English* or *family style* of service is more practical. All the food is served at the table by the host and hostess instead of being served from the kitchen in individual servings.

A third type, usually called *"compromise"* service, is also used especially for semiformal meals and is described below.

### THE SEMIFORMAL DINNER

This is the most formal meal most homemakers are likely to give. Invitations may be partially engraved, with names, dates, and hours filled in by hand; or they may be extended in an informal letter or by telephone. The time is usually eight or eight-thirty. Men are usually expected to wear dinner jackets, black or, in warm weather, white, rather than business suits; and women usually wear informal evening dress or dinner dresses. The considerate hostess will include a hint of the degree of formality in her invitation.

The dinner itself consists of only four or five courses — soup, fish (usually in the form of a cocktail), meat and vegetables, salad, and dessert, and of these either the fish course or the salad is often omitted. After-dinner coffee is usually served in the living room.

Service of a semiformal dinner is known as "compromise" service and is a combination of English and Russian style, sometimes called American. It is suited to the home with one maid or with a part-time waitress, and means that while the first course, salad, and dessert are served by the maid, the host or the host and hostess participate in serving the main course. The host generally carves the meat and places it on

**147**

plates, which may be passed by the maid or handed down the table by the guests. The hostess sometimes serves the potatoes and vegetables; or the serving dishes may be offered to the guests by the maid. When there is no man of the house, the carving may be done by a close friend; or the hostess may do all the serving.

### THE INFORMAL DINNER

Invitations to the most frequent and most intimate form of dinner may be issued personally, by telephone, or by informal letter. The guests will seldom number more than ten, especially if there is no maid. The guests' dress is dictated by custom; it is perfectly proper for the men to come in business suits and the women to dress accordingly. If the meal is a real "party" on a non-business day, dinner jackets and dinner dresses are quite in order.

The menu may consist of only two or three courses — either soup or fish, meat and vegetables, and dessert; or casserole, salad, and dessert. After-dinner coffee in the living room is still a pleasant custom, but coffee may be served at the table. The "family-style" service may be assisted by a maid, or by a member of the family or a guest, but the hostess will probably do most of the serving. And the hour may be any time from six to eight-thirty.

### TABLE SETTING

The hostess's common sense as well as her knowledge of tradition will be called upon in setting the table for dinner. Everything should be correctly planned in an orderly manner.

The first step is to lay the cloth. For a really formal dinner a pure white or pale cream-colored cloth of linen damask is traditional, though a handsome lace cloth may be used. At least 9 inches of overhang should be allowed at each end. For less formal dinners, pastel damask, lace, linen edged with lace, or place mats may be used. A silence cloth or felt is always used under damask or linen.

Next, the dinner plates are placed. These should be spaced equidistant from each other, and one inch from the edge of the table. To allow the guests elbow room, a minimum of twenty inches must be allowed for each place—twenty-five or thirty inches is better.

The flat silver is arranged next. Only pieces actually needed for the food to be served should be put on the table, and these should be arranged in the order in which they will be used, starting from the outside. Forks (except cocktail forks) are placed to the left of the plate; knives, spoons, and cocktail forks to the right. All should be parallel to each other and at right angles to the edge of the table, with the handles an inch from the edge. Butter knives are placed on the butter plates, either parallel or at right angles to the table edge. Dessert forks or spoons are usually brought in with the dessert, though at an informal dinner they may be placed on the table.

The water glass is set at the tip of the dinner knife. Other glasses (for wines) are placed to the right and slightly in front of the water glass. The butter plate occupies the position at the tip of the dinner fork. Folded napkins are placed on the dinner plate if it is empty when the guests come to the table, or at the left of the forks; the folding should display the monogram, if there is one, and the open edges should be parallel with the fork and edge of the table and next to the fork. Individual ashtrays with matches and a few cigarettes should be supplied at each place. Iced water should be poured at the last moment; there should be no ice in the glasses.

Any centerpiece should be low enough to permit conversation across the table. Candles should be tall enough to burn above eye level.

### SEATING OF GUESTS

When dinner is announced, at a semiformal dinner, the hostess leads the way in to the dining room, followed by the ladies and then by the gentlemen, with the host. Only at very formal dinners does the host enter first with the lady guest of honor on his arm; then the hostess goes in last with the gentleman guest of honor. The host is always seated at one end of the table with the lady of honor at his right, and the hostess at the opposite end with the gentleman guest of honor at her left. If there is no difference in age, rank, or distinction among the guests, the lady at the host's right and the gentlemen at the hostess' left have the positions of honor. Ladies and gentlemen alternate along the sides of the table, with husbands and wives usually not seated side by side.

A thoughtful hostess will make her seating plan with her guests' interests and tastes in mind, and try to place together those who will find one another interesting and congenial. In a large party, place cards will be helpful, but at a smaller dinner she may indicate to each guest where he or she is to sit.

### SERVING PROCEDURE

Whatever the degree of formality, the lady seated at the host's right is always the first to be served. The hostess is never served first, unless she is the only lady present. Nor should the hostess ever be the first to help herself from an untouched serving dish. The classic sequence of serving goes clockwise around the table, starting with the lady guest of honor, but other sequences are also possible and correct; *i.e.*, one course clockwise, the next counter-clockwise, so that a different gentleman is last to be served in each case. When several have been served, guests may begin eating without waiting for the hostess, but the considerate hostess will lay her fork on her plate as a signal if she sees that the guests are waiting for her to begin. She should always be the last to finish.

All plates are placed and all serving dishes offered to guests from the left. The plates are always removed from the right. Ideally, the dishes offered should be held in the waitress's left hand, but in the interest of saving time, she may bring in two dishes at once, or present two dishes on a tray. Water and wine should both be poured from the right, by the waitress's right hand.

Dishes are always removed singly, never "stacked" on the table. When the main course is finished, serving dishes are removed first; then each place is cleared; then the maid takes away the pepper and salt shakers and the breadbasket on a tray, and crumbs the table, using a folded napkin and a clean plate. Dessert plates and silver are then put on the table.

Serving after-dinner coffee in the living room is a practical as well as a pleasant custom. It may be done in three ways, according to the size and character of the group, the formality of the occasion, and the service available. One way is to pour the coffee in the kitchen and have it brought in to the living room on a tray by the maid. Another way is to carry in to the living room a tray containing the silver coffee pot, creamer, sugar bowl, and the cups; the hostess then pours and hands the cups to guests who are nearby, or the host or other member of the family, who will hand them to more distant guests. The hostess may ask each guest for his cream and sugar preference, or they may help themselves. And the third way, perfectly acceptable at informal gatherings, is for the hostess to make the coffee freshly in the presence of the guests, using an electric coffee maker on a tray.

## SOME FACTORS IN A SUCCESSFUL DINNER

Formal or informal, any dinner party will be more successful if it has been planned in detail. Whether the hostess expects to have a regular or part-time maid for part of the service or to handle it all herself, writing down the work schedule will help to prevent last-minute confusion. A maid brought in for the occasion will work more smoothly if time can be given to rehearsal beforehand.

Since the food is still the most important part of the dinner party, its quality should be safeguarded. Hot foods must be piping hot when they are brought from the kitchen, and cold foods should be served very cold. Serving platters and dishes for hot meats and vegetables should be warmed and plates for salads and for refrigerator or frozen desserts chilled.

More important than the observance of every rule of etiquette is that the dinner party should be enjoyed by everyone, guests and hostess alike. This happy result is more easily attained if the hostess has invited no more guests than she can comfortably seat and serve, and if her planning has been such that everything goes smoothly without visible effort. A dinner is a challenge for any hostess, and it can be fun too.

## THE COCKTAIL HOUR

The hour before dinner is, in many homes, the cocktail hour—a pleasant interlude during which guests may relax from the cares of the day and become better acquainted before they dine.

The appetizers that are served with the cocktails should be

**151**

both delicious and attractive. One or two kinds are enough—perhaps a piquant dip served with crisp crackers or potato chips, and a tiny hot appetizer such as cheese balls. Hot appetizers are better served with before-dinner cocktails than at a cocktail party, because the hostess can be reasonably sure they will be eaten before they cool.

As always, when cocktails are served, a nonalcoholic beverage should be provided for guests who prefer it. It may be a well-seasoned tomato juice, a fruit juice or tart fruit punch.

## Buffets

Buffet service fits perfectly into the relaxed, informal pattern of contemporary living. If you have limited dining space, or if you are a do-it-yourself hostess, buffet service permits you to entertain with more ease than any other type of service, and just as graciously and pleasantly.

Your buffet table may be set against a wall, or in the center of the room. For only six or eight guests, it is often placed with the long side against a wall; a larger number may need both long sides for sufficient elbow room when serving themselves. Because it presents all the food to the guests at one time and is thus the center of interest, the table should be arranged with care and artistry—and with common sense too, for the buffet table is functional and its arrangement is as important as its beauty.

The table itself should be dressed as attractively as possible, in lace, linen, or pretty place mats. And this is the time for bringing out your beautiful serving trays and plates. Flowers have an important role to play on the buffet table. If the table is against the wall, the flower arrangement may be a background for the foods; if in the center of the room, it will probably be a centerpiece. Since guests will all be standing, there is no need to keep it low. If candles are used for lighting the table, be sure to use plenty of them, placed so they really illuminate.

For the convenience of your guests, plan the arrangement of the table carefully. Confusing traffic plans should be avoided in order to help the serving line progress with ease and speed. Place a stack of large dinner plates at the point where guests are to start—probably at one end of the table. Napkins and silverware should be where they will be picked up last, after the plates are filled. Unless the guests are to eat at small tables, it is customary to serve only foods that can be eaten with a fork, since use of a knife is difficult. Rolls are usually buttered before they are put on the buffet. If you serve a tossed salad, tongs are far more easily handled than the conventional salad fork and spoon, when one hand is occupied by a plate. Since seasoning is so largely a matter of individual preference, individual salt and pepper shakers should be provided on snack tables or other convenient surfaces near the guests' chairs rather than on the buffet. A side table may hold a tray with goblets or glasses and a pitcher of iced water.

When guests have served themselves, partially emptied serving dishes should be refilled and empty ones removed from the buffet. Second servings may be passed by the hostess, or she may ask the guests to return to the buffet to serve themselves. When the first course is eaten, the buffet table is cleared, and dessert and the dishes in which it is to be served are then brought out.

The basic pattern of buffet service is varied in many ways. For the most informal type of service, guests may serve themselves with everything, even pouring their own coffee. At a semiformal buffet party, the hostess or a friend may pour the coffee at one end of the table; sometimes another friend may be asked to serve the main hot dish, if it is a casserole. Ornamental trays large enough to hold the plate and coffee cup, napkin and silverware, and water glass may be provided for the guests; the trays may be held on the guests' laps, or they may be mounted on folding legs; if trays are not provided, snack tables or card tables should be provided to set things on while guests deal with their plates on their laps. Plates and silver used in the first course may be returned by the guests (either to the kitchen, if the party is very informal, or to a table set up near the kitchen), or cleared away by the hostess or the host, or a friend. On some occasions, when space allows, a partial buffet may be preferred. Under this arrangement, guests select their food and seat themselves at

smaller tables, such as card tables, where a place is set for each one.

Courses for a buffet meal are usually limited to just two—a main course with salad and rolls, and a dessert. Dishes should be chosen that are easy to serve and that stand up well. Casserole dishes are better than delicate soufflés which need to be served immediately. A chafing dish is a great convenience on a buffet table; heat-retaining casseroles are also an aid in keeping hot food hot. Mixtures should not be too thin and runny, salads not too juicy. Tossed or molded salads are always good; fruit salad mixtures may be served in lettuce cups which can be transferred to plates.

Remember to consider eye appeal of foods as well as their taste appeal. The colors of the foods themselves as well as their arrangement on serving dishes and their garnishings are important, for a buffet meal provides almost the only opportunity for guests to see the whole menu at once. In planning for your party, be sure to estimate quantities generously, for there is something about a buffet which is irresistible to the appetite!

Larger, heartier buffet meals are sometimes served. For one such, a roast turkey may be placed at one end, and a handsomely garnished baked tender ham at the other; both of these may be set out either hot or cold, and sliced or partly sliced beforehand, or else sliced and served by the hostess's helpers. To complete this particular meal, little hot Southern biscuits are delicious, with a big relish tray of carrot sticks, celery curls, olives, cranberry jelly to go with the turkey and spiced crab apples or peaches for the ham, a platter of sliced tomatoes drizzled with French dressing, cauliflower polonaise, and lemon meringue tarts. Sumptuous!

### THE COCKTAIL PARTY

The cocktail party is a special kind of buffet party. The purpose of hors d'oeuvres at this party is a little different from the before-dinner cocktail hour, since no other food is ordinarily to be provided. A variety should be served, allowing at least five or six "pieces" for each guest. Hot hors d'oeuvres should not be attempted unless they can be served piping hot. Tiny and attractively garnished canapés are very much in order. One non-alcoholic beverage should be provided.

In keeping with the delicate and fine quality of cocktail glasses, other serving equipment and the service itself will tend to be formal rather than informal. A beautiful tablecloth, flowers, and candles form an attractive background for the hors d'oeuvres trays. Small plates may or may not be provided, but plenty of cocktail napkins should be placed at both ends of the table.

### SMÖRGÅSBORD

Best-known of all Scandinavian dining customs is the smörgåsbord—usually the prelude to the feast, but on some occasions the whole feast itself. In Sweden, where the custom is believed to have originated in the festivities of country people, the smörgåsbord is served as a first course. A small number of appetizers, which invariably include herring, are presented buffet-style to guests who relax and nibble, exchange toasts and conversation, and then assemble around the dining table with appetites pleasantly stimulated but unimpaired. In other countries, and especially in America, the character and function of the smörgåsbord have altered and it may comprise the principal part of a meal. A

155

munificent variety of fish, meat, cheese, egg, and vegetable dishes is arranged on a necessarily commodious buffet or table and guests visit it as often as they please. A dessert (by recommendation, simple) and good strong coffee bring the feast to a close.

A time-tried ritual is prescribed for the proper enjoyment of either a small smörgåsbord or the full-scale, panoramic affair. First, and always first if one is to observe the Scandinavian spirit of the occasion, the herring! Then one adventures (with clean plate in hand) through dishes in which fish is combined with other ingredients, then cold meats, the delicious hot dishes, the salads and aspics, and finally, for digestion's sake and to soothe a possibly jaded palate, a bit of cheese.

In Norway, the smörgåsbord is also called *koldt bord*. It usually consists of a few appetizers—fish, meat, and cheese —but on special occasions may be elaborate and bountiful, including roasts of meat and several kinds of fish. Roast beef tenderloin, for example, and loin of pork served with prunes and apple slices; boiled lobster with mayonnaise, whole baked or boiled salmon with sour cream; and a whole cold ham. Include parsley potatoes in the more elaborate type of smörgåsbord. Rum pudding usually rounds out these heroic collations.

A Swedish adaptation of the smörgåsbord is the gracious *supé*—a late supper served after the theater or an evening of dancing. The supé too is governed to some extent by tradition. Hot dishes are always served. They may be croustades with creamed filling, an omelet or soufflé, new potatoes with fresh dill. Breads, especially the fragrant limpa, accompany the dishes. Fish and a relish, such as sliced tomatoes, are included as a matter of course. Amounts served are not lavish. The dishes are kept small, but always garnished with the flair for beauty that characterizes Scandinavian cuisine. Cookies are sometimes included in supé and coffee is always served. To precede a Swedish dinner, a plate of three (it must be three) canapés is placed before each individual. Canapés would not be served with a smörgåsbord.

The American homemaker can make a respectable gesture toward a smörgåsbord with herring, sardines, anchovies or other small canned fish, a platter of ready-to-serve meats and cheese, and a relish or two—all of which may also be included in a much more elaborate buffet.

A word about bread and cheeses: Custom dictates that only the dark breads belong to the smörgåsbord and that knackebrod (hardtack in American parlance) should be among them. Cheese may be Swiss, Danish Bleu, Edam, goat cheese, or bond ost, but it is never proffered in slices. Guests cut it to individual preference.

### Dessert Parties

Most feminine of all forms of entertaining is probably the dessert party. There are a dozen excuses for it: a club meeting in the home, an afternoon of bridge, a shower for bride- or baby-to-be, the introduction of a newcomer in the neighborhood to your friends. It's a gay sort of affair, usually given in the afternoon when the men are away, but occasionally late of an evening when they may possibly be persuaded to participate. And it calls for your most special magic to produce a really breath-taking pièce de résistance.

The dessert's the thing—for a dessert party is not and should not be a meal, but merely a gesture of dainty, delectable hospitality. The whole menu served at the dessert party need consist of no more than the dessert itself— eye-appealing, taste tempting, and irresistibly delicious— with, of course, a beverage of distinction. Include salted nuts and mints if you wish.

Service for the dessert party should be of the simplest. You may have your card table or tables spread with dainty cloths and set with silver and napkins when your guests arrive; this permits your guests to finish eating and you to clear the tables before the business or pleasure of the meeting gets under way. Or finish the business first, and then set the tables, so guests may relax over your dessert masterpiece. The dessert itself may either be served and prettily garnished in the kitchen; or if the dessert is particularly beautiful, by all means display the attractively garnished platter before you serve it with a flourish.

## Serving Wine with Your Meal

Wine through the years has meant many things to many people around the world. To the average Frenchman or Italian, wine, along with bread, is almost as important as life itself and is a daily requisite at family meals.

Probably due to increased travel to foreign countries where wine is a familiar commodity, large numbers of Americans have been added to the list of wine-lovers. Today the domestic wines grown in California, New York, and Ohio compete strongly with the traditionally more famous but much more expensive imports from France, Italy, and Spain. There is one basic fact, however, which one should keep in mind—that choosing a wine is a matter of personal taste plus a consideration of the money available for purchasing it.

## WINE & FOOD CHART

| Wine Class | Best-Known Types | Wine and Food Combinations |
|---|---|---|
| Appetizer Wines | Sherry<br>Vermouth<br>Flavored wines | Serve at cocktail time, chilled, without food, or with hors d'oeuvres, nuts, cheeses |
| White Table Wines | Sauterne<br>Chablis<br>Rhine Wine | Serve well chilled with lighter dishes such as chicken, fish, shellfish, omelets, any white meat |
| Red Table Wines | Burgundy<br>Chianti<br>Claret<br>Rosé<br>"Vino" types | Serve at cool room temperature with hearty dishes such as steaks, chops, roasts, game, cheese dishes, spaghetti (Rosé with all foods) |
| Dessert Wines | Muscatel<br>Angelica<br>Cream (sweet) Sherry<br>Port<br>Tokay | Serve at dessert, chilled or at cool room temperature, with fruits, cookies, nuts, cheese, fruit cake, pound-cake |
| Sparkling Wines | Champagne<br>Pink Champagne<br>Sparkling Burgundy<br>Cold Duck | Serve well chilled with any food —appetizers, the main course, or dessert (especially good in party punches) |

## Wine-serving tips

• Wine-serving etiquette requires that the host be served first for a very practical reason—to sniff or taste the wine to check on its quality before offering it to guests.
• Wine is appreciated most when served with food, so make it easily available by placing it on the dining table.
• If served in its own bottle and if it is a wine that has to be chilled, place it in a wine cooler. If it is a red wine that should be served at room temperature, place it in a wine basket in which the bottle lies on its side. The slanting position of the bottle keeps any sediment in the bottom.
• Covering the bottle with a napkin is unnecessary as many people like to see the label to know what they are drinking. The purpose of the napkin is to keep the bottle, if iced, from

slipping in your hand, also to absorb drops of wine that might fall. If a napkin is used, hold a small one in your left hand while pouring with your right. For an elaborate table setting one might stand the bottle in an antique silver holder designed for serving wine at the table.

• The familiar rule of serving white wine with white meat and red wine with red meat should not be considered a binding one. It often needs modification, and it is the individual who must decide which wine gives him the most enjoyment with certain foods. For instance, there are wine connoisseurs who find the full red wines of Bordeaux perfect with roast chicken or some of the red wines of Burgundy good with roast turkey. A not-too-dry white wine is delightful with roast ham or a vin rosé with roast pork. A rather light red Bordeaux or a Beaujolais is a perfect foil for veal or sweetbreads. A red Bordeaux also goes well with roast leg of lamb and a full-flavored red Burgundy adds to the enjoyment of a good lamb stew.

• Vins rosé are in a class by themselves and are pink in color and rather light-bodied. They are usually considered to be compatible with all types of food, but this, too, is just a generalization.

• There is an old saying that no aged wine should ever be served over 72°F. Today, it is customary to serve red wines at room temperature (meaning 65° to 75°F), dry wines and vins rosé cooled, and sweet wines and champagne cooler still. It is said that no wine should be icy-cold as it deadens the taste. Here again one must add that many wine drinkers find white wines and rosés much more refreshing when thoroughly chilled.

• Wine left in the bottle after a meal may be "held over" as long as it is used within a week and provided the wine, if it had been chilled, remains chilled. If there is no sediment in the bottom of the bottle the wine may be used also for cooking.

• The so-called cooking wines obtainable at the market should be avoided unless their quality is comparable to a good table wine. As wine users know, the alcohol in the wine, also the water, evaporates during the cooking process and all that remains in the food is the flavor. Since that is the reason for adding the wine in the first place one must be sure the flavor is a pleasant one. It should be added here that wine labeled "cooking wine" indicates that salt has been added. Therefore, if this type is used in recipes, it is often necessary to adjust the amount of salt called for in the recipe. Wine with

**159**

salt added is unpalatable for drinking, and it is said that the practice developed in restaurants to discourage the employees from drinking wine intended for cooking.

• When serving more than one wine at a meal a dryer wine should precede a sweeter one and a lighter wine come before a heavier one.

### Wine Glasses

To play up the beautiful color and the delightful bouquet of good wine to best advantage, use a stemmed glass made of clear crystal, at least 6-ounce capacity and tulip-shaped. A large bowl enables the taster to swirl the wine around in the glass which should not be filled more than half. The tapering of the glass at the top serves as a sort of chimney allowing the wine bouquet to rise up to the nose as one sniffs the wine. Many connoisseurs still prefer to serve wine in the traditional Rhine wine römer. If your budget and storage space are limited, select one wine glass appropriate for most types of wine. Champagne, however, requires a special type of glass. Be sure that wine glasses are always sparkling clean and free of any detergent odors.

Written by
RICHARD EKSMED

# Basic
# Tools

# Contents

**STARTING YOUR TOOL COLLECTION** .......... **163**
    Your Most Valuable Tools ................... **163**
    Tool Storage ............................ **164**

**CERTAIN BASIC SAFETY TIPS** ................. **164**

**YOUR FIRST TOOLBOX** ..................... **165**

**BUYING TOOLS** .......................... **165**
    Hammers ............................. **165**
    Nails and Screws ...................... **166**
    Nailsets ............................. **166**
    Screwdrivers ......................... **167**
    Pliers ............................... **168**
    Handsaws ............................ **170**
    Hand Drills .......................... **171**
    Wrenches ............................ **171**
    Utility Knife ......................... **173**
    Putty Knife .......................... **173**
    Chisels ............................. **173**
    Measuring Tools ...................... **174**
    Try Square .......................... **174**
    Levels .............................. **174**
    Force Cup ........................... **175**
    Planes .............................. **175**
    Paintbrushes ......................... **176**
    Electric Drill ........................ **177**
    Files ............................... **178**
    C-Clamp ............................ **178**
    Other Tools ......................... **178**

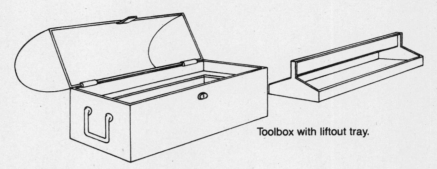

Toolbox with liftout tray.

## Starting Your Tool Collection

All the how-to talent in the world won't help you if you don't have a proper set of tools. Don't make the mistake of going out and investing a small or large fortune in whatever the local hardware store has in stock, but—if you are new to the do-it-yourself game—have on hand a few basic items. You can buy others as the need arises.

When you inhabit a furnished room or an apartment, your tool needs are few. But when you own your own home, you will find that you need a small arsenal of basic tools to take care of the place.

Never bargain-shop for tools. Don't settle for a lesser type or smaller size than you really need. And don't skimp on quality. A penny saved can mean a dollar lost—or worse. Whatever the tool, look for a sturdy body and smooth finish. Metal surfaces should be coated for rust prevention; wood parts should be varnished, waxed, or lacquered for durability and protection against splinters.

Check all moving parts of a tool before purchase to make sure that they work smoothly and easily but are free of any play or wiggle. Look for tools that are permanently marked with the manufacturer's name or symbol as an indication of careful construction and quality materials. Some quality tools even have performance warranties.

### Your Most Valuable Tools

What would you pay for the most valuable tools in the world? These tools can help you grip, grasp, push, twist, and help you operate equipment. They can distinguish temperature variations and are sensitive to touch. It is impossible to purchase such tools—they are your hands.

These fabulous tools are subject to injury by being caught in machines, cut by a variety of sharp-edged tools, crushed by whatever objects fall on them. They can be damaged by being burned, fractured, or sprained unless you are always alert.

Protect these most valuable tools, because you cannot replace them.

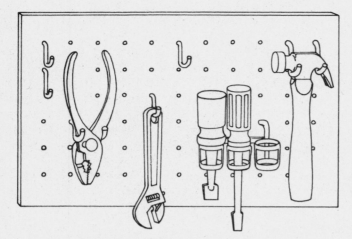

Hanging tools on perforated hardboard.

## Tool Storage

You are going to need a place to keep all those shiny new tools. The kitchen "junk" drawer might be okay to start with, but you'll soon find that the screwdriver is hopelessly entangled with string when you want it most. One of the first things you should do in your new home is to make some sort of plan for tool storage. In the beginning, as long as you have only a few tools, or if you are an apartment dweller, a simple toolbox might do. It will keep your tools in good condition, help to protect them from dust and moisture, and provide a convenient organizer, storage space, and carrying case as well.

A good start toward tool storage is also a piece of perforated cardboard (popularly known as Pegboard, a trade name). When you buy the board get one of the kits that contain hardware for attaching it to the wall as well as the hooks, hangers, and assorted accessories for accommodating various tools. Hang it in the basement or garage. Later on, you'll probably want a workbench, so make sure there is room for one underneath your storage wall.

---

### CERTAIN BASIC SAFETY TIPS

They apply to tool usage, regardless of what the tool may be.

• Never use a tool with a dulled cutting blade or bit or a loose part.
• Use tools only for the work they were intended to do. Never use a screwdriver to pry, chip, or pound; a wood bit to drill masonry or metal; pliers to pound or cut taut wire, or a wrench to hammer.

• Never expose pliers, screwdrivers, or wrenches to extreme heat; they could become weakened and suddenly give way during use.
• Do not try to repair a tool yourself unless you know what you are doing. Either buy a new one or take the crippled tool to an expert.

## Your First Toolbox

In this booklet you'll find a great number of tools described and illustrated. Which ones you need depends on how ambitious a do-it-yourselfer you are and what kinds of jobs you plan to do. If you live in an apartment we recommend a toolkit that contains: A claw hammer • Pliers • A Phillips screwdriver and a regular one • A hand drill and bits • An awl • An adjustable wrench • A plane • A utility knife • A nailset • A crosscut saw • A steel tape measure • A level • Assorted screws and nails • Glue • A paintbrush • An assortment of sandpaper grades and a holder • Assorted faucet washers • Liquid drain cleaner • A toilet plunger.

## Buying Tools

Does a devoted fisherman buy a cheap rod and reel? Does a dentist buy a bargain-basement drill? Of course not. The same attitude should apply to any tool. A good hammer is precisely tooled, properly weighted, and has maximum strength so that it will drive a nail straight, true, and fast. A cheap hammer will slip off the nail, drive it crookedly, and require more strokes. Often the head is poorly attached so that it might fly off at a crucial moment and possibly even become a lethal missile. It just isn't worth it. The same applies to all tools. So let's remember this principle and shop for:

### Hammers

There are many kinds of hammers: ball peen for metalwork, tack for upholstery, mason's for brickwork, mallets with heads of wood, plastic or rubber to drive chisels without marring the surface, sledge hammers to break up cement or blacktop, to name just a few. What most laymen, however, mean by a "hammer" is the common claw,

Ball peen hammer.

Tack hammer.

Sledge hammer.

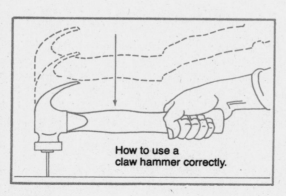

How to use a
claw hammer correctly.

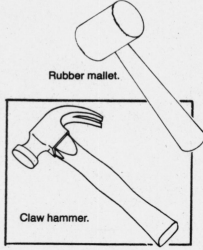

Rubber mallet.

Claw hammer.

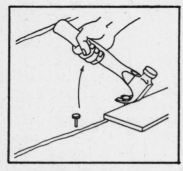

Pulling out nails with
a claw hammer.

or nail, hammer. The claw hammer is the basic hammer for jobs like whacking wood into place, but it is designed primarily for driving in or pulling out nails. The best claw hammer for general use has a 16-ounce head that is firmly attached to a wood handle, either with a solid wedge or glue on top, or both, or forged in a single piece with the handle, which is then covered with rubber, plastic, or leather for a firm grip.

To use a hammer correctly, grip it at or near the end of the handle and swing it from your shoulder. You may miss the nail at first, but keep trying (on scrap wood) until you get the "swing" of it. It's well worth the practice.

## Nails and Screws

Box nail.

Finishing nail.

Screws.

Nails come in two shapes: box nails and finishing nails. Box nails have large heads. Use them for rough work when appearance doesn't matter. Finishing nails have very small heads. You can drive them below the surface with a nailset or another nail, and cover them. Use them where appearance is important, as in putting up paneling or building shelves.

Screws are best where holding strength is important. Use them to install towel bars, curtain rods, to repair drawers, or to mount hinges. Where screws work loose, you can refill the holes with matchsticks or wood putty and replace them.

## Nailsets

A nailset is used to drive finishing nailheads below the surface of woodwork (paneling, floorboards, etc). After the nailhead disappears below the surface, the hole is filled with putty or cement. Nailsets are made to suit different sizes of nailheads, ranging from $1/32$ inch to $5/32$ inch. The nail is usually driven with a nail hammer up to slightly above the surface to prevent possible marring of the wood with the hammer; then the nailset, which has a tip slightly smaller than the head of the nail, is used.

Driving finishing nails
with nailset.

## Screwdrivers

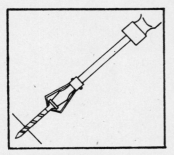

Screwdriver with clip
to hold screws.

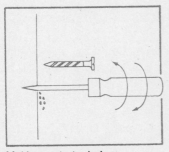

Making a starter hole
with an awl.

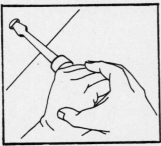

Use two hands on screwdriver.

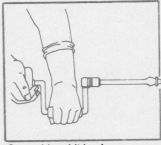

Screwdriver bit in place.

Another familiar tool is the screwdriver, designed to provide good turning leverage for driving and removing screws. It comes in two basic styles. The flat-tip style is for the single slot screws used in walls, woodwork, and furniture. The Phillips fits the cross-slotted screws found on many home appliances. If you don't own at least one of each, you should buy them, keeping the following points in mind.

The most generally useful flat-tip model has a wedge-shaped end about ¼ inch wide and a blade about 6 inches long. A No. 2 Phillips with a 4-inch blade works on most cross-slotted screws. Either style should have a large, fluted handle with a gently rounded butt end for firm, comfortable gripping. If compact storage is desirable, look for a model with a detachable, reversible blade — flat-tipped at one end and Phillips style at the other.

Assorted tip sizes and blade lengths may be a good investment if you use tools often. A flat-tip driver wider than the screw will scar the surrounding surface; a tip too narrow gives poor leverage and may damage the screw slot. Shorter blades are helpful in cramped quarters. Either prepackaged sets or three flat-tipped drivers — 4, 6, and 8 inches — plus No. 1 and No. 2 Phillips meet most household needs.

A screwdriver is simple to use once the screw is started. Many novices try to use the screwdriver without starting the hole first. This may sometimes work in soft wood but is virtually impossible in hard wood. Use an awl, a nail, or a tool specifically designed for starting screws. Many old-timers start the screw by banging it in with a hammer, but this often results in damage and hard-to-work screw slots. It is helpful to hold the blade and screw head together in the beginning. This is not always possible, however, and some screwdrivers have metal clips over the blade that hold the screw head to the blade for use in hard-to-reach areas. Firm pressure should be applied against the screw during driving to keep the blade in place. When the wood is very hard, it is wise to predrill the entire hole. Special drill bits are available for this purpose, matching screw sizes. It sometimes helps to use both hands once the screw is started, one turning the handle, and the other held flat against the end of it to apply more pressure.

It is easy to remove screws once you get them loosened. The trouble, again, is getting them started, or "broken." Don't forget

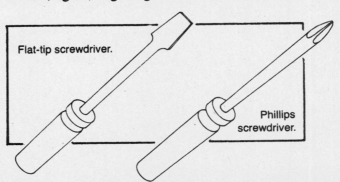

Flat-tip screwdriver.

Phillips screwdriver.

Multipurpose pliers.

Locking pliers.

Water-pump pliers.

that screws are driven in clockwise and removed counterclockwise. If a screw won't budge, give it a quick twist in both directions. For larger stubborn screws, a screwdriver bit in a brace provides extra leverage.

## Pliers

Pliers are probably the most misunderstood and misused of all tools. They are used as substitutes for hammers, wrenches, bottle openers, and who knows what else. When properly applied they can perform many holding and gripping operations.

There are numerous types of pliers, most of them used by specialists such as electricians and electronics workers. The kind the homeowner uses most often is the slip-joint pliers. It performs numerous holding tasks — and is often the wrong tool for the job. Pliers are not really designed for tightening and loosening nuts — wrenches are. Yet this is a common household use, and it will do if you don't have the right wrench in your toolbox.

The slip-joint pliers *is* the right tool for grasping, turning, bending, or pulling bolts, wires, broken glass, and sharp or small objects. The term "slip-joint" is applied because the tool has two slots in which the center fastener pin can be located. In one slot, the pliers grip small objects with the forward jaws tight and parallel. When the pin is in the other slot, the concave inner jaws can go around larger objects. Some pliers have cutting jaws just inside the curved portion. These are for cutting wires, small nails, etc.

When shopping for pliers, choose ones that have been drop-forged and have either a polished surface or a bluish-black sheen. The pin should be solidly fastened so that you can't remove it. The outer parallel jaws should have fine grooves or cross-hatching, the inner ones sharp, rugged teeth. Handles should be scored or tooled so that you can grip them firmly.

Specialized pliers for plumbing repairs are water-pump pliers, channel-lock pliers, and locking pliers.

The water-pump pliers are designed for tightening or removing water-pump packing nuts. One jaw is adjustable to several different positions. The inner surface of the jaws consists of a series of deep grooves adapted to grasping cylindrical objects.

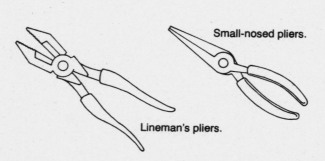

Small-nosed pliers.

Lineman's pliers.

Channel-lock pliers.

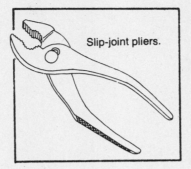

Slip-joint pliers.

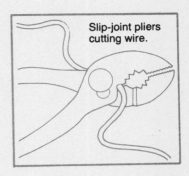

Slip-joint pliers cutting wire.

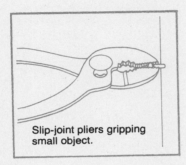

Slip-joint pliers gripping small object.

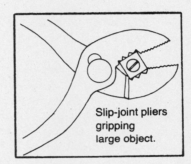

Slip-joint pliers gripping large object.

Channel-lock pliers are similar to water-pump pliers, but the jaw-opening adjustment is different. Lands (raised areas) on one jaw fit into grooves on the other. Channel-lock pliers are less likely to slip from the adjustment setting than water-pump pliers, but they are less effective as a wrench and should be used only where it is impossible to fit a wrench.

Locking pliers are very useful when working with small-diameter pipe. They can be clasped on an object and will stay by themselves, leaving your hands free for other work. The jaw opening is adjusted by turning a thumbscrew at the end of one handle.

Specialized pliers for electrical repairs are small-nosed pliers, lineman's pliers, and multipurpose pliers.

Small-nosed pliers (sometimes called needle-nosed pliers) have narrow, tapered jaws to make it easy to bend wire into loops around terminals and to reach into such tight quarters as switch and outlet boxes. The better ones have insulated handles to help protect against shock.

Lineman's pliers are heavy-duty pliers used for firmly gripping cable, connectors, and the like. They also have side jaws that are used for cutting wire.

There are several varieties of multipurpose electrician's pliers. All have as their purpose the combining of as many operations as possible into one tool. The tool usually operates as a pliers, stripper, crimper, and cutter. It may also do other jobs, depending on the model.

## Handsaws

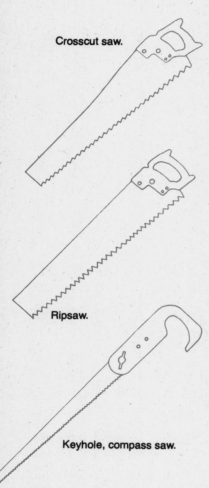

Crosscut saw.

Ripsaw.

Keyhole, compass saw.

Saws, too, come in a wide variety of sizes and types. The homeowner should purchase an 8- or 10-point crosscut saw for all-around work. The "8-point" means that there are 8 teeth per inch. "Crosscut" means that the teeth are beveled slightly outward and knife-shaped, designed for cutting across the grain of the wood — the most common type of cut.

A ripsaw has squarish, chisellike teeth, and it cuts with the grain. Most do-it-yourselfers have little need for a ripsaw. If you must do a lot of ripping, a power saw of some kind is preferred.

A hacksaw is used for cutting metals and some plastics. It has a wide U-shaped frame with devices on each end for holding the removable, fine-toothed saw blade. A thumbscrew draws the blade taut.

A coping saw is somewhat similar in design to a hacksaw, except that the blade is much thinner and has larger teeth. A coping saw blade can be turned to various angles for making curving cuts in wood.

Keyhole and compass saws are similar, with the keyhole blade being thinner and finer. Both are used to make curving cuts and small cuts when only one side of the work is accessible, such as in paneling, wallboard, and similar materials that are already nailed up.

The backsaw is made in 10- to 16-inch lengths, usually with 12 or 13 teeth per inch. It is designed for joint-cutting work, for smooth cuts with or across the grain. A longer version of the backsaw with 11 teeth per inch is the miter box saw.

When buying a saw, look for a tempered steel or chrome-nickel blade. Handles should be removable hardwood or high-impact plastic. Better saws have taper-ground blades, and some have a Teflon coating for rust resistance and less binding.

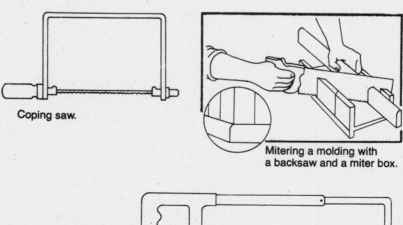

Coping saw.

Mitering a molding with
a backsaw and a miter box.

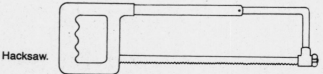

Hacksaw.

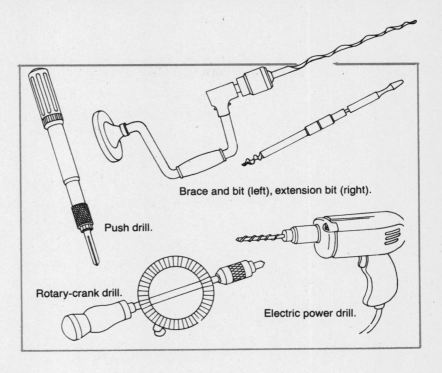

Push drill.

Brace and bit (left), extension bit (right).

Rotary-crank drill.

Electric power drill.

## Hand Drills

To insert long screws or bolts into or through wood or wallboard, you first need to make neat, straight holes for them. Either a rotary cranking or a push-style hand drill can do the job. Each is sold with interchangeable bits for making holes at least ¾ inch deep and up to ¼ inch wide. The handles are hollow for bit storage, and replacement bits are available at most hardware stores.

The rotary-cranking style is easy to control and versatile. By turning a crank you set gears in motion to activate the bit at any speed you want. The drill chuck holds bits of many sizes and types. However, a quality model is nearly a foot long and weighs several pounds; it is bulky to store.

The push drill is generally less than a foot long and under a pound in weight. Forward or downward pressure on the handle activates an inner spiral, or ratchet, that turns the bit. Some have a reverse mechanism that allows a bit to be backed out of a deep hole or one in which it is stuck.

The use of an electric drill makes jobs go faster and easier (but also noisier). However, it's not much good if electricity is not available. In that case, or if you do not yet have an electric drill, a brace and bit can do the same job as a power drill because it provides more leverage than any other hand drill.

## Wrenches

There are probably more types of wrenches than of any other tool. There are open-end and box wrenches, some with a combination of each, and some with half-boxes. (A box wrench completely encloses the nut.) There are ratchet wrenches that are turned like a crank, pipe wrenches, chain wrenches, and countless others.

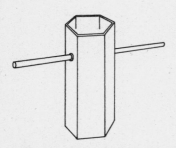

Packing nut socket wrench.

Your first wrench acquisition should be an adjustable wrench. These come in various sizes, but one about 8 inches long, with jaw capacity up to an inch, is a good starter. This wrench has one fixed jaw and another that is moved away from or toward the fixed jaw by means of a knurled knob.

The adjustable open-end wrench is used on square or hexagonal nuts and for working on the interior parts of many types of faucets and valves. If you buy more than one wrench, a 12-inch one is good for most minor plumbing jobs and a 6-inch wrench comes in handy for smaller work.

Place the wrench on the nut so that you pull the handle toward the side with the adjustable jaw. This will prevent the jaw from opening and slipping off the nut. Be sure that the nut is all the way into the throat of the jaws, and that the jaws are adjusted to fit snugly around the nut. Otherwise, you may damage the nut or valve.

A monkey wrench is used for the same purpose and in the same way as the adjustable open-end wrench. Force is applied to the back of the handle — the side of the wrench opposite the jaw opening.

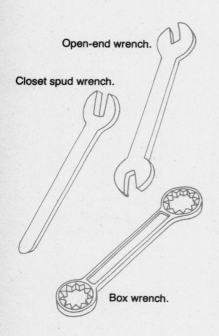

Open-end wrench.

Closet spud wrench.

Box wrench.

In buying a wrench, look for a drop-forged, alloy steel wrench with a chrome-polished or blue-black sheen. The jaws should be exactly parallel and not loose (check that by wiggling the movable jaw). Some have a locking device that holds the adjustable jaw in a constant position.

Fixed wrenches (open-end and box) are of a specific size and cannot be adjusted. When you buy fixed wrenches, get a quality set of graduated sizes. For working in tight places, special thin open-end wrenches, called closet spud wrenches, are particularly helpful.

Packing nut socket wrenches come in various sizes to fit tub and shower faucet assemblies. Hexagonal in shape and with a hollow core, this type of wrench fits over the faucet stem to remove the valve packing nuts and stem assembly. Since these parts are made of brass, ordinary wrenches should not be used on them. Application of too much pressure will bend or break the fittings, which are very difficult to replace since they are inside the wall. It is far cheaper to buy and use the right wrench for the job than to have to tear apart the wall.

Right and wrong way to use an adjustable open-end wrench.

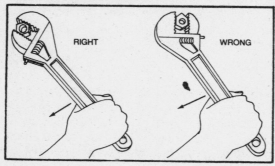

RIGHT    WRONG

Right and wrong way to use a monkey wrench.

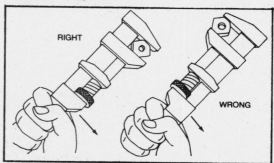

RIGHT    WRONG

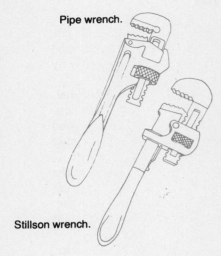

Pipe wrench.

Stillson wrench.

Pipe wrenches are adjustable wrenches designed to grip round surfaces. There are several types: the strap wrench for working with brass, aluminum, soft metal, or plastic pipe, the chain wrench used on large-diameter pipe, such as cast-iron drain pipe, and many others. In a narrower sense, the term "pipe wrench" is used to designate one particular type. This type of wrench has hardened steel jaws that provide excellent bite and grip. It is often called a Stillson wrench, which is only a slight misnomer. The main difference between a pipe wrench and a Stillson wrench is that the latter has a separate housing in which the adjusting nut operates. In both types the movable jaw is pivoted to permit a gripping action on the work. Both are used for working with steel or iron pipe.

Pipe wrenches come in many sizes. For small pipe work, a 6-inch or 8-inch length is best. For pipe in the ½-inch to 1½-inch range, a 12-inch or 14-inch wrench should be used. For pipe up to 2 inches, the wrench should be 18 inches long.

Two wrenches are needed in most applications, unless the work is held in a vise. One is used to hold the pipe, the other turns the fitting. Pipe wrenches work in one direction only, so they are placed on the work in opposing directions.

## Utility Knife

The small, sharp blade of the utility knife held firmly by a sturdy handle can save you time and effort in cutting twine, trimming carpet, tile or wallpaper, and opening cartons. It is specially designed to lessen the chance of cutting accidents during handyman jobs and is an excellent safety investment for your toolbox.

Look for a utility knife with a single-edge, replaceable blade held securely by a screw at the throat of the handle. The handle should be shaped to fit your hand and hollow for the storage of extra blades. Some handles have a push-button to retract the blade or extend it for conveniently cutting different thicknesses.

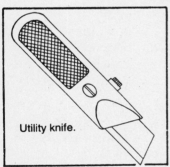

Utility knife.

## Putty Knife

A putty knife helps you attain a smooth finish when spreading spackling compound into chipped spots or small holes in walls, applying putty to window frames, or inserting grout between tiles. Those with stiffer blades can also be used for minor scraping of paint, plaster, or adhesive.

The thin, polished blade should have a blunt end and no sharp edges; it should be firmly attached to the handle by two rivets or eyelets. A good style for general use has a blade about 3 inches wide and is about 7 inches long.

## Chisels

A wood chisel consists of a steel blade usually fitted with a wooden or plastic handle. It has a single beveled cutting edge on the end of the blade. According to construction, chisels are divided into two general classes: tang chisels, in which part of the chisel enters the handle, and socket chisels, in which the handle enters into a part

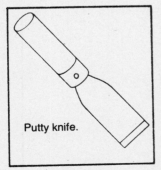

Putty knife.

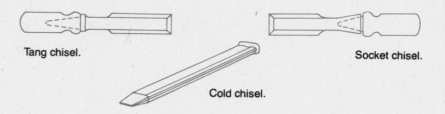

Tang chisel.

Socket chisel.

Cold chisel.

of the chisel. A socket chisel is designed for striking with a wooden mallet (never a steel hammer), whereas a tang chisel is designed for hand use only.

Wood chisels are also divided into types, depending on their weight and thickness, the shape or design of the blade, and the work they are intended to do. For general household use, a ½-inch or ¾-inch paring chisel is probably best. It has a relatively thin blade and is beveled along the sides.

Another type of chisel for exterior work is the cold chisel. This is made of hardened, tempered alloy steel and is used for striking steel, concrete, stone, and other hard materials. A cold chisel is struck with a ball peen or other heavy hammer.

## Measuring Tools

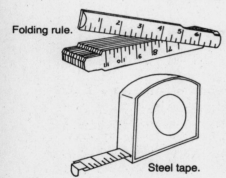

Folding rule.

Steel tape.

A 6-foot folding rule is a good all-around measuring device. The readings are large and easily read, and some have red markings every 16 inches (the standard "centering" for framing).

A steel tape that is rigid when extended but flexible enough to retract into a small case is especially convenient if you work without a helper. A 10-foot model with a ½-inch blade is useful for home purposes. The tape is marked in inches and $1/16$-inch intervals and ends in a hook that holds onto objects being measured. The case should prevent the extended tape from turning over and should have measuring marks that can be read as an extension of the tape. Many cases have a friction lock to hold the tape at a desired length.

## Try Square

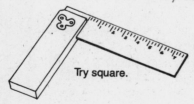

Try square.

The try square consists of two parts at right angles to each other: a thick wood or iron stock and a thin steel blade. Most try squares are made with the blades graduated in inches and fractions of an inch. The blade length varies from 2 to 12 inches. This tool is used for setting or checking lines or surfaces that have to be at right angles to each other.

## Levels

The carpenter's level is a tool designed to determine whether a plane or surface is true horizontal or true vertical. It is a simple instrument consisting of a liquid, such as alcohol or chloroform, partially filling a glass vial or tube so that a bubble remains. The vial is mounted in a frame of aluminum, magnesium, or wood. Levels

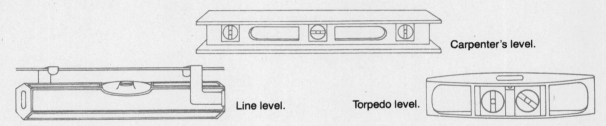
Carpenter's level.

Line level.

Torpedo level.

Bell-shaped force cup.

are usually equipped with two or more vials. One vial is built into the frame at right angles to another. The vial is slightly curved, causing the bubble always to seek the highest point in the tube. On the outside of the vial are two sets of gradation lines separated by a space. Leveling is established when the air bubble is centered between the gradation lines.

There are several other types of level. A torpedo level is useful in tight places. It has a top-reading vial so that you can place it on a low or deep surface and tell whether it's level without bending way down to look at it. A line level hooks onto a piece of twine or string and is useful when working with concrete forms, brick, and similar jobs where lines are used.

## Force Cup

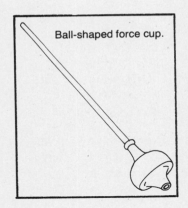
Ball-shaped force cup.

Aptly called "the plumber's helper," a force cup is the well-known tool of first defense against clogged sink or bathtub drains and overflowing toilets. By providing pressure and suction into stopped-up pipes, it can help you avoid water damage or costly plumber's bills.

Force cups are available with either a bell- or ball-shaped flexible cup screwed onto a wood handle. A ball-shaped style with a 2-foot handle is satisfactory for most households. It has a smaller end opening than the more conventional bell-shaped model for easier insertion in toilet discharge pipes, but it can also be conveniently used on drains.

## Planes

The plane is the most extensively used of the hand shaving tools. Most of the lumber handled by anyone working with wood is dressed on all four sides, but when performing jobs such as fitting doors and sash and interior trim work, planes must be used.

Bench and block planes are designed for general purpose smoothing and squaring. Other planes are designed for special types of surface work.

For your basic toolbox buy a block plane, the smallest (about 6 inches long). Its blade is mounted bevel up at a low angle, and it is used for smoothing all plane surfaces on very small work. It can also be used for cross-grain squaring of end-stock. The angle of the blade can be adjusted with the adjustment screw. Make sure before starting to plane that the iron is sharp.

Block plane.

# Paintbrushes

Flagged bristles.

Wall brushes.

Pressing the brush on a surface to test for bounce.

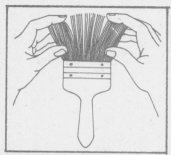
Fan brush to check for loose bristles.

Your basic toolbox should contain at least one good brush. If you should, however, decide to paint your house, rooms, or furniture, one brush certainly won't do the job.

Quality is a very important factor in selecting a brush, regardless of the size or style needed for a particular project. A good brush will hold more paint and enable you to apply the paint more smoothly and with less effort.

All good brushes have bristles that are "flagged," a term denoting splits on the bristle end. The more "flags" the better, as they help retain paint. Hog bristle is naturally flagged; synthetic bristle is artificaly flagged or split.

Test for "bounce" by brushing bristles against the back of your hand. In a good brush, the bristles will feel elastic and springy. When the brush is gently pressed on any surface, the bristles will not fan out excessively.

Check the setting. Bristles should be solidly set to prevent any chance of fallout during painting. Jar the brush and fan the bristles. Any loose bristles will be apparent. The metal band holding the bristles is called a ferrule. Stainless steel and aluminum are generally used on better-grade brushes for greater resistance to corrosion.

Both the surface area and type of paint determine the size and style of brush to be used. Calcimine brushes with very long, tough, and elastic gray hog bristles are best for applying water-thinned paints to large areas. Enamel and varnish brushes, both flat and chisel-shaped, are best for applying oil-based paints and lacquers. The shape and length of the latter type help secure a smoother flow and prevent lap marks.

The following brush styles and sizes are recommended for most painting projects around the home:
• Flat wall brushes: sizes vary from 3 to 6 inches in width with thicknesses of ¾ to 1½ inches and bristles from 2 to 7 inches long. They are best suited for painting large surfaces such as walls, ceilings, and floors.
• Varnish brushes: sizes range from 1 to 3½ inches in width, with

Flat, chisel-shaped varnish brushes.

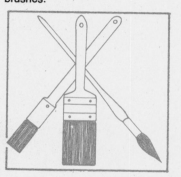
Sash, trim, artist's brushes.

bristles from 2 to 4½ inches long. They are ideally suited for painting baseboards, window frames, narrow boards, or enameling and varnishing furniture and small panels.
• Round sash and flat trim brushes: sizes range from 1 to 1½ inches in width. Trellises, screens, small pipes, toys, and all small areas are best painted with sash, trim, or even artist's brushes.

In addition to these general styles, most dealers carry special brushes for bronzing, roofing, stippling, and stenciling.

A quality brush is a fine tool and should be properly used and cared for. For example, a wide brush should never be used to paint pipes and similar surfaces. This causes the brush to "fishtail." A brush should never be left standing on its bristles. The weight causes the edge to bend and curl, ruining the fine painting tips.

Always clean a brush while it is still soft after painting. Once it is thoroughly cleaned it should be properly stored. For long-term storage, make sure that the bristles are completely dry, then wrap the brush in foil or heavy paper. Hang by the handle in an out-of-the-way place.

## Electric Drill

An electric drill can do so many jobs that it is almost a must in the do-it-yourselfer's toolbox. With it you can make holes in almost any material. By using its accessories and attachments you can sand, polish, grind, buff, stir paint, and drive screws.

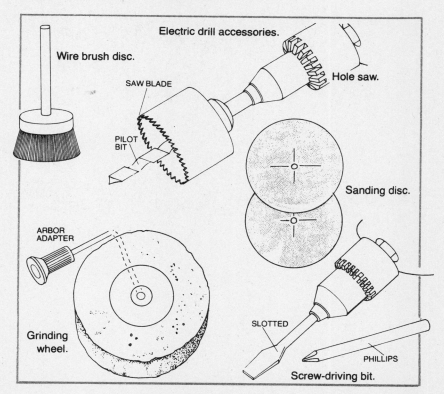

Electric drill accessories.

Wire brush disc.

SAW BLADE

Hole saw.

PILOT BIT

Sanding disc.

ARBOR ADAPTER

Grinding wheel.

SLOTTED

PHILLIPS

Screw-driving bit.

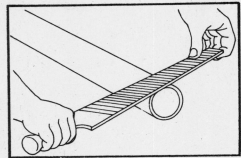

Filing burrs from
end of a cut pipe.

## Files

A toolkit is not complete unless it contains at least one if not an assortment of files. A number of different types of files are in common use, and each type may range in length from 3 to 18 inches.

Files are graded according to the degree of fineness and according to whether they have single- or double-cut teeth. The selection of files calls for matching the file to the job and to the material on which it is used.

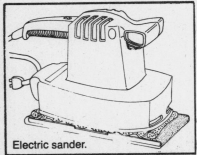

C-clamp.

## C-Clamp

Named for the shape of its frame, the C-clamp holds work in place or presses two pieces together for gluing. It is handy when you use adhesive to repair furniture or objects made of metal or plastic.

A 6-inch, light-duty type with an extra-deep opening can accommodate fairly large items but adjusts by means of a screw for smaller work. A sliding handle turns the screw to tighten the clamp, and a swivel button prevents the screw end from marring the work surface. For many jobs you will need a pair.

## Other Tools

There are literally hundreds of specialized tools that you may use for specific tasks. Buy these as the need arises, as your skills increase, and as you undertake more detailed work around the house — especially if you begin making improvements as well as routine repairs. Power tools will make your work easier and the results better. The ones you will probably buy are: a saber saw, for fast cutting of curved and straight lines in wood and other materials; a circular saw for extensive cutting of straight lines and invaluable for major jobs such as installing wood siding; and an electric sander, for smooth, speedy removal of wood, paint, or anything else removable by regular sandpaper.

Electric sander.

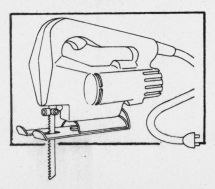

Circular saw.

Saber saw.

**Written by**
**DONALD F. LOW**

# Interior
# Home
# Repairs

# Contents

**FIX-IT-YOURSELF!** . . . . . . . . . . . . . . . . . . . . . . . . . . . **181**

Leaky Faucet . . . . . . . . . . . . . . . . . . . . . . . . . . . **181**

Noisy Faucet . . . . . . . . . . . . . . . . . . . . . . . . . . . **182**

Clogged Toilet . . . . . . . . . . . . . . . . . . . . . . . . . . **183**

Frozen Pipe . . . . . . . . . . . . . . . . . . . . . . . . . . **184**

Clogged Sink Drain . . . . . . . . . . . . . . . . . . . . . **184**

Blown Fuse . . . . . . . . . . . . . . . . . . . . . . . . . . . **186**

Damaged Electric Plug or Cord . . . . . . . . . . . . . **187**

Broken Electric Bulb . . . . . . . . . . . . . . . . . . . . **189**

Damaged Cord of a Table Lamp . . . . . . . . . . . . **190**

Damaged Lamp Socket . . . . . . . . . . . . . . . . . . **191**

Broken Window . . . . . . . . . . . . . . . . . . . . . . . . **192**

Damaged Screen . . . . . . . . . . . . . . . . . . . . . . . **194**

Sticking Window . . . . . . . . . . . . . . . . . . . . . . . **195**

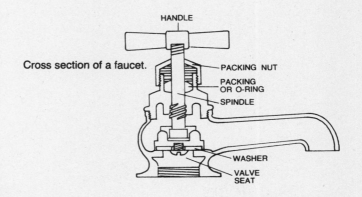

Cross section of a faucet.

HANDLE

PACKING NUT

PACKING
OR O-RING

SPINDLE

WASHER

VALVE
SEAT

## Fix-It-Yourself!

No matter how well your house or apartment is built or how well made and expensive the fixtures are, things will go wrong occasionally. "Fix-it-yourself " has become a way of life for a generation of Americans. Some of them derive pleasure from working with tools; for most, however, it has become a necessity because the neighborhood handyman-for-hire either doesn't come or has become prohibitively expensive.

In this booklet is a selection of simple home repairs that can be executed with the most basic tools.

Every effort has been made to insure the accuracy of the information and instructions. However, we are not infallible, and neither are you. We cannot guarantee that there are no human or typographical errors herein, nor can we guarantee that you will not err in following our directions. We only hope that, if this happens, it will not discourage you from trying again.

### LEAKY FAUCET

**The problem:** A leaky faucet wastes water • The dripping water may discolor the sink • The noise of a dripping faucet can cause daytime irritation and nighttime insomnia.

**Tools you need to fix it:** A screwdriver • An adjustable wrench • Assorted sizes of washers.

Fig. 2

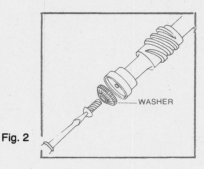

WASHER

Fig. 3

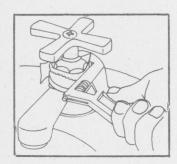

Fig. 1

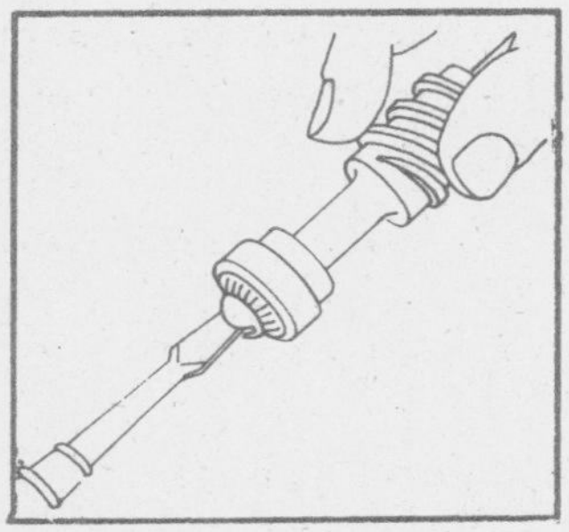

**The basic steps:**

1. Shut off the water supply at the supply stop in the line below the faucet (the valve nearest to the faucet to be repaired). Then turn on the faucet until the water stops running.

2. Loosen packing nut with wrench (fig. 1). Wrap the nut with tape or rags to protect the chrome finish before you start.

3. Remove the faucet stem or spindle (fig. 2). Use the handle to pull out the unit.

4. Remove the screw that holds the washer at bottom of the valve unit (fig. 3).

5. Put in new washer and replace screw (fig. 4).

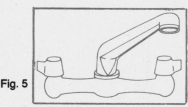

Fig. 4

6. Put valve unit back in faucet and turn the handle to the proper position.

7. Turn on the water at the shut-off valve.

**Note:** Mixing faucets, used on sinks and bathtubs, are actually two separate units (fig. 5) with the same spout. If leaking occurs, each unit must be repaired separately.

Fig. 5

## NOISY FAUCET

If a faucet squeals or chatters when you turn it on or off, take it apart as described above and check whether the washer is tightly screwed to the stem. Replace the washer if it is worn, even if the faucet does not leak.

If the stem of the faucet can be moved up and down, the threads are probably worn and the old stem must be replaced with a new one.

# CLOGGED TOILET

**The problem:** When you flush the toilet, the water level in the bowl rises rather than recedes.

**Tools you need to fix it:** A plunger • A closet auger • An adjustable wrench.

**The basic steps:**

1. Place the plunger over the discharge opening in the toilet bowl and work it vigorously up and down. This should clear the stoppage (fig. 1).

2. If this does not help, try the auger, commonly called a snake. (Be careful not to scratch the inside of the toilet bowl.) Work the snake into the trap and crank it in one direction until it becomes tight (fig. 2). Pull it back; often it will bring the obstruction with it. If it doesn't, try again, cranking the snake until it pushes through and clears the stoppage.

3. If this also fails, bail out as much water as possible from the bowl and soak up the rest with rags.

4. Remove the toilet from the floor, using the wrench to loosen the bolts (fig. 3).

5. Put the toilet (upside down) on a piece of paper to the side.

6. Work the obstruction out through the discharge opening.

7. If it has already passed into the waste line and is stuck there, work it out with the snake (fig. 4).

8. Put the toilet back in place.

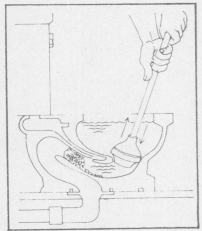

Fig. 1

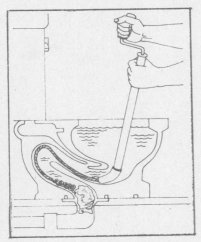

Fig. 2

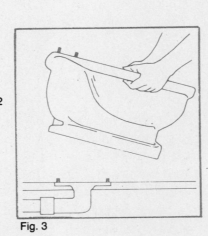

Fig. 3

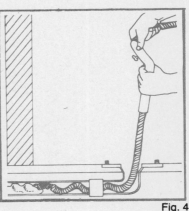

Fig. 4

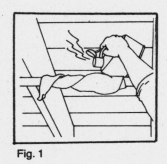

Fig. 1

Fig. 2

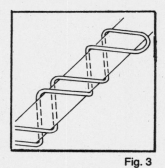

Fig. 3

## FROZEN PIPE

**The problem:** No water runs through the pipe • Pipes may burst • The joints may be forced open.

**Tools you need to fix it:** A kettle with boiling water • A piece of burlap or cloth • A blowtorch • Electric heating cable.

**The basic steps:**
1. Open all faucets in the frozen line.
2. Wrap cloth or burlap around the pipe and pour boiling water over it (fig. 1). Keep on doing so until the water in the line is flowing freely.
3. The use of a blowtorch or propane torch (fig. 2) might be faster, but use it only if the pipe is in an absolutely safe location away from flammable walls or other materials.
4. If you use a torch, don't concentrate on a single spot; rather move it along the pipe toward an open faucet, so that steam generated within the pipe can escape.
5. Use of electric heating cable is the best method of thawing frozen pipes, because the entire length of the pipe is thawed at the same time (fig. 3).

## CLOGGED SINK DRAIN

**The problem:** The sink may overflow.

**Tools you need to fix it:** Dry or liquid chemical drain cleaner • A plunger or a force pump • An auger • An adjustable wrench.

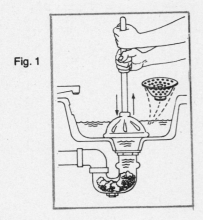

Fig. 1

**The basic steps:**

1. If the drain is not completely clogged, try running scalding water into it for several minutes.

2. If this doesn't work, use a chemical drain cleaner, following manufacturer's instructions.

3. If this helps, flush the drain for several minutes with hot water.

4. If the chemical doesn't work, remove the strainer from the drain and use the plunger. Make sure there is enough water in the sink to cover the plunger, providing a good seal. Work the plunger up and down until the drain is cleared and the water runs out normally (fig. 1).

5. If you prefer to use a force pump rather than the plunger, place it squarely over the drain, covered with enough water to make a firm seal.

6. Pump the handle to clear away the obstruction by air pressure (fig. 2).

7. If neither plunger nor force pump does the job, look for the cleanout plug under the sink. Place a pail below it to catch the water. Remove the plug and try to clear away the obstruction (fig. 3).

8. If that doesn't work, or if there is no cleanout plug, loosen the slipnuts with the wrench and remove the trap (fig. 4).

9. If the stoppage is in the trap, remove it. If not, use the drain auger, feeding it into the drain line.

10. Rotate the auger repeatedly until the obstruction is cleared (fig. 5).

11. Reassemble the trap and run scalding water down the drain for several minutes.

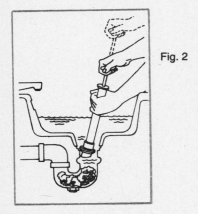

Fig. 2

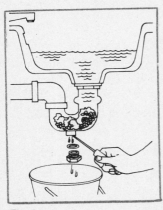

Fig. 3

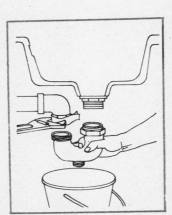

Fig. 4

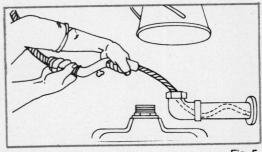

Fig. 5

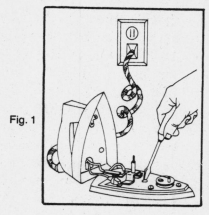

Fig. 1

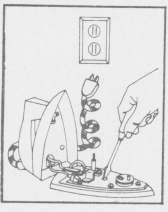

Fig. 2

**Note for electrical repairs:** When you make a mistake in plumbing repairs, you might get wet, you might flood the basement or even the house, but it's unlikely that you would drown. Making electrical repairs, however, leaves no margin for error. If you mess up here it could result in fire, serious injury, or worse.

Always exercise a healthy respect and never "play around" with electricity.

Never work on an appliance that is plugged in (fig. 1); always disconnect the appliance first (fig. 2).

## BLOWN FUSE

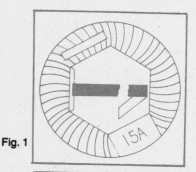

Fig. 1

Fig. 2

**The problem:** A portion of your electrical system is off
• Lamps or appliances do not work.

**Materials you need to fix it:** A set of fuses of the same amperage that you have in your entrance panel.

**The basic steps:**
1. Check the entrance panel for a blown fuse.
2. If the copper strip in the center of the fuse is melted apart (fig. 1), the cause is probably overload.
3. If the window of the fuse is darkened, perhaps so much that you can't even see the copper strip, a short circuit is the prime suspect (fig. 2).
4. If it is overload, disconnect some appliances. If it is a short, try to find where it is located.
5. If you have removed the possible source, replace the fuse, but always with one of the same amperage.
**Note:** It is not impossible that the temporary aberration may

have been caused by a sudden power surge. In this case merely replace the blown fuse or flip the breaker switch if you have a circuit breaker box. If the fuse does not blow again, your troubles are over.

If the entire house is plunged into darkness, either it is a general blackout or something is seriously wrong and the main fuse of the house has blown. If your neighbors *do* have light, you can exclude a general power failure and you had better call an electrician; the trouble that causes a main to blow is nothing for a do-it-yourselfer to fix.

## DAMAGED ELECTRIC PLUG OR CORD

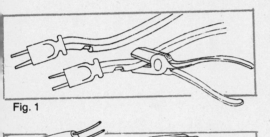

Fig. 1

**The problem:** A lamp or appliance does not work properly • A damaged plug is dangerous • A damaged or loose cord in a plug can cause a short circuit.

**Tools you need to fix it:** A new plug (if the old one cannot be used anymore) • A screwdriver • A knife or a wire stripper • A needle-nose pliers • A lineman's pliers.

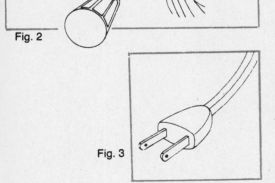

Fig. 2

**The basic steps if the plug is attached to thin, flexible cord:**
1. Cut the cord beyond the break (fig. 1).
2. Bare the wires at the end of the cord and reinstall the plug (fig. 2).
3. If the original plug was a molded one (fig. 3), do not bare the ends of the wires after having cut the cord; replace the original plug with a lever-type snap-on plug (fig. 4).

**Note:** As an alternative to the snap-on plug, you can use a squeeze-type plug: Slip body over cord (fig. 5), squeeze prongs together (fig. 6), and pull body over prongs (fig. 7).

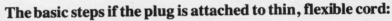

Fig. 3

Fig. 5

Fig. 6

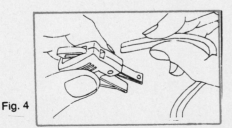

Fig. 4

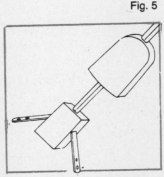

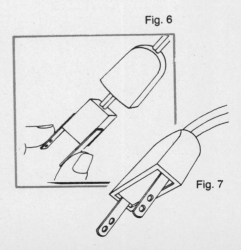

Fig. 7

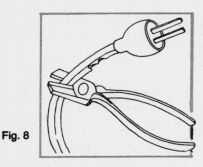

Fig. 8

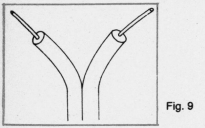

Fig. 9

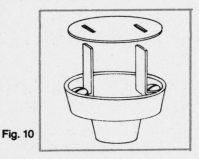

Fig. 10

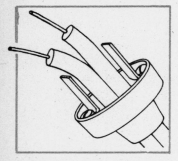

Fig. 11

## The basic steps if the plug is attached to heavy appliance cord:

1. Cut the cord above the molded plug or break in the wire (fig. 8).
2. Separate the wires at the end of the cord, and strip off about ⅝ inch of insulation of each (fig. 9). A wire stripper is the best tool for the job; if you use a knife, be careful not to cut into the wire.
3. Remove the fiber insulating cover from the prongs of the plug if it is not a molded one (fig. 10).
4. Loosen the terminal screws to release the wires, then pull off the plug.
5. Untie the Underwriter's knot, if there is one.
6. Remove the old plug and slip the new one over the cord (fig. 11).
7. Tie an Underwriter's knot: separate about 3 inches of wire. Loop the black wire behind itself and the white wire (fig. 12). Loop the white wire over the end of the black and bring it up through the black loop (fig. 13).
8. Tighten the knot and pull it down snugly into the plug body (fig. 14).
9. Bend loops in the ends of the bared wires with needle-nose pliers (fig. 15).
10. Fit the wires inside the plug and place the loops clockwise around the terminal screws (fig. 16), black to brass, white to chrome.
11. Tighten the screws and replace the fiber insulating cover over the prongs of the plug.

**Note:** Replacement of a three-prong plug is similar. Follow all steps as above. Instead of the Underwriter's knot, tie the 3 wires together in a tight knot and pull the cord until the knot is

Fig. 12

Fig. 13

Fig. 14

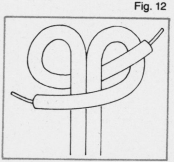

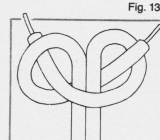

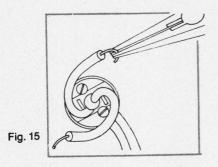

Fig. 15

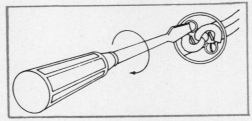

Fig. 16

snug against the plug. Loop the green wire clockwise around the green or dark-colored screw, the black wire around the brass screw, and the white wire around the chrome screw. Tighten the screws.

## BROKEN ELECTRIC BULB

**The problem:** The base of the broken bulb is stuck in the socket of the lamp.

**Tools and materials you need to fix it:** A wad of newspaper • Needle-nose pliers • A screwdriver.

**The basic steps:**
1. Unplug the lamp.
2. Wad up newspaper, press it down firmly on the broken bulb, and turn it counterclockwise until the bulb base is removed (fig. 1).
3. If this does not work because the glass is broken off right down to the base, try turning it out with needle-nose pliers (fig. 2).
4. If it still won't come out, wedge a screwdriver inside the base, pressing it against the sides while turning until the base is removed (fig. 3).

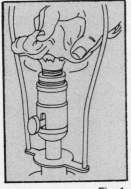

Fig. 1

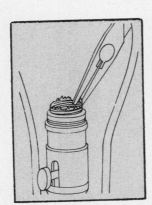

Fig. 2

Fig. 3

**The problem:** Lamp does not light or flickers • Damaged cord might cause a short circuit or even a fire.

**Tools you need to fix it:** A screwdriver • A knife • An open-end wrench.

**The basic steps:**

1. Unplug the lamp.
2. Remove shade and bulb from the lamp (fig. 1).
3. Pry off felt pad on lamp base carefully with a knife (fig. 2).
4. If the base contains a weight, remove the nut holding it in place and take the weight out (fig. 3).
5. Lift the tube that runs through the lamp body about 6 inches out of the top (fig. 4). Turn the tube counterclockwise or loosen the setscrew (or both, depending on the installation) to remove the tube from the lamp socket.
6. Press in at bottom of the socket's metal outer shell (fig. 5).
7. Lift the outer shell straight up (fig. 6).
8. Loosen the terminal screws and remove the wire (fig. 7).
9. Pull out the old cord at the bottom of the lamp (fig. 8).
10. Thread new cord through the tube.

Fig. 1

Fig. 2

Fig. 3

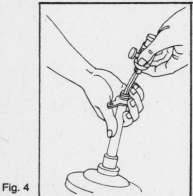

Fig. 4

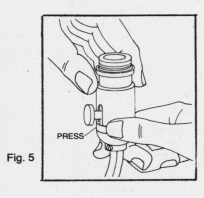

PRESS

Fig. 5

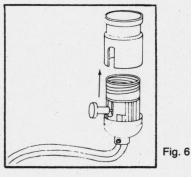

Fig. 6

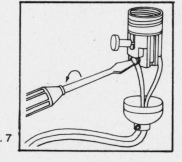

Fig. 7

Fig. 8

11. Strip the ends of the wires and attach them to the terminals on the socket, then reassemble (fig. 9).

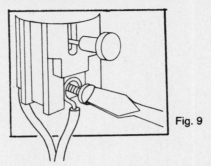

Fig. 9

## DAMAGED LAMP SOCKET

**The problem:** The lamp switch, incorporated in the socket, is worn and the lamp cannot be turned on or off properly.

**Tools you need to fix it:** A screwdriver.

**The basic steps:**
1. Unplug the lamp, remove shade and bulb.
2. Remove the socket as described above and shown in Figures 5, 6, 7.
3. Buy a new socket (take the old one with you to get a replacement of the same type).
4. Remove the outer and the insulated shell from the new socket and loosen the terminal screws.
5. Fit the cord through the new socket cap and install the wires on the screws, looping them around so that, as the screws are tightened, the ends of the wires are tightened around them (fig. 1).
6. Fasten new socket cap on tube (fig. 2).
7. Pull the wire through the lamp bottom until the socket sits firmly in the cap (fig. 3).
8. Place the insulated shell over the socket (fig. 4).
9. Press the bottom into the cap; it should snap securely in place (fig. 5).
10. Reassemble the lamp.

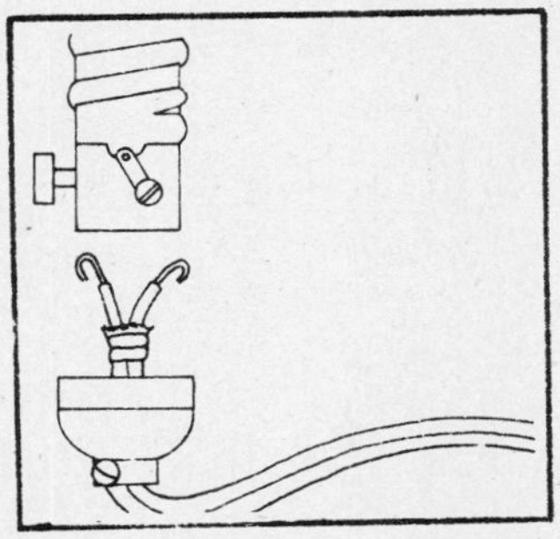

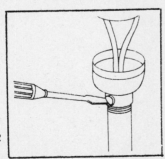

Fig. 1

Fig. 2

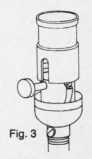

Fig. 3

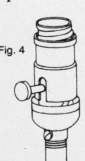

Fig. 4

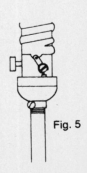

Fig. 5

**191**

**The problem:** Loss of heat in winter • Loss of cool air in summer • Rain and snow may ruin draperies and carpets.

**Tools and materials you need to fix it:** Window glass • A glass cutter • A putty knife • A small wood chisel • Putty or glazing compound • Pliers • A hammer • Glazier's points.

**The basic steps:**
Work from the outside of the window.
1. Remove broken pieces of glass from the frame, wearing heavy work gloves (fig. 1).
2. Clean out old putty with a small wood chisel (fig. 2). Be careful not to damage the frame.
3. Extract glazier's points with pliers (fig. 3).
4. Mark replacement glass with a sharpened crayon. It should be $1/16$ inch smaller all around than the frame opening.
5. Score the glass with a glass cutter, using a steel straightedge to guide the cut (fig. 4).
6. Lay the glass over the edge of the work table and apply pressure on both sides of the score to break it cleanly (fig. 5).
7. If the piece to be broken off is very narrow, snap it off with the slotted head of the cutting tool (fig. 6).
8. Paint the groove in the frame with linseed oil to prevent drying out and cracking of the body (fig. 7).
9. Apply $1/8$ inch thickness of putty all around the frame (fig. 8).
10. Press the glass into place, making sure it lies flat against the shoulders of the frame (fig. 9).
11. Insert glazier's points. Tap them in carefully to avoid breaking the glass. Points should be placed all around the frame every 4 to 6 inches (fig. 10).
12. Roll some more putty into a "rope" about ½ inch thick. Use your fingers to press it against the wood and glass around the frame.
13. Smooth and bevel the putty with the blade of a putty knife (fig. 11). The putty should form a smooth seal around the window.

**Note:** For metal windows special clips are used instead of glazier's points (fig. 12). If there are metal strips screw them back into place.

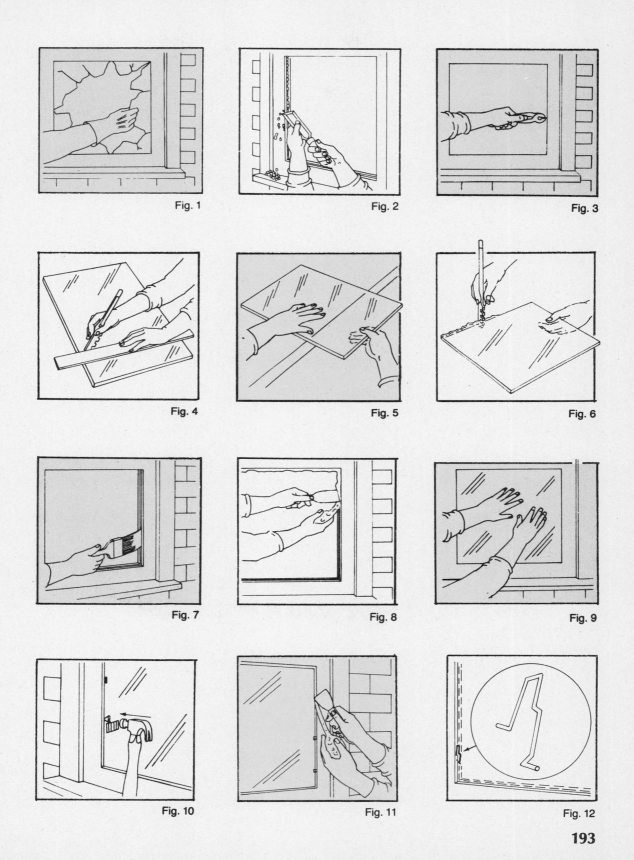

Fig. 1

Fig. 2

Fig. 3

Fig. 4

Fig. 5

Fig. 6

Fig. 7

Fig. 8

Fig. 9

Fig. 10

Fig. 11

Fig. 12

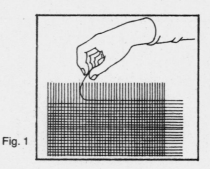

Fig. 1

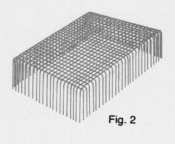

Fig. 2

## DAMAGED SCREEN

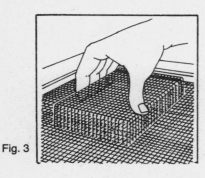

Fig. 3

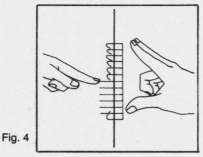

Fig. 4

**The problem:** Insects come through holes in the screen • Small holes tend to become larger • New screens are expensive.

**Tools and materials you need to fix it:** Heavy-duty scissors • A ruler or a small block of wood with straight edges • Screening or ready-cut screen patches • Waterproof cement.

**The basic steps:**
1. Trim the hole in the screen to make smooth edges.
2. Cut a rectangular patch of wire screen material ½ inch larger than the hole.
3. Unravel two wires at each side of the patch (fig. 1).
4. Bend the ends of the wires at a right angle on all four sides (fig. 2); use the block of wood or the edge of a ruler to do this.
5. Put the patch over the hole from the outside. Hold it tight against the screen so that the bent wire ends go through the screen (fig. 3).
6. From the inside, bend the ends of the wires toward the center of the hole (fig. 4). You may need someone outside to press against the patch while you do this, to secure the patch firmly.

**Note:** If the hole in the screen is very small, a drop or two of waterproof cement will do the job (fig. 5); the cement hardens into a film that covers the hole.

Fig. 5

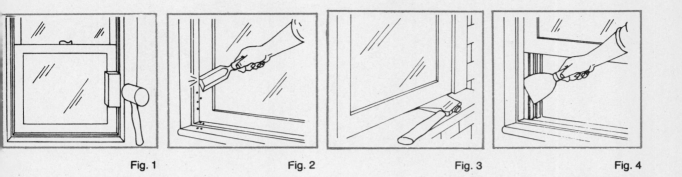

Fig. 1    Fig. 2    Fig. 3    Fig. 4

## STICKING WINDOW

**The problem:** You cannot open the window.

**Tools and materials you need to fix it:** A hammer or a mallet • A hatchet • A screwdriver • A chisel • A paint scraper • A wood block • Lubricating oil.

**The basic steps to repair a paint-stuck window:**
1. Tap along both sides of the window with a hammer or mallet on a block of wood (fig. 1).
2. If this does not free the window, insert the blade of a paint scraper or a broad, thin chisel between the sash and the stop molding (fig. 2).
3. Tap the blade in with a hammer, then rock the tool back and forth gently to force the sash back from the molding. Repeat this at several points on each side of the sash until the window moves freely again. Never use a screwdriver for this purpose, as it will leave marks in the wood.
4. If all this doesn't help, hammer a hatchet or any broad, hard metal wedge along the bottom of the sash. Pry as you go along (fig. 3). Do this from the outside, to avoid damaging the finish of the window and windowsill.
5. Once the window is free, scrape off any crust of paint at the back face of the stop molding (fig. 4).
6. Sand the molding lightly and touch up the window track.

**The basic steps to repair a window that is permanently swollen out of shape:**
1. Cut a block of wood that will fit snugly into the channel between the inside and outside window stops above or below the sash.

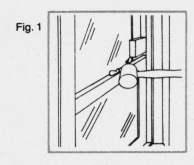
Fig. 1

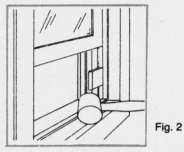
Fig. 2

Fig. 3

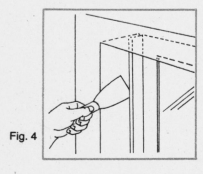
Fig. 4

2. Give the block several taps with a hammer at both sides of the window (fig. 1).

3. This should free the sash so that it can be raised (or lowered) at least partially. Repeat the procedure at the exposed channels at the bottom or top (fig. 2).

4. Apply a lubricant such as paraffin or candle wax to the channels.

5. If this doesn't help, take out the window (fig. 3).

6. Remove stop molding on a window that has sash cords (fig. 4).

7. Disengage sash cord at both sides (fig. 5).

8. Keep sash cord from slipping past pulley with a nail or a strip of wood (fig. 6).

9. If the pulley is stiff, lubricate it with a few drops of oil (fig. 7).

10. Sand or plane the wood of the sash to make it fit.

11. Reassemble the window.

**Note:** If a window has tension strips, try first to adjust them by turning their mounting screws (fig. 8). If this doesn't do the trick, remove the tension strips and proceed as in Steps 10 and 11.

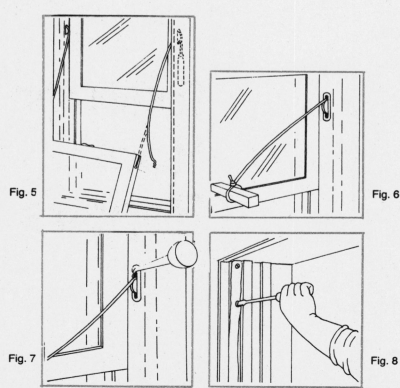
Fig. 5

Fig. 6

Fig. 7

Fig. 8

Written by
DONALD F. LOW

# Exterior
# Home
# Repairs

# Contents

**EMERGENCY REPAIRS** ....................... 199
  Broken Window ......................... 199
  Roof Leak ............................ 200
  Burst Water Pipe ...................... 201
  Icy Walks ............................ 201

**ASSUMING THE ROLE OF "HANDYMAN"** ..... 201
  Damaged Porch Floorboards ............. 201
  Deteriorated Porch Railing ............ 203
  Worn Porch Steps ..................... 203
  Heaved or Settled Brick in Brick-in-Sand Patio . 203
  Heaved or Settled Brick in Mortared
    Brick Patios ....................... 204
  Heaved, Settled, or Broken Stones in Flagstone
    Patio ............................. 205
  Heaved Sidewalk ...................... 206
  Cracked Blacktop Driveways ........... 206
  Defective Mortar Joints in Brick Walls ....... 208
  Loose or Badly Damaged Brick .......... 209
  Damaged Wood Siding ................. 209
  Loose or Cracked Asbestos Cement Shingles ... 210
  Calking Air Leaks Around Windows, Doors, Faucets,
    Chimneys, etc. ..................... 211
  Clogged or Leaking Gutters and Downspouts .. 213

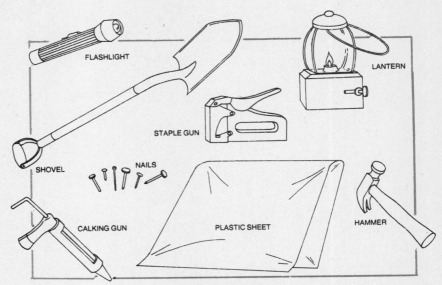

Emergency arsenal.

## Emergency Repairs

When the wind starts to howl and the snow is piling up, the home owner should be prepared and be aware that just about anything might happen. He has to be armed with at least enough emergency tools to have a fighting chance. The emergency tool kit should include a claw hammer, an assortment of nails, a screwdriver, pliers, a knife, a staple gun with a good supply of staples, and at least one flashlight. Also included in the emergency supplies should be a couple of kerosene lanterns, a supply of candles, a loaded calking gun, a can of asphalt cement, a shovel, a couple of large plastic sheets, a roll of masking tape, wire and rope, and several lengths of 1 x 2 or 1 x 3 lumber. It's handy to have rock salt and/or an electric heating cable to attack ice buildup.

### BROKEN WINDOW

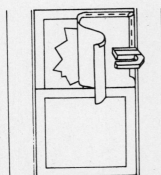

Fig. 1

**The problem:** Loss of heat in winter • Loss of cool air in summer • Rain and snow may ruin drapes and carpets • Weather conditions at the moment prevent you from making a permanent repair.

**Tools and materials you need:** A staple gun • Plastic sheets • Masking tape.

**The basic steps for temporary repair:**
1. Staple the sheeting around the window frame (fig.1).
2. Double it at the edges for additional strength.
3. Seal the edges with masking tape.

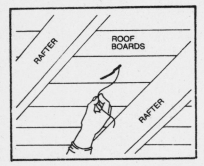

Fig. 2

**The problem:** Rain or snow will seep into the house • It would be foolish to attempt to go on the roof to make repairs when it is wet or covered with ice or snow.

**Tools and materials you need:** A claw hammer • A piece of wire • Asphalt roofing cement • A piece of wood • Nails.

**The basic steps for emergency repairs from the inside:**
1. If the leak is not easily visible because water flows along the roofboards or rafters before dripping down, probe with a wire until you find it (fig.2).
2. Coat the leaking area with asphalt roofing cement (fig.3).
3. Cut a 1 x 6 or similar board to fit between the rafters, and toenail it in place beneath the asphalt patch (fig.4).
**Note:** After the storm subsides it may be possible to make a temporary repair from above provided the leak is close enough to the edge of the roof so that you can reach it from a ladder:
1. Slip a plastic sheet under the course of shingles above the leaking area and staple it to the roof (fig.5).
2. Calk around the edges (fig.6).
3. Nail 1 x 2 strips around the exposed edges. Later, when you make a permanent repair, the nail holes will have to be filled, but this is certainly better than having water pour through the leak.

Fig. 3

Fig. 4

Fig. 5

Fig. 6

## BURST WATER PIPE

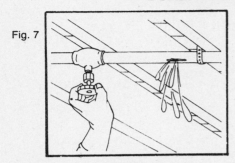

Fig. 7

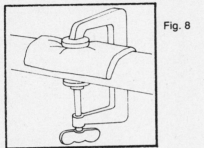

Fig. 8

**The problem:** Flooding • Ruining of floors, ceilings, and walls.

**Tools and materials you need:** A piece of sheet rubber or a section of garden hose • Hose clamps or C-clamps.

**The basic steps for temporary repair:**
1. Close shutoff valve nearest leak (fig. 7). If there is no shutoff nearby, turn off the main intake valve.
2. If the water is still running, because of a worn or damaged valve, wrap a piece of sheet rubber firmly around the leaky section and clamp it tightly; special clamps for this are available in various pipe sizes (fig. 8).
3. Instead of sheet rubber you can cut a section of garden hose, slit it, and place it over the leak, holding it in place with a C-clamp.
**Note:** Permanent repairs should be made as soon as possible.

## ICY WALKS

**The problem:** An invitation to injuries and lawsuits.

**Materials you need:** Rock salt • Clean sand.

**The basic steps:**
1. Sprinkle plenty of rock salt on the icy walks. This chemical melter has the disadvantage that it may do some damage to concrete as well as corrosion to cars that are driven over it (small consequences compared to the alternatives).
2. You might also consider keeping a large supply of clean sand and using it to skidproof walks and driveways.

# Assuming the Role of "Handyman"

## DAMAGED PORCH FLOORBOARDS

**The problem:** Boards or planks are broken • Boards or planks have holes or are badly splintered.

**Tools and materials you need:** A framing square • An electric drill or a brace and bit • A wood chisel • A mallet • Aluminum or galvanized flooring or finishing nails • A nailset • Replacement flooring • Wood filler.

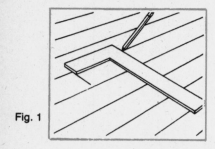

Fig. 1

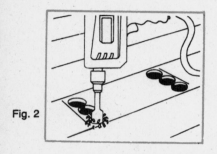

Fig. 2

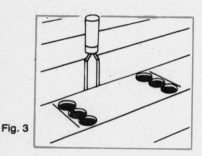

Fig. 3

**The basic steps:** (The damaged section must be cut away over the nearest joists. Be very careful not to mar the surrounding boards).

1. With a framing square, mark off the section of board to be removed at an exact right angle to the boards (fig.1).
2. Drill large, interconnected holes inside the lines on both sides of the damaged section with an electric drill or a brace and bit (fig.2).
3. Break out the damaged portion with a wood chisel by striking along the grain (fig.3).
4. Remove the pieces, being particularly careful not to damage the tongue or groove of the boards on either side.
5. Chisel out the remainder of the board on the outside of the drilled holes, making sure that you cut exactly on the line (fig.4), pull out any remaining nails, and clean away all debris.
6. Put a replacement board along the removed section and mark carefully where the damaged section was, again at an exact right angle, using the framing square (fig.5).
7. Saw along the lines and chisel off the *bottom* of the grooved edge (fig.6) so that the board will slip into the open space. (Leave the top portion of the grooved edge.)
8. Slip the board into place (fig.7).
9. Nail through the top with aluminum or galvanized flooring or finishing nails. Use two nails on each end.
10. Set the nails with a nailset (fig.8) and cover with wood filler.

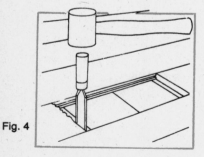

Fig. 4

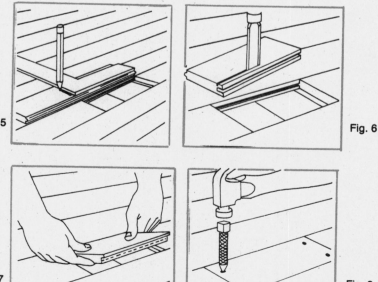

Fig. 5

Fig. 6

Fig. 7

Fig. 8

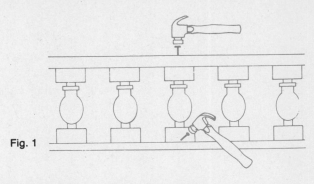

Fig. 1

## DETERIORATED PORCH RAILING

**The problem:** Rail and/or baluster has rotted.

**Tools you need:** A hammer • Nails • Replacement rail and/or baluster.

**The basic steps:**
1. Knock out the deteriorated pieces with a hammer.
2. Replace rotted rail with a new one, nailing it to the baluster.
3. Replace baluster if you can find a matching piece, or take the old one to a millworking shop and have a new one turned.
4. Without complicated joinery, nail through the rail into the baluster or toenail the baluster to the rail (fig.1).

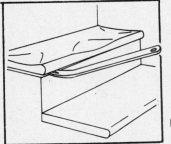

Fig. 1

## WORN PORCH STEPS

**The problem:** Treads or risers are loose, sagging, broken, or warped.

**Tools and materials you need:** A wrecking bar • A hammer • Aluminum or galvanized finishing nails • A nailset • A rasp • Sandpaper • Wood putty.

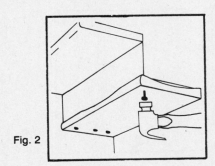

Fig. 2

**The basic steps:**
1. Pry up worn tread with a wrecking bar (fig.1).
2. Turn it over and nail it in place, bottom side up, with aluminum or galvanized finishing nails (fig.2).
3. Set the nails and fill the holes with wood putty.
4. Duplicate rounded edges with a rasp and sandpaper.

**Note:** When new treads or risers are needed, take an old one to the lumberyard and try to find a match. Apply wood preservative to new wood before nailing in place.

## HEAVED OR SETTLED BRICK IN BRICK-IN-SAND PATIO

**The problem:** Uneven surfaces are dangerous.

**Tools and materials you need:** An old screwdriver • A shovel • A broom • Sand.

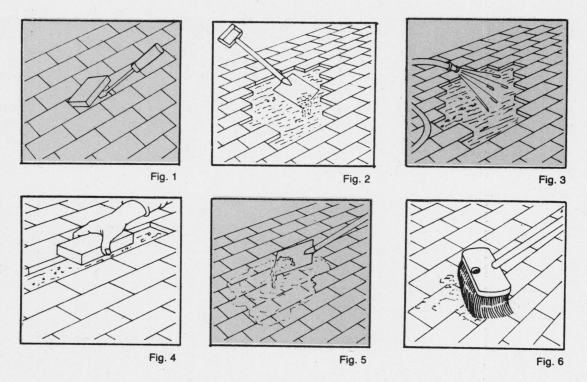

Fig. 1     Fig. 2     Fig. 3

Fig. 4     Fig. 5     Fig. 6

**The basic steps:**

1. Dislodge the first heaved or sunk brick with an old screwdriver (fig.1).

2. Lift out the adjacent bricks by hand.

3. If the brick has settled, lay in some extra sand—any sand will do for this, even beach sand (fig.2)—and tamp it down well.

4. Watering helps to settle the sand and compact it (fig.3).

5. When the bed is satisfactory, reinstall the bricks the same way they were laid before, butted tightly against one another (fig.4).

6. When all have been replaced, spread more sand over the top (fig.5).

7. Work the sand down between the cracks with a stiff-bristled broom (fig.6).

8. Spray the patio with a hose, then sweep in more sand. (It may take three or more similar applications before the brick is again locked into position and no more sand can be worked in.)

## HEAVED OR SETTLED BRICK IN MORTARED BRICK PATIOS

(Since mortared brick patios should be set on top of a concrete base slab, heaving or settling of the brick itself should be relatively rare.)

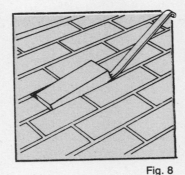

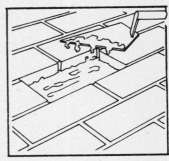

Fig. 7             Fig. 8             Fig. 9

**The problem:** Uneven surfaces are dangerous.

**Tools you need:** A brick chisel or a cold chisel • A wrecking bar • A trowel • Mortar.

**The basic steps:**
1. Chip out mortar (fig.7).
2. Pry up settled brick (fig.8).
3. Lay in enough new mortar to bring the surface level with the rest (fig.9). Standard or common brick is nominally 2¾ inches in depth, counting mortar, with the actual brick size 2¼ inches. But not all brick is alike, so measure what you have. For mortar, it is easiest to purchase premixed mortar from a masonry or building supply dealer.
4. When the brick is heaved, the brick and mortar must be removed and the concrete base chipped off to bring it down to the surrounding level.
5. Then proceed as above.

## HEAVED, SETTLED, OR BROKEN STONES IN FLAGSTONE PATIO

(Flagstone patios, whether they are built with random shaped and colored stones or with matched rectangular stones, are constructed the same way as brick patios.)

**The problem:** Uneven surfaces are dangerous.

**Tools you need:** A piece of pipe, or a wood dowel, or a steel rod • A pry bar • A trowel • A cold chisel • A mash hammer.

**The basic steps:**
1. Place a piece of pipe or a wood dowel or a steel rod next to the stone to be removed.
2. Lift the stone with the pry bar just enough to rest a corner on the rod.

3. Shove the stone onto the rod and roll it away so that you can work beneath.

4. If the stone has been broken badly, it must be replaced. The replacement is easier to find with random shaped and colored stones, since they don't have to match their mates in either size or shape. It can be somewhat smaller but not larger.

5. Fill in the surrounding spaces with mortar.

6. If you can't find a matching rectangular stone as a replacement, ask a stone dealer to cut one to your specifications — it is difficult to do this yourself. If you have to cut it yourself, it can be done with a cold chisel and a heavy mash hammer. First score a line on all sides with the chisel, then keep banging at it on one side and then the other until it breaks.

## HEAVED SIDEWALK

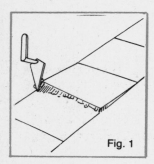
Fig. 1

**The problem:** Small cracks in sidewalks are becoming larger • It can cause accidents to you and your family • You are responsible if strangers are hurt.

**Tools and materials you need:** A sledgehammer or a jackhammer • An ax • A trowel • Wire reinforcing mesh • Vinyl or epoxy patching mix.

**The basic steps:**

1. If weather conditions prevent a complete repair, it will help to avoid accidents if you create a slope around the heaved portion of walk. Use vinyl or epoxy patching mix to smooth the section as best you can (fig.1). But vow to do a complete repair job in the not-too-distant future.

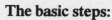

2. For permanent repair, break up the old section using a sledgehammer or, if you can rent or borrow one, a jackhammer (fig.2).

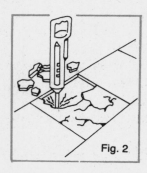
Fig. 2

3. When the old concrete has been removed, you can determine whether or not tree roots are the cause of the trouble. If so, take an ax and cut off the offending roots

4. If no roots are found, you can assume that Jack Frost did the dirty deed. In that case, it is wise to install wire reinforcing mesh (fig.3) before pouring the new section.

## CRACKED BLACKTOP DRIVEWAYS

Fig. 3

**The problem:** The potholes can damage your car • You can hurt yourself • Water and oil can seep through and attack from underneath.

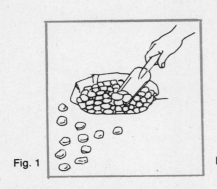

Fig. 1

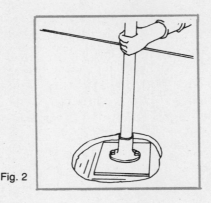

Fig. 2

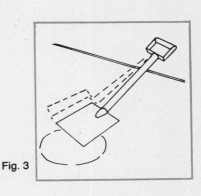

Fig. 3

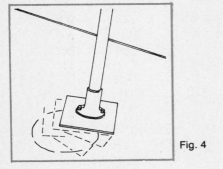

Fig. 4

**Tools and materials you need:** A shovel • A metal tamper • Blacktop patch • An applicator for sealer.

**The basic steps:**
1. Remove the deteriorated sections when blacktop starts to crack and break up.
2. Dig out the area underneath (fig.1).
3. Fill in with the old broken-up blacktop.
4. Tamp down the subgrade thoroughly (fig.2) and fill with gravel or other solid material if the depth is more than 2 inches.
5. Pour in new blacktop patch (available at reasonable cost from most building supply dealers) and smooth over the top with a shovel (fig.3).
6. Tamp down thoroughly again (fig.4). A metal tamper is a necessity. You should be able to rent one.
7. Keep tamping until the patch is smooth and level, then run over it a few times with your car's tires (fig.5). Do this as gently as possible. Your car is merely acting as a roller.
8. Let the patch dry and harden for a few days.

**Note:** To prevent cracking, a good sealer should be applied every year or two.
   Blacktop must not be applied when the temperature is likely to fall below 50° F.

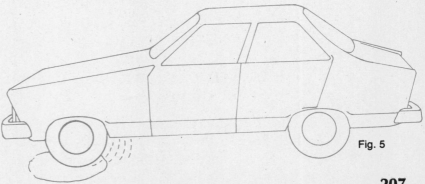

Fig. 5

207

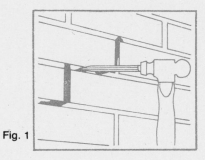

Fig. 1

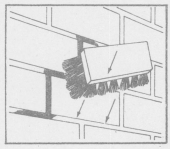

Fig. 2

## DEFECTIVE MORTAR JOINTS IN BRICK WALLS

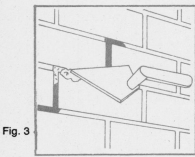

Fig. 3

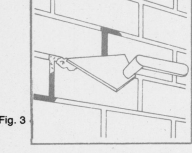

Fig. 4

**The problem:** Joints may become porous • Bricks may become loose • Air and moisture enter the wall.

**Tools and materials you need:** A ballpeen or mash hammer • A cold chisel • A pointed trowel • A wire brush • A dowel • Mortar mix.

**The basic steps:**
1. Chisel out loose or crumbling mortar (fig.1).
2. Clean the joint with a wire brush and wet it thoroughly (fig.2).
3. Mix the mortar, following the directions on the package (you can buy a prepared mortar mix at your hardware or building supply store).
4. Force the mortar into the joint with the trowel (fig.3).
5. Form it with the point of the trowel to match the surrounding mortar joints (fig.4).
6. A concave joint can be formed by using a dowel or a small piece of pipe to finish off the new mortar (fig.5).
7. If the mortar joints of an entire wall become porous, either because of age or of poor original workmanship, apply a clear waterproofing compound, available at masonry and building supply stores, to each joint (fig.6).

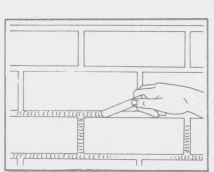

Fig. 5

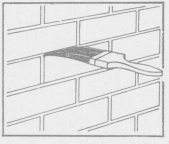

Fig. 6

208

## LOOSE OR BADLY DAMAGED BRICK

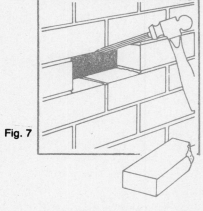

Fig. 7

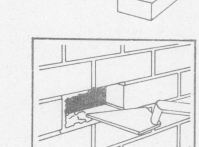

Fig. 8

**The problem:** Other bricks may be affected • Air and moisture enter the wall.

**Tools and materials you need:** A ballpeen or mash hammer • A cold chisel • A pointed trowel • Mortar.

### The basic steps:

1. Chisel out the mortar all around the loose or damaged brick (fig.7). Be careful not to damage the surrounding bricks.
2. Take out the loose or damaged brick.
3. Chisel away any remaining mortar in the opening and clean away dust and debris.
4. Wet down the opening.
5. Apply mortar to the sides and back of the opening (fig.8).
6. Dampen the replacement brick.
7. Coat it with mortar and press it into place (fig.9).
8. Finish the mortar joint with a trowel.

**Note:** In brick veneer walls, the brick is laid against a wood-sheathed wall behind it, attached by small metal clips (fig.10). To allow proper drainage of this cavity, there are usually weep holes along the base of the wall to permit water to run off. Make sure that these holes are not blocked, either by dirt or fallen mortar, and clean them out occasionally with stiff wire or a masonry drill (fig.11).

## DAMAGED WOOD SIDING

**The problem:** Boards are loose, warped, or split • Cracks have developed • Air and moisture enter the wall.

**Tools and materials you need:** A putty knife • A chisel • A claw hammer • Nails • Waterproof glue • Lead-base putty.

Fig. 9

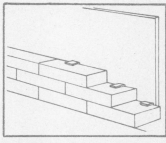

Fig. 10

Fig. 11

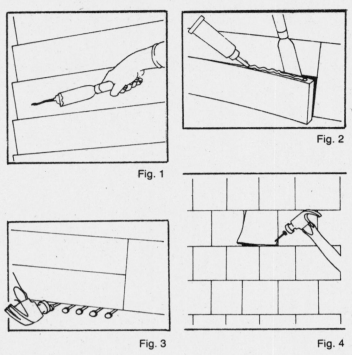

Fig. 1

Fig. 2

Fig. 3

Fig. 4

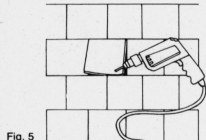

Fig. 5

## The basic steps:
1. Fill small cracks with lead-base putty.
2. Work putty into the crack with the putty knife (fig.1).
3. If a board has split along the grain, pry up the loose portion of the board and apply waterproof glue along the split (fig.2).
4. Press the split together and drive galvanized nails beneath the board to hold the edges together until the glue is dry (fig.3).
5. Remove the nails and fill the holes with putty.

**Note:** Loose wood shingles can be secured with galvanized or aluminum serrated nails driven along the edges (fig.4).

## LOOSE OR CRACKED ASBESTOS CEMENT SHINGLES

**The problem:** Air and moisture seep in, causing more deterioration.

**Tools you need:** An electric drill • A claw hammer • Nails • A nailset • A chisel • Pliers • A hacksaw.

**The basic steps:**
1. Drill pilot holes for the nails when you are repairing a material such as asbestos cement shingles, which are very brittle (fig.5).
2. Countersink nails (fig.6).
3. Fill holes with putty.

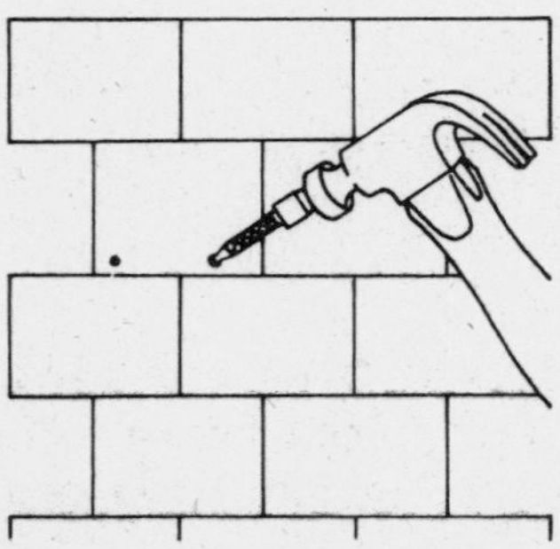

Fig. 6

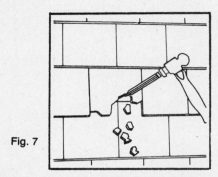
Fig. 7

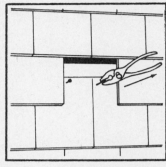
Fig. 8

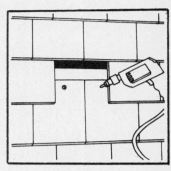
Fig. 9

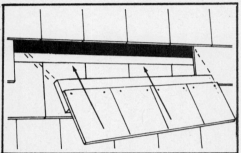
Fig. 10

4. Paint over putty.

5. Break off cracked or otherwise damaged shingles piece by piece, striking them with a hammer and chisel (fig. 7); be careful not to damage the surrounding siding.

6. Exposed nails can be pulled out with pliers (fig. 8).

7. Cut the nails of the shingle above with a hacksaw.

8. Another method is to drill the nails through the outside (fig. 9), slip the replacement shingle of the same size into position, and drill pilot holes for nails.

9. Use a nailset to drive the nails home so that the hammer does not damage the new shingle.

10. Some asbestos shingles are attached to boards, usually about 4 feet in length. When one of these is damaged, it is generally advisable to replace the entire panel (fig. 10). This is done in the same way as replacing individual shingles.

## CALKING AIR LEAKS AROUND WINDOWS, DOORS, FAUCETS, CHIMNEYS, ETC.

**The problem:** Big heating and cooling bills • Moisture, dust, and dirt come through cracks • Insects enter the house through them • Water seeps through cracks around the chimney.

**Tools and materials you need:** A calking gun • A putty knife or other scraping tool • A screwdriver • Calking compound (polyvinyl acetate type, in both rope and bulk form) • Cleaning fluid • A ladder.

Calking gun
and cartridge.

**The basic steps:**

1. Load the calking gun and make a thorough examination of the outside of the house, looking for any area where air could leak in (wherever two different materials or parts of the house meet).

Fig. 1

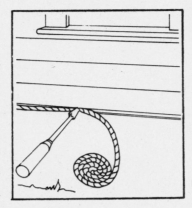

Fig. 2

Fig. 3

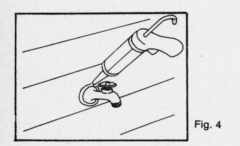

Fig. 4

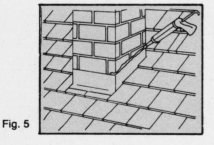

Fig. 5

2. Before applying calking compound, clean the area of paint buildup, dirt, or deteriorated calk, using solvent and a putty knife or other scraping tool (fig.1).

3. For extra long cracks, use calking compound that comes in rope form. Force it into the cracks with the fingers or a screwdriver (fig.2).

4. Draw a good bead of calk with the gun, and make sure the bead overlaps both sides for a tight seal around windows (fig.3), around water faucets that penetrate the outside house surface (fig.4), around the chimney (fig.5), and between the main body of the house and the porch (fig.6).

**Note:** Estimating the number of cartridges of calking compound needed is difficult, since the number will vary greatly with the size of the cracks to be filled. If possible, it's best to start with a half dozen cartridges and then purchase more as the job continues and you need more.

Calking a house usually requires the use of a ladder. Be sure you use it safely. Carry the calking gun in a sling (fig.7) so that you can use both hands climbing the ladder, and don't try to reach for that extra bit (fig.8). Get down and move the ladder.

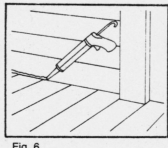

Fig. 6

Fig. 7

Fig. 8

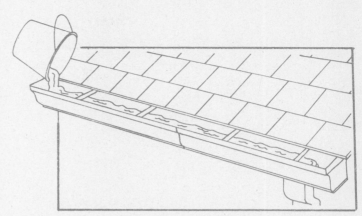

Fig. 1

## CLOGGED OR LEAKING GUTTERS AND DOWNSPOUTS

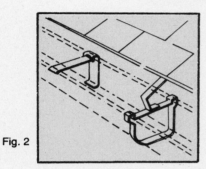

Fig. 2

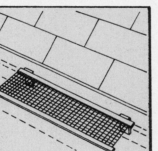

Fig. 3

**The problem:** Water stands in the gutter • Water overflows or spills over the edge of the gutter • Water leaks from the gutter or downspout and seeps into the earth around the building, causing wet basements, wood decay, peeling paint, and even termite damage.

**Tools and materials you need:** A pail • A putty knife • A hammer • A screwdriver • Gutter hangers • Galvanized nails • Galvanized screws • Gutter guards • Electric heating cable • A garden hose • Wood preservatives • Exterior paint • Roofing cement • Tarpaper • Asphalt cement.

**The basic steps:**
1. Inspect and clean gutter and downspouts at least twice a year.
2. Remove all leaves and other debris from the gutter and check for loose joints.
3. Check gutter pitch by pouring a pail of water in the end of the gutter opposite the downspout or leader end (fig.1). Because water seeks its own level, a slight downward pitch to the drainage end of the gutter is necessary.
4. Make note of the areas where water accumulates.
5. To increase the pitch or elevate a sagging length of gutter, install gutter hangers (fig.2). They are available at most hardware stores.
6. If gutter hangers are already in place, check them for tightness; if loose, renail with a galvanized nail or tighten with a galvanized screw.
7. Install gutter guards (fig.3), which will prevent leaves and debris from accumulating.
8. Check the gutter outlet opening where the water flows into the downspout. It should have either a leaf guard or a leaf

213

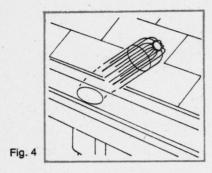

Fig. 4

strainer (fig.4); clean debris from the guard or strainer and replace in position.

9. With a good strainer properly installed, downspouts rarely become clogged. Nonetheless, it is a good idea to flush them out once a year with a garden hose (fig.5), thus forcing out small particles that could accumulate and become a clogging problem.

10. All gutters should slant outward (fig.6).

11. Check that the outsides of the gutters are hung lower than the edge of the roof eaves. In winter this allows ice to slide off without taking the gutter along.

12. If this does not prevent snow or ice buildup, install electric heating cables where accumulation is a problem (fig.7).

**Note:** Wood gutters, rare today, should be treated with wood preservatives and then coated with exterior paint. Lining the inside of these gutters with roofing cement will further prevent decay. Small holes in wood gutters can be patched with pieces of tarpaper and asphalt cement (fig.8).

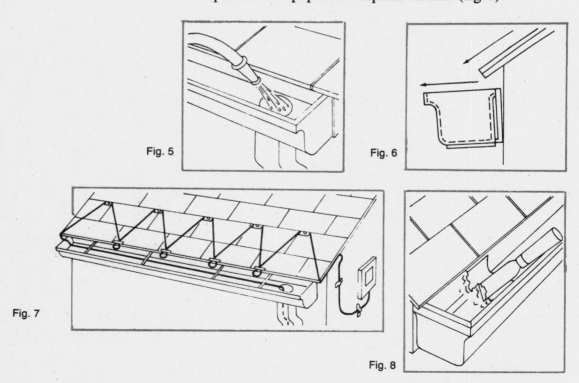

Fig. 5

Fig. 6

Fig. 7

Fig. 8

Compiled by
CHRISTOPHER SETON

# Credit
## WHAT YOU SHOULD KNOW ABOUT IT

# Contents

**QUICK CREDIT GUIDE** ...................... 217

**WHAT YOU SHOULD KNOW ABOUT CREDIT** . 218
**Buying on the Installment Plan** .............. 219
**How Credit Charges Are Figured** ........... 219

**SHOPPING FOR CREDIT** .................... 222
**Compare Costs** ......................... 223
**Truth in Lending: Annual Percentage Rate** ..... 225
**Protection Under Truth in Lending** .......... 226
**Compare Other Terms** .................... 227

**YOUR CREDIT RATING** .................... 228

**SHOULD YOU OR SHOULDN'T YOU?** ........ 231

**MIND MADE UP?** ......................... 232

**IN CASE YOU GET INTO CREDIT TROUBLE** .... 233

# Quick Credit Guide

**A. Spend wisely • B. Know the cost of credit • C. Before you sign • D. Understand the annual percentage rate.**

## A. SPEND WISELY

- Wise use of consumer credit begins with wise spending.
- Must you buy now? Can you wait a little and pay more of it in cash?
- Is having something NOW worth the extra cost of credit?
- Does your decision fit into your family's budget and plans?
- Can you meet the new payments, plus all other existing payments? Will you have money left for emergencies?

## B. KNOW THE COST OF CREDIT

- Credit comes from stores, dealers, finance companies, credit unions, and banks.
- Do you know how much you are paying for the use of credit?
- The Truth in Lending law requires that you be told the dollar amount of finance charge — total cost of the credit including interest, service, and carrying charges, plus any charges for required insurance — and the annual percentage rate.

## C. BEFORE YOU SIGN

- Read and understand the contract. Don't rush.
- Never sign a contract with spaces left blank.
- Be sure the contract tells:
  - Exactly what you are buying.
  - Purchase price.
  - Down payment and trade-in allowance.
  - Amount borrowed.
  - Total amount due.
  - Interest and service charge in dollars and the annual percentage rate.
- Know to whom you make payments, and when payments are due.
- What if you can't pay on time? Or if you pay ahead?
- What are seller's commitments for maintenance, service, or replacement?
- Be sure you get a copy of the contract to keep.
- How much cash will you actually get?
- How much will you have to repay?
- What are the interest, service, and other charges?
- What is the annual percentage rate?
- What if you miss a payment?
- How does the lender figure the balance due if you refinance?
- If you pay ahead of time is there a penalty? Will you get a refund?

## D. UNDERSTAND THE ANNUAL PERCENTAGE RATE

- If you borrow $100 for one year for a finance charge of $6 and at the end of the year repay $106, the annual percentage rate is 6 percent. You have use of the $100 all year.
- If you repay the $100 plus $6 finance charge (total of $106) during the year in equal monthly payments, the annual percentage rate is 11.1 percent. You have use of only about half the $100 for the full year.

• The annual percentage rates for typical charges based on amount borrowed and repaid in 12 equal monthly installments are:

| Finance Charge | Annual Percentage Rate |
| --- | --- |
| $6 per $100 per year | 11.1% |
| $8 per $100 per year | 14.8% |
| $10 per $100 per year | 18.5% |
| $12 per $100 per year | 22.2% |

• Some interest rates are quoted on a monthly basis; for example, 1½% per month on the unpaid balance. But remember that this is only for one month. The annual percentage rate would be 12 times the monthly rate, or 18 percent.
• The annual percentage rates for typical monthly rates are:

| Rate Per Month | Annual Percentage Rate |
| --- | --- |
| ¾ of 1% | 9% |
| 1% | 12% |
| 1¼% | 15% |
| 1½% | 18% |
| 2% | 24% |
| 2½% | 30% |

• If the monthly percentage rate is based on unpaid balance, you will pay a lower dollar finance charge than if based on the previous month's balance (before any payment is deducted).
• Use ony the annual percentage rate when comparing the cost of credit from different lenders and creditors.

## What You Should Know About Credit

Credit has many forms: installment buying, revolving accounts, credit cards, charge cards, buying on time. Whatever it is called, credit is an arrangement to receive cash, goods, or services now and pay later. For example, if a lender hands you money, if a store lets you take a washing machine to keep, or if a garage repairs your car and you pay later, you are using credit.

Whether you will pay more by using credit rather than cash depends on how soon you pay. Many stores and bank credit cards allow you to pay within 25 or 30 days without an extra charge. Unless you pay all that you owe, you will be billed for an extra amount of money called a finance charge. The Federal Consumer Credit Protection Act, popularly known as the Truth in Lending law, requires lenders to express interest or carrying charges with the words "finance charge."

When you remember that the bank, store, or garage has to pay its bills such as wages, heat, electricity, and insurance while it is waiting to receive payments from you, you should not be surprised when credit costs you extra money in the form of a finance charge.

Credit can be a help or a hindrance, depending on how you use it. It has helped many families to furnish a home, buy a car, and meet all kinds of financial emergencies. It also has caused many families worry, hardship, and loss.

You are urged to use installment credit by merchants who want to sell their goods and by banks and loan companies that want to lend their money. You are encouraged with promises of "loans on your

signature," "no money down," and "very easy payments." You can easily be carried away by such promises. It is wise to learn the facts about installment credit so that you can make sensible decisions about it.

Consumers can obtain installment credit in a number of places. Retail merchants offer credit in the form of deferred payments for goods you take and use while you are paying for them. Banks, credit unions, finance companies, and small loan companies lend money, which you repay in small amounts at a time.

## Buying on the Installment Plan

When you buy goods on the installment plan, you pay more than when you buy for cash. When you get an installment loan, you pay back more than you receive. The installment seller or lender adds a charge to cover such costs as investigating to find out if you are a good credit risk; the work of making out the contract, collecting the installments, and keeping the records; and interest on his money while you have the use of it. He may also add the cost of filing fees, insurance to protect him from loss should you die before the debt is paid, and other charges.

Some merchants and lenders charge more for credit than others. Charges for different kinds of loans differ, too. The credit rate is usually higher for small than large loans and for unsecured than for secured loans.

For example, the rate is higher when the lender has only your signature or promise to assure him of getting his money back (this is an "unsecured" loan) than when you put up a car, refrigerator, bonds, or some other security he can take if you do not pay.

## How Credit Charges Are Figured

Lenders use different methods of figuring credit charges on installment purchases and loans. There are two common methods. One is to calculate the amount you owe for credit each time you pay an installment. It is figured as a percentage of the debt you owe at that time (the "unpaid balance"), so it gets smaller as the debt decreases.

The lender quotes the charge as a certain percentage of the unpaid balance per month. Notice that this is per month and not per year. If you want to know the rate per year, multiply the monthly rate by 12. Here are some typical monthly rates and corresponding yearly rates:

| If the Monthly Rate Is | The Rate Per Year (Annual Percentage Rate) |
|---|---|
| ¾ of 1% | 9% |
| 1% | 12% |
| 1½% | 18% |
| 2% | 24% |
| 2½% | 30% |
| 3% | 36% |

Spend wisely.

This method of calculating credit charges is generally used by credit unions and small loan companies. Retail merchants use it for revolving or budget charge accounts.

Another way of figuring credit charges is to calculate the credit charge all at one time, when you get the loan or make the installment purchase. It is figured as a percentage of the total amount you borrow or the price of the item you buy. The charge for the entire loan period is added to the loan by some lenders and subtracted from it by others. Then the total is divided into installments.

The lender may quote the charge as a certain number of dollars per $100 per year — say, $8 or $10 per $100. Take a loan at $8 per $100 as an example. If the lender adds the charge ("add-on" method), you receive $100 and pay back $108. If he subtracts it ("discount" method), you receive $92 and pay back $100.

A credit charge of $8 or $10 per $100 per year on these loans appears to be 8 or 10 percent a year, and the lender sometimes quotes it that way. Actually, however, since you do not have the use of the entire $100 for a whole year, the true annual rate is much higher than that. In fact, it turns out to be about double. *(See Table 1.)*

Usually banks and sales finance companies use either the add-on

| Table 1 | | | |
|---|---|---|---|
| **THE ANNUAL RATES ON LOANS REPAID IN 12 MONTHLY INSTALLMENTS** | | | |
| If the Credit Charge per Year Is: | The Quoted Rate per Year Is: | The True Rate per Year Is: | |
| | | For "add-on" | For "discount" |
| $ 4 per $100 | 4% | 7.4% | 7.7% |
| $ 6 per $100 | 6% | 11.1% | 11.8% |
| $ 8 per $100 | 8% | 14.8% | 16.1% |
| $10 per $100 | 10% | 18.5% | 20.5% |
| $12 per $100 | 12% | 22.2% | 25.2% |

or the discount method of calculating credit charges when they make loans for buying cars and other consumer durable goods. The retail dealer usually figures your debt by the add-on method when you buy equipment or furniture on time. He is likely to quote you the total credit charge in dollars rather than the credit rate.

You should also be aware that lenders sometimes add more charges on top of the add-on or discount rates they quote. These may include charges for investigation of your credit rating, credit insurance, filing fees, and others. Watch for these extras, for they make the true annual credit rate higher.

You may have to pay very high rates for credit, especially when you compare them with the rate of interest you receive on your savings. Think of this if you have savings you could use instead of credit.

Credit costs may be easier to understand if you see them in dollars rather than percentages. Here is how the dollar cost of a loan on a new car worked out for one buyer—a fairly typical case. He bought a car priced at $5,575, received $1,275 for his old car as a trade-in, and made a cash down payment of $800. He financed the rest of the cost through the dealer (who probably turned it over to a sales finance company), who added $141 to cover insurance for the loan. The buyer agreed to pay 36 monthly installments of $119.

Calculations to find out the dollar cost were:

(1) Price of the car . . . . . . . . . . . . . . . . . . . . . . . . . . . . . . . . . $5,575
(2) Value of trade-in . . . . . . . . . . . . . . . . . $1,275
(3) Cash down payment . . . . . . . . . . . . . $  800
(4) Total down payment (2) + (3) . . . . . . . . . . . . . . . . . . . . $2,075
(5) To be financed on car cost (1) − (4) . . . . . . . . . . . . . . . $3,500
(6) Loan insurance . . . . . . . . . . . . . . . . . . . . . . . . . . . . . . . . . $  141
(7)          Total to be financed (5) + (6) . . . . . . . . . . . . . . . $3,641
(8) 36 payments of $119 each . . . . . . . . . . . . . . . . . . . . . . . . $4,284
(9) Dollar cost of credit (8) − (7) . . . . . . . . . . . . . . . . . . . . . $  643
(10) Annual percentage rate . . . . . . . . . . . . . . . . . . . . . . . . . 11.74%

This buyer paid $643 more for his car than if he had bought it for cash. This is not an unusually large amount to pay for credit on a major purchase like an automobile.

Here is an example of how dollar costs can add up on smaller purchases. Many families equip their homes (or replace household equipment) by buying pieces one by one on the installment plan.

Let's say a family plans to buy a washing machine, a dryer, a refrigerator, an electric range, and a vacuum cleaner. Buying them from a mail-order company, one after the other, the family would pay about $400 more for them on the company's installment purchase plan than by paying cash. The credit price would be about $2,060; the cash price, $1,660. By planning and saving ahead, the family could pay cash and save enough to buy another convenience —perhaps an air conditioner, a TV set, or a piece of furniture.

Table 2 gives the dollar cost of credit charges on a debt of $1,000, at different credit rates. It shows how the cost mounts when you take longer to pay off a debt. Take a loan of $1,000 at an add-on rate of $8 per $100 per year as an example. The credit charge would cost $80 if you repaid the debt in 12 monthly payments, but $240 if you took 36 months to pay it. It would be to your advantage to choose as short a repayment period as you could manage.

| Table 2 | | | | | | |
|---|---|---|---|---|---|---|
| **DOLLAR COST OF CREDIT CHARGES ON A $1,000 LOAN AT DIFFERENT CREDIT RATES, REPAID IN DIFFERENT NUMBERS OF INSTALLMENTS** | | | | | | |
| **Credit Rate** | **Dollar Cost of Credit Charges When Number of Monthly Installments Is:** | | | | | |
| **"Add-on" rate (added to beginning amount of debt):** | **12** | **18** | **24** | **30** | **36** | **42** |
| $ 4 per $100 per year ......... | $ 40 | $ 60 | $ 80 | $100 | $120 | $140 |
| $ 6 per $100 per year ......... | $ 60 | $ 90 | $120 | $150 | $180 | $210 |
| $ 8 per $100 per year ......... | $ 80 | $120 | $160 | $200 | $240 | $280 |
| $10 per $100 per year ......... | $100 | $150 | $200 | $250 | $300 | $350 |
| $12 per $100 per year ......... | $120 | $180 | $240 | $300 | $360 | $420 |
| **Percent of unpaid balance** | | | | | | |
| ¾ of 1% per month ............ | $ 49 | $ 73 | $ 96 | $120 | $145 | $169 |
| 1% per month ............... | $ 66 | $ 98 | $130 | $162 | $196 | $230 |
| 1½% per month ............... | $100 | $149 | $198 | $249 | $301 | $355 |
| 2% per month ............... | $135 | $201 | $269 | $340 | $412 | $488 |
| 2½% per month ............... | $170 | $254 | $342 | $433 | $528 | $627 |

## Shopping for Credit

You should shop for credit the way you shop for anything else. It's best to shop at more than one place, and it's best to know what to look for. A typical household with a good credit rating can save enough for an annual vacation by shopping for the money it "rents" in order to buy now and pay later.

Here are some pointers to help you shop for money for installment buying through contracts and through credit cards and other kinds of revolving charge plans.

## Compare Costs

Credit can cost you pennies or dollars. It depends on your character, your capital and your capability to repay, the money market, and other economic factors.

Two choices you frequently have are closed-end and revolving transactions. Under the closed-end plans you ordinarily sign a promissory note, if you are borrowing cash, or a retail installment contract, if you are using sales credit. You agree in advance on the specific amount to borrow, the number and size of weekly or monthly payments, and a due date.

On the other hand, the revolving charge plan is open-ended. A top limit is agreed upon, but purchases are added as they are made and finance charges are figured on the unpaid balance each month. A monthly interest rate is quoted — usually 1 or 1½ percent a month, which is a 12 or 18 percent annual rate.

Revolving charges come in many forms. There are credit cards from stores and gasoline and other companies for charging at branches. Bank credit cards (such as Visa and Master Charge) and those issued by "travel and entertainment" groups (Diners Club, Carte Blanche, American Express) allow you to arrange a line of credit and to charge at many participating retailers, or even to borrow cash.

Credit cards are conveniences we've all come to rely on, but they charge some of the highest interest rates around — 18 percent annually, or 1½ percent monthly. (If you itemize your tax returns, you can deduct this interest.)

If you keep money in a savings account earning only, for example, 5 percent, why should you pay 18 percent per year for interest on credit card purchases just to avoid touching your savings? Of course, to many people, saving is a matter of discipline, but is it worth the 13 percent you end up paying? Why not buy only what you really can afford — use credit cards to get free use of that money until the bill is due, then pay the bill on time and avoid finance charges.

Banks and some credit unions also offer books of special checks or drafts indicating preapproved loans. As you spend the checks or

**223**

## To finance $2,000 for 2 Years:

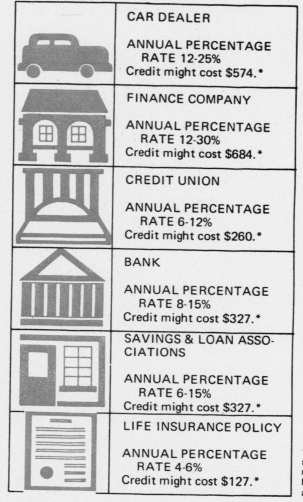

| | |
|---|---|
| | **CAR DEALER**<br><br>ANNUAL PERCENTAGE<br>RATE 12-25%<br>Credit might cost $574.* |
| | **FINANCE COMPANY**<br><br>ANNUAL PERCENTAGE<br>RATE 12-30%<br>Credit might cost $684.* |
| | **CREDIT UNION**<br><br>ANNUAL PERCENTAGE<br>RATE 6-12%<br>Credit might cost $260.* |
| | **BANK**<br><br>ANNUAL PERCENTAGE<br>RATE 8-15%<br>Credit might cost $327.* |
| | **SAVINGS & LOAN ASSO-<br>CIATIONS**<br><br>ANNUAL PERCENTAGE<br>RATE 6-15%<br>Credit might cost $327.* |
| | **LIFE INSURANCE POLICY**<br><br>ANNUAL PERCENTAGE<br>RATE 4-6%<br>Credit might cost $127.* |

Finance with the lender that offers you the lowest annual percentage rate (APR).

*Figured on highest rate shown. These are estimates of national averages. Maximum rates vary, according to state laws.

drafts, interest begins. For occasional credit, many people now have checking accounts with overdraft privileges, which allow them to write a check for more than their balance. But overdraft privileges (usually limited to $700 or so) may cost as much as store credit. Before signing up for an overdraft account, be sure to find out the interest rate. Banks may charge anywhere from 10 to 18 percent for overdrafts. Some banks also charge a fee per transaction in addition to regular interest rates.

Banks make overdraft advances either for the exact amount or in multiples. Therefore, if the bank lends only in multiples of $100, you would have to borrow $100 and pay interest on it even though you only wanted $10. Some banks charge a monthly fee for overdraft privileges in addition to interest. Find out whether deposits to your checking account automatically apply to an overdraft balance or whether you must specifically repay the overdraft account.

What you pay for credit depends a good deal on whether you use closed-end or revolving charge plans and where you arrange for them. In buying a car, for instance, what you would pay for the use of $2,000 for two years might vary from $127 to $684, which is from a 4 percent (available on some insurance loans) to a 30 percent annual rate, depending on where you financed it and the plan you used.

The kind of security the lender or dealer requires from you also affects the cost. Sometimes the word collateral is used instead of security. Both words mean "something having money value." As a general rule, the more security you can offer, the lower the cost of credit. A cosigner or comaker may lower the cost for you.

You may have other borrowing options. Does your life insurance policy have a loan clause? If you have paid-up insurance, can you risk short-changing your protection? If so, some insurance loans run at a 4 to 6 percent annual rate.

Another option might be borrowing on passbook savings you have at a savings and loan association.

## Truth in Lending: Annual Percentage Rate

Annual percentage rate, which is the unit pricing of money, is the key to cutting your cost of credit. It's a relatively new approach made possible by the Truth in Lending law. Here is how you use the annual percentage rate approach in shopping for closed-end credit.

All merchants and lenders are required under the Truth in Lending law to show the unit price for money on all consumer credit contracts. They do this by stating the cost in terms of the annual percentage rate (APR), the cost of buying an item or service on time, expressed as a percentage figured on the unpaid balance.

Just as consumer sense has taught you to shop for the lowest cost per pound on grocery items, economy dictates that you shop for money by looking for the lowest annual percentage rate.

Here's how it works in closed-end credit shopping. Often each lender you approach offers you a different loan amount, for a different time period, with a different sized payment. For his special package, he works out the finance charge. This is the dollar cost including interest and other charges for extending the credit. He converts the finance charge into the annual percentage rate he can offer for his transaction.

You can quickly tell which deal offers you the most credit for the money. It's the one with the lowest annual percentage rate. Meanwhile you compare total dollar cost through the finance charge. Be sure to ask the lender specifically for annual percentage rate. Some lenders might make loan rates sound lower by quoting some other rate.

With regard to revolving charge, you simply look for the lowest annual percentage rate to compare cost. To save the most when using revolving credit, join the one-third of all consumers who pay within the 25 or 30 days allowed without any finance charges. This gives you the convenience at the same cost as paying cash.

The Truth in Lending law does not fix interest rates or other credit charges. Your state may have a law setting a limit on interest rates, which would still apply.

Chances are that if the monthly statements and other materials you receive from companies giving you credit look different now, it doesn't mean they've changed their rates, only their way of showing them to comply with the Truth in Lending law. Your department store bills, for example, should now list both a monthly rate (for example, 1 percent, 1½ percent, or some other number) and the annual percentage rate. This may be 12 percent, 18 percent, or some other percentage, but it will usually be 12 times the monthly rate.

## Protection Under Truth in Lending

The law also gives a new look to the advertising of credit terms. It says that if a business is going to mention one feature of credit in its advertising, such as the amount of down payment, it must mention all other important terms, such as the number, amount, and period of payments that follow. If an advertisement states "Only $2 down," it must also state, for example, that you will have to pay $10 a week for the next two years. Here again, the intent is to provide you with full information so that you can make informed decisions.

One other important provision of the law is designed for your protection in case you use your home as collateral in a credit transaction. This frequently occurs when you are having a major repair or remodeling job done on your home. Today, when you enter into a credit transaction in which your home is used as collateral, the law gives you three business days to think about it and to cancel the transaction during that period if you wish. The creditor must give you written notice of your right to cancel, and if you decide to cancel the transaction, you have to notify him in writing.

Under this right of cancellation, the contractor cannot start work until the three days are up. You may give up your right to cancel and get the work started without the three-day wait if you notify the creditor in writing that you face a real financial emergency and need the credit immediately to finance repairs necessary to avoid danger to you, your family, or your property.

The right of cancellation does not apply when you sign a first mortgage to finance the purchase of a home.

The law, and the regulations issued by the Board of Governors of the Federal Reserve System to carry it out, contain many other detailed provisions. Businessmen extending credit should familiarize themselves with all of these, to make sure they are complying with the law. You as an individual may sue if a businessman fails to make the required disclosures. You may sue for twice the amount of the finance charge—for a minimum of $100, up to a maximum of $1,000—plus court costs and reasonable attorney's fees.

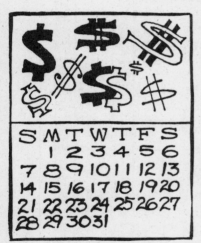

Pay within the 25 or 30 days allowed without any financial charges.

You may sue for twice the amount of the financial charge.

If you cannot meet your payments, you may have to give back the merchandise.

## Compare Other Terms

There are things to consider other than cost in shopping for closed-end credit. When you buy on credit, you make many promises. If you cannot meet your payments, you may have to give back the merchandise, pay damages, and continue to make the payments you owe. You may even have to forfeit personal belongings right down to your silverware.

Closed-end contracts vary a good deal from one lender to another. Let's say you want to buy a $600 stereo. You've found just the right one. You know that you do not have to finance it through the dealer and that closed-end credit may be less expensive than letting the salesperson charge it on your revolving account or your bank credit card.

You must know the size of payment that you can handle each week or month without risking disaster. Let's say that you have talked to three lenders and found the deal with the lowest annual percentage rate. But the payment was too high, so you have just about decided to borrow on a plan that allows you to pay less each time by stretching out the payments for a longer period. You recognize that credit will cost you more this way, but there is less risk that you will be unable to meet the payments.

Before you sign the contract, it's important to weigh the other risks. This checklist should help you:

• **Down payment:** A larger down payment can help cut the cost of the credit. But beware of borrowing the down payment from a second lender. This means two payments instead of one.

• **Size of Payments:** Are they all the same? Watch out for a larger final payment or "balloon clause." Even if you make all but the balloon payment, you may lose everything.

• **Your home as security:** Is it included? If so, the seller should give you a cancellation form. The Truth in Lending law allows you three days to change your mind and rescind.

• **Repayment in advance:** Is there any refund of the finance charge?

• **Missing a payment:** What happens? Penalty charges? Entire debt due? Immediately?

• **Default:** What if you can't pay and have to default? Collection charges? Storage or court costs? Can you reclaim the item? If it's sold but doesn't cover your debt, must you pay the difference?

**227**

- **Faulty work or merchandise:** Is there a time limit for your complaints? To whom should you complain? Your installment contract probably will be sold to another company; will the new creditor stand behind your purchase?
- **Moving the merchandise:** Can you remove it from the state?
- **Insurance:** Is it involved? On the item? On you, to assume full payment of the debt in case of accident, illness, death? Who collects? Can you get cheaper coverage from your own insurance company?
- **Waiving your rights:** Must you sign away other rights? Avoid signing a statement that work has been completed or an item received when it hasn't been.
- **Add-on contract:** Think twice before you add an item to a contract you already have with a store. A missed payment can mean you lose all the items even though you've paid for the first ones.

If there are contract terms you do not want, ask the lender to strike them out. If he agrees, you and he both must initial the modifications on his copy and on yours. It's only the written agreement that counts, not verbal promises.

If you cannot understand the contract, ask for a blank, unsigned copy. Compare terms other than cost, and discuss it with someone (a friend or a relative) who can help you. Avoid signing any statement or contract that is not completely filled out. Such action allows the lender to fill in amounts and terms that you did not agree to in conversation.

The foregoing checklist is useful primarily for closed-end credit but can be used for revolving plans. Here are more pointers on revolving credit.
- Notice how much you are paying each month. Total all the finance charges from your bills for a typical month. Multiply by 12 for the yearly cost. Is the credit worth it?
- When amounts outstanding become sizable, would you do better to pay them off by arranging a closed-end credit deal? Or by arranging a less expensive revolving plan? Some credit unions offer annual percentage rates lower than 18 percent on their "draft" preapproved loans. Some banks offer less than 18 percent on their check credit plans.
- In considering which system might be less costly, keep in mind these variables among revolving plans: Some require an initial or annual fee. Some do not. Some allow more time than others between date of purchase and due date. And some have a way of figuring the finance charge so that their credit costs you less than others.

## Your Credit Rating

If you have a charge account, a mortgage on your home, life insurance, or have applied for a personal loan or even a job, it is almost certain that there is a "file" existing somewhere that shows how you pay your bills, if you have been sued or arrested, if you

It's only the written agreement that counts.

have filed for bankruptcy. Some of these files include your neighbors' and friends' views of your character, general reputation, or manner of living.

The companies that gather and sell such information to creditors, insurers, employers, and other businesses are called "consumer reporting agencies," and the legal term for the report is a "consumer report."

If, in addition to credit information, the report involves interviews with a third person about your character, reputation, or manner of living, it is referred to as an "investigative consumer report."

The Fair Credit Reporting Act was passed by Congress to protect consumers against the circulation of inaccurate or obsolete information, and to insure that consumer reporting agencies exercise their responsibilities in a manner that is fair and equitable to consumers.

Under this law you can now take steps to protect yourself if you have been denied credit, insurance, or employment, or if you believe you have had difficulties because of a consumer report on you. Here are the steps you can take. You have the right:

1. To be told the name and address of the consumer reporting agency responsible for preparing a consumer report that was used to deny you credit, insurance, or employment or to increase the cost of credit or insurance.

2. To be told by a consumer reporting agency the nature, substance, and sources (except investigative-type sources) of the information (except medical) collected about you.

3. To take anyone of your choice with you when you visit the consumer reporting agency to check on your file.

4. To obtain all information to which you are entitled, free of charge, when you have been denied credit, insurance, or employment within 30 days of your interview. Otherwise, the reporting agency is permitted to charge a reasonable fee for giving you the information.

5. To be told who has received a consumer report on you within the preceding six months, or within the preceding two years if the report was furnished for employment purposes.

6. To have incomplete or incorrect information re-investigated, unless the request is frivolous, and, if the information is found to be inaccurate or cannot be verified, to have such information removed from your file.

7. To have the agency notify those you name (at no cost to you) who have previously received the incorrect or incomplete information that this information has been deleted from your file.

8. To have your version of a dispute placed in the file and included in future consumer reports when a dispute between you and the reporting agency about information in your file cannot be resolved.

9. To request the reporting agency to send your version of the dispute to certain businesses for a reasonable fee.

10. To have a consumer report withheld from anyone who under the law does not have a legitimate business need for the information.

11. To sue a reporting agency for damages if it wilfully or negligently violates the law and, if you are successful, to collect attorney's fees and court costs.

12. Not to have adverse information reported after seven years; one major exception is bankruptcy, which may be reported for 14 years.

13. To be notified by a business that it is seeking information about you that would constitute an investigative consumer report.

14. To request from the business that ordered an investigative report more information about the nature and scope of the investigation.

15. To discover the nature and substance (but not the sources) of the information that was collected for an investigative consumer report.

The Fair Credit Reporting Act does not:

1. Give you the right to request a report on yourself from the consumer reporting agency.

2. Give you the right, when you visit the agency, to receive a copy of or to physically handle your file.

3. Compel anyone to do business with an individual consumer.

4. Apply when you request commercial (as distinguished from consumer) credit or business insurance.

5. Authorize any federal agency to intervene on behalf of an individual consumer.

If you want to know what information a consumer reporting agency has collected about you, either arrange for a personal interview at the agency's office during normal business hours or telephone in advance for an interview.

The consumer reporting agencies in your community can be located by consulting the Yellow Pages of your telephone directory under such headings as "Credit" or "Credit Rating or Reporting Agencies."

If you decide to visit a consumer reporting agency to check on your file, the following checklist may be of help. Did you:

1. Learn the nature and substance of all information in your file?

2. Find out the names of each of the businesses (or other sources) that supplied information on you to the reporting agency?

3. Learn the names of everyone who received reports on you within the past six months (or the last two years if the reports were for employment purposes)?

4. Request the agency to re-investigate and correct or delete information that was found to be inaccurate, incomplete, or obsolete?

5. Follow up to determine the results of the re-investigation?

6. Ask the agency, at no cost to you, to notify those you name who received reports within the past six months (two years if for employment purposes) that certain information was deleted?

Request the agency to re-investigate.

7. Follow up to make sure that those named by you did in fact receive notices from the consumer reporting agency?

8. Demand that your version of the facts be placed in your file if the re-investigation did not settle the dispute?

9. Request the agency (if you are willing to pay a reasonable fee) to send your statement of the dispute to those you name who received reports containing the disputed information within the past six months (two years if received for employment purposes)?

## Should You or Shouldn't You?

You now have information about where you can get installment credit and how much it costs, and your credit rating is such that you will have no trouble getting a loan. The next question is whether you want to get into this sort of thing at all.

If you have in mind some particular item to buy, you might consider such questions as: Could you pay cash for it without using too much of your savings? Is having it now worth the extra cost of buying it "on time"? Can you handle this much debt?

Perhaps you have read the rule of thumb that a family should not commit itself for installment payments amounting to more than 20 percent of its income. The truth is that many families would be unwise to commit as much as 15, 10, or even 5 percent of their income to installment payments. Some, on the other hand, might pay installments amounting to more than 20 percent of their income — for a time, at least — without hardship.

Each family has different financial resources, as well as different needs, wants, goals, future prospects, and management skills. These are the things that will determine how much installment debt they can handle.

Instead of searching for a rule to tell you how much installment debt you can safely assume, take stock of your own financial situation. Have a family budget session to review your spending plan, your accounts, assets, and liabilities.

Considering these questions will help you to make a decision:

• How much do you have left from your income each month now, after you have paid all your living expenses, made the payments on your presents debts, put the planned amount into your savings account, and taken care of other obligations? (It makes sense not to take on another installment payment larger than this amount.)

• Is it always easy to make the payments on your present debt? (If it sometimes means scraping and squeezing or skipping a payment, better think twice before taking on another debt.)

• How much do you have in savings accounts, bonds, or other funds that you can easily draw on? (Unless it is enough to pay living expenses and keep up debt payments for at least a month or so in case of illness or layoff from work, go slow.)

• Will some debt be paid off soon, so you can use the money you now pay on that for installments on a new debt? (A "yes" here may be a go-ahead indicator.)

• Will another installment debt mean you have to postpone or give up some goal you have planned for? (If the answer is "yes," weigh the pros and cons carefully.)

Taking time to think things through like this may save you from the kind of impulse installment buying that gets families into trouble. Every installment payment you promise to make has to fit into the budget somewhere. The time to make sure it does is before you sign on the dotted line.

## Mind Made Up?

Once you have made up your mind to buy or borrow on the installment plan, keep the price you pay for credit as low as possible.

First, shop around for a good credit deal. If you are considering credit from a retailer, compare prices on the item you are buying as well as the credit charges. Sometimes merchants who sell on time charge more for the goods they sell.

Also, look into the possibility of getting a loan from a bank or credit union instead. Either way, be sure you are doing business with an established dealer or lending agency — one with a good reputation.

Do not be taken in by the unknown door-to-door salesman who offers to sell on the installment plan. Merchandise sold door-to-door is often overpriced and may be of poor quality. Take two days to think it over. Any honest salesman will be happy to come back. Compare prices of similar merchandise in stores before you buy from a door-to-door salesman. Don't sign any papers promising to pay unless you know the total cost. (High interest, credit insurance, and other service charges may double the price.)

Make as large a down payment as you can without reducing your savings to the danger point.

Finally, make monthly payments as large as your budget will allow. This way, you can pay the debt in the shortest possible time and save dollars.

When you buy things on time or get an installment loan, you have to sign a contract. Be sure you get a copy. Keep it in a safe place so you can refer to it if you need to.

Before you sign the contract:

To avoid credit trouble, estimate first the regular income and obligations you have.

• Read and understand everything in it, including the fine print.
• See that there are no blank spaces left when you sign.
• Be sure the contract tells exactly what you are buying: the purchase price, or the amount of cash you will receive from the loan; all the credit charges; the down payment and trade-in allowance, if any; the total amount you have to pay; the amount you have to pay for each installment; the number of installments to be made, and the dates due.
• Find out to whom you are to make the payments.
• Know what will happen if you cannot pay, and if you want to pay ahead.
• Know what the seller's responsibility is for maintenance, service, or replacement of the goods purchased.

Once you have made a credit deal, it's up to you to see that the installments are paid regularly. If you fail to make the payments, the creditor can take the washing machine, car, or whatever it is you owe for. This means you lose the money you have already paid on it. In some states, you can be required to pay more, too, if the creditor cannot sell the washer or the car for as much as you owe.

Your rating as a credit risk depends on how prompt you are in paying your debts. Because you will probably want credit again, it will pay you to keep this rating good.

## In Case You Get Into Credit Trouble...

### FEDERAL WAGE GARNISHMENT LAW

**Basic Provisions:** Limits amount of employee earnings that may be withheld for garnishment in any workweek or pay period and protects employee from being fired if pay is garnisheed for only one debt (regardless of number of levies made to collect).

**Authority and Enforcement:** Title III, Consumer Credit Protection Act; enforced by Wage and Hour compliance officers located across the U.S.

**Coverage and Earnings:** Law protects everyone receiving personal earnings; i.e., wage, salary, commission, bonus, and income from pension or retirement program. (Tips are generally not considered earnings for purposes of this law.)

**Restrictions on Garnishment:** Amount of total pay subject to garnishment is based on employee's "disposable earnings," the amount left after legally required withholdings for federal, state, and local taxes and for social security. Deductions such as those for union

dues, health and life insurance, and savings bonds are not considered required by law.

In any workweek, garnishment is limited to the lesser of: 1) 25 percent of disposable earnings, or 2) the amount by which disposable earnings for that week exceed 30 times the highest current federal minimum wage. However, employee is protected by garnishment law, even if not covered by minimum wage.

**Exceptions:** Law does not apply to: 1) court orders for support of any person; 2) court orders in personal bankruptcy cases; or 3) state or federal tax levies. Wage assignments are not generally within the law's scope.

**State Laws:** When state garnishment laws conflict with federal, the law resulting in smaller garnishment applies.

**Further Information:** Available from local Wage and Hour offices, listed in most phone directories under U.S. Government, Department of Labor, Employment Standards Administration.

## AVOIDING CREDIT PROBLEMS

The best way to avoid credit problems is not to use credit. However, you probably will need to borrow money or to use credit accounts for some expensive items during your life. You can avoid many difficulties with credit by using the following guides:

• Make a list of each monthly payment you have already agreed to make, for example:

| | |
|---|---|
| rent | $280 |
| washing machine | $ 32 |

Compare the total of these payments and other living expenses with the take-home paychecks you expect for the same months. Try to allow some income for emergencies and savings.

• Use credit only for the higher-priced purchases you must have now.
• Shop for the lowest finance charges you can get.
• Make your payments only as large as you can meet regularly.

## EQUAL CREDIT OPPORTUNITY ACT

The Equal Credit Opportunity Act starts all credit applicants off on the same footing. The law does not guarantee that you will get credit; you must still pass the creditor's tests of creditworthiness. But the creditor must apply these tests fairly, impartially, and without discrimination against you on any of the following grounds: age, sex, marital status, race, color, religion, national origin, because you are on welfare or social security, or because you exercise your rights under federal credit laws. This means that a creditor may not use any of those grounds as an excuse to:

• discourage you from applying for a loan;
• refuse you a loan if you qualify;
• lend you money on terms different from those granted another person with similar income, expenses, credit history, and collateral.

Under the Equal Credit Opportunity Act, you must be notified within 30 days after your application for a loan has been completed whether it has been approved or not. If credit is denied, this notice must be in writing and it must explain the specific reasons for denying credit or tell you of your right to request an application. You have the same rights if an account you have had is closed.

If you think you can prove that a creditor has discriminated against you for any reason prohibited by the Act, you may sue for actual damages plus punitive damages — that is, damages for the fact that the law has been violated — of up to $10,000 if the violation is proved to have been intentional. In a successful suit, the court will award you court costs and a reasonable amount for attorney's fees.

Written by
RICHARD ARLEN

# Buying Insurance

# Contents

**INSURANCE, PROTECTION AGAINST RISK** .... 237

**HEALTH INSURANCE** ....................... 237

**AUTOMOBILE INSURANCE** ................. 241

**LIFE INSURANCE** .......................... 244

**HOMEOWNER'S INSURANCE** ............... 248

**INSURANCE FOR THE RENTER** .............. 253
  Costs ................................... 253

## Insurance, Protection Against Risk

"There's no one with endurance like the man who sells insurance." We all know that. But what about those of us who must buy it? Do we have the endurance to persevere through the Clauses, Provisions, Endorsements, Exceptions—all written in legalese jargon that would tax the talents of the cryptographers who broke the Imperial Japanese Code in World War II? Still, we all need a basic understanding of insurance, since it is our first line of defense against many of life's problems and catastrophes.

How would your family react to the emotional and financial impact of a long-term illness? A legal suit brought against you because of inadequate car insurance? The death of the breadwinner of your family?

An insurance policy, whether it be health, car, home, or life, is protection for you and your family against risk. A policy is the document given to you by the insurance company to explain the protection and the conditions under which payments or indemnities (compensations) will be made in event of loss or damage.

## Health Insurance

Good health is one of the most valuable things in life, but good health does not remain the same throughout life. By having adequate health insurance, the risk of financial disaster from a long-term illness can be largely reduced.

It is often difficult to sort out the facts and obtain the kind of health insurance you are seeking because health insurance contracts are detailed and difficult to understand. A policy that satisfactorily addresses the following six items will be most likely to provide you with the essentials necessary for a sound health insurance plan:

• What types of expenses are covered by the policy?

Every policy covers certain kinds of expenses, and these expenses will be subject to certain conditions. Hospital indemnity, which is one of the simplest forms of health insurance, will pay only a fixed amount while you are hospitalized. If you receive outpatient treatment, you probably will collect nothing.

• How much will the policy pay?

The glowing ads give the maximum payments possible, but few policyholders receive the top payment. To be certain what the policy does and does not cover, get a copy of the actual policy and read it carefully.

When the ad for a health insurance plan says, "Up to $40,000 extra cash when you're in the hospital" and "Get $200 tax-free each week," stop and do some thinking and figuring. To collect the $40,000 at the benefit rate of $200, you would have to be hospitalized for almost four years!

Excluding maternity, mental and TB cases, only 15 out of 100 people are hospitalized during any one year. The average hospital stay is 5 days. Those with the highest hospitalization rate stay an average of 12 days.

Examine the clauses designed to limit payment. These might include deductibles, co-payment provisions requiring you to pay a portion of the expenses, and the specified amount allotted for various kinds of operations.

Always find out what the limits and restrictions are in any policy. If, for example, you are paying $200 a day for your room, plus drugs, X rays and operating room expenses, and the indemnity policy pays $50 a day, you are going to be left with the remainder of the hospitalization expense.

• Is there a waiting period before the policy goes into effect?

Usually, individual policies (in contrast to group policies) have a clause stating that you can't collect during the first year or two years for an illness that was treated before you enrolled in the plan, or you may not receive benefits even though you didn't know the condition existed at the time.

Be alert for such clauses as "benefit builder" period. Be sure you get the details. In some policies there may be more than one kind of waiting period.

• Is the policy renewable?

If a policy is stated as non-cancellable, the company can't cancel unless the premium payment on the policy lapses. However, the company can refuse to renew the policy. Few companies offer a truly non-cancellable policy.

When reading the ads and policies you will find that the company can cancel, refuse renewal, or raise premiums if it does so for all policyholders of the same "class." What is a "class"? It can mean all people in the same state with the same coverage, or all people in the same age group. Some companies guarantee renewal but maintain the right to raise rates on a class basis.

• Does the coverage supplement Medicare?

Medicare does not cover services such as dental treatment, eyeglasses, medical appliances, and drugs not supplied by a hospital. (See Tables 1 A and B.) If the policy being considered to supplement Medicare concentrates its benefits on hospitalization or on services covered by Medicare, it still isn't going to provide the coverage needed. The policyholder will have to pay for the uncovered costs.

• Is the company licensed in your state?

To some extent, you can protect yourself more adequately and efficiently by insuring with companies licensed by your state. If you have a complaint against a company licensed in your state, the state insurance department can proceed against the company more easily.

When considering a given company, be sure to find out if the company is licensed. Your state insurance department will be able to provide this information.

When starting your health insurance program, begin with basic coverage. No policy will cover all the potential costs.

# BASIC HOSPITAL COVERAGE—PART A

| TYPE OF SERVICE | TIME LIMIT | PATIENT PAYS | MEDICARE PAYS | QUALIFICATIONS | EXCLUSIONS |
|---|---|---|---|---|---|
| **HOSPITAL (a) CONFINEMENT** Semi-private room and board unless a private room is required for medical reasons. Covers general nursing, drugs, and normal services, including operating & recovery rooms. | First 60 days each benefit period **(b)**. | First $144 | | Age 65 and: (1) Entitled to Social Security (or Railroad Retirement) benefits; or (2) is *not* entitled, a citizen or permanent resident for 5 years, may enroll by paying $63 per month plus 10% to 40% more if you did not sign up when you were first eligible, plus Part B (cost below). Under 65 when: (1) Social Security (or Railroad Retirement) disability benefits payable for 24 consecutive months, or (2) any worker (or dependents) with chronic kidney disease who need dialysis, or (3) disabled widow (or disabled widower between 50 & 65, or (4) children (of retired, disabled or deceased workers) disabled before age 22. | First three pints of blood, private duty nurses, non-covered levels of care, and services covered under Part B. |
| | Next 30 days continuous hospital confinement. | $36 each day | Balance | | |
| | Lifetime aggregate reserve of 60 additional days. | $72 each day | | | |
| **SKILLED NURSING FACILITIES (a)** following hospital confinement. | First 20 days each benefit period **(b)**. | Nothing | 100% | Must require care within 14 days (may be extended to 28 days) after hospital confinement which lasted at least 3 days. | Same as above: unskilled medical care (such as "Old Age Homes" and Custodial Care). |
| | Next 80 days continuous confinement. | $18 each day | Balance | | |
| **HOME HEALTH CARE (a)** by visiting nurses, aides, therapists following hospital confinement. | 100 visits during the 1 year following confinement. | Nothing | 100% | Must require care for same or related causes as hospital stay, within 14 days after hospital stay, plus home confinement. | Full time (private duty) nursing, self-administered drugs, services covered under Part B. |
| **PSYCHIATRIC CONFINEMENT CARE** | Same as Hospital Confinement Benefits with a lifetime | | maximum limit of 190 days. | | |

# SUPPLEMENTAL MEDICAL COVERAGE—PART B

| TYPE OF SERVICE | TIME LIMIT | PATIENT PAYS | MEDICARE PAYS | QUALIFICATIONS | EXCLUSIONS |
|---|---|---|---|---|---|
| **PHYSICIANS AND SURGEONS** services at home, hospital or office. | No Time Limit | First $60 **(d)** per calendar year, then 20% of reasonable charges. | Balance of reasonable charges **(c)** (pays *full* reasonable charges for radiology and pathology services while hospital confined). | Voluntary enrollment, costs $8.20 or more a month, depending on date of enrollment, and subject to change each July. | Services covered by Workmen's Compensation, private duty nurse, eye-glasses, routine physicals, dental work, hearing aids, orthopedic shoes, non-skilled nursing care, plastic surgery, charges made by a relative, first 3 pints of blood in a calendar year, vaccinations, self-administered drugs, services in a foreign country. |
| **MEDICAL SERVICES & SUPPLIES** diagnostic tests, surgical dressings, casts, splints, braces, artificial limbs and eyes, rental or purchase of medical equipment, ambulance, X-ray therapy, professionally administered drugs, some chiropractic services, non-routine footcare. | | | | | |
| **HOSPITAL CARE** Outpatient. | | | | | |
| **HOME HEALTH CARE** visiting nurses, aides, therapists. | 100 visits per year (may be in addition to Part A). | First $60 **(d)** | 100% | Home confinement required but prior hospital care not required. | |
| **PSYCHIATRIC OUTPATIENT CARE** | Per calendar Year | First $60 **(d)** | 50% of charges | paid up to a maximum of $250 | |

**(a)** Hospital or Skilled Nursing Facility or Home Health Care Agency must be qualified and have signed Participation Agreement with U.S. Department of H.E.W.

**(b)** Each benefit period begins with first day of hospital confinement and ends after having been discharged from a hospital or Skilled Nursing Facility for 60 consecutive days.

**(c)** Reasonable charges are determined by the Medicare administration in the recipient's area. The charge approved will be either the customary charge, the prevailing charge, or the actual charge, whichever is lowest.

**(d)** All Part B expenses (i.e. Medical Services & Supplies or Home Health Care or Psychiatric Outpatient Care), including expenses incurred during last 3 months of previous year, can be counted toward the $60 deductible.

This chart is a brief description, further details can be found in Social Security literature. For use by MacArthur Insurance Companies Agents only. Includes changes effective 7-1-78.

## TABLE 1

Table 1. If you are over 65 — and in some instances, if you become disabled before you are 65 —

Medicare pays a major part of most medical bills, as shown in the Table. You may want to purchase "add-on" insurance from a private company to cover the rest.

Begin with an insurance that pays for a range of major costs —hospitalization and surgery. Then choose a reliable "major medical" policy that is designed to cover the costs of serious illness.

Before buying any insurance, whether it is through a group protection or an individual policy, carefully review the insurance coverage you already have. Remember, group protection usually provides more comprehensive coverage at a lower rate.

If you are nearing 65, it is particularly important to review your existing coverage, because many policies reduce benefits when you qualify for Medicare. If you are interested in learning more about the Medicare program, ask for a free copy of *Your Medicare Handbook* at the Social Security Administration office in your area.

## Automobile Insurance

Shopping for automobile insurance can present many problems and leave you very distraught. However, if you know the basic features to look for, you can shop with more confidence and are likely to get more for your money.

Auto insurance can be bought in the form of package coverage, or each section can be purchased separately.

Liability is the core of an auto policy. With liability coverage the insurance company pays for bodily injury and property damage to others when you are legally responsible for an accident.

Claims against you may be settled out of court, but if court action is brought against you, the company will defend you. The protection covers you, resident members of the family, and others who drive with your approval. You and members of your family are also covered when driving another car with the owner's consent.

Liability coverage is listed separately for bodily injury and property damage. The maximum coverage is generally stated in a form such as 10/20/5. This means that the company is liable for up to $10,000 for any one person injured; up to $20,000 for all injuries in the same accident; and up to $5,000 for damage to the other car, fences and private property. You are responsible for damages exceeding these amounts.

Liability coverage pays for other people's injuries—not yours. Medical payments cover you and your passengers'

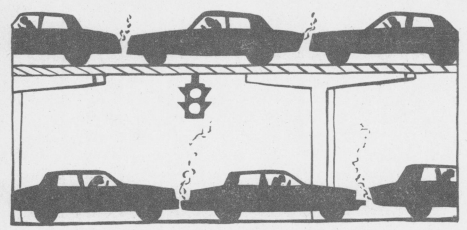

medical fees regardless of who was to blame for the accident. Medical payments coverage is sold in amounts ranging from $1,000 up. The limit is for each person injured, so with a $1,000 plan, four people would collect a total of $4,000.

Uninsured motorist coverage offers protection to you, your spouse, and resident children if you are injured by an uninsured or hit-and-run driver while driving or walking. (See Table 2 at the end of the book.)
• The coverage applies only when the other driver was to blame for the accident.
• Bodily injury payments generally are limited to minimums of state liability regardless of the face value of the basic policy.

Collision insurance pays for damage to your car when you hit another vehicle or an object such as a tree or a telephone pole.

Collision coverage is usually sold in the forms of $50, $100, and $200 deductible. If you hit a tree, do $150 damage to your car, and have a $50 deductible, the company will pay $100.

The larger the amount of the deductible, the lower the premium. In most instances, by buying a $100 deductible collision policy rather than $50 deductible, you can cut about 20 percent of the collision premium.

The company restricts its responsibility to the "actual cash value" of the car. This means that if your car is worth $1,600, that is the most you can expect to collect on a collision claim. No matter how dear to your heart the "old crate" is, the company will not spend $1,800 to repair it. Consider the book value of your car. It is often economically unwise to buy collision coverage for an old car.

Losses caused by fire, wind, theft, vandalism, collision

with animals, explosions, flood, and lightning are covered by the comprehensive coverage feature. Comprehensive provides limited coverage for personal property left in the car. If you have a homeowner's insurance policy (explained later in this booklet), there may be additional coverage. Discuss this with the agent who sold you the homeowner's policy.

Accidental death and dismemberment coverage pays a lump sum for death in a car accident, loss of a limb, blindness, fractures, and dislocations, plus a disability benefit each week. This accidental death coverage often overlaps coverage from liability and other insurance. Therefore, you may be spending premium money for overlapping coverages.

Premium rates vary by locality and state and according to the loss experience of the company. But these factors are heavily weighted according to:
• The purposes for which your car is used: pleasure, business, or farm work. Business receives the highest rate and farm work the lowest.
• Age (teenagers are considered a high risk).
• Marital status (a young married man is considered a better risk than a young bachelor).
• Whether you drive to work, and the distance to work if you do.
• Total mileage. A car driven more than a certain distance in a year is often subject to a higher insurance rate.

Special rating factors can help trim premiums. Some of the examples for you to explore are the following:
• If your son or daughter ranks in the top 20 percent of his or her class, or is on the dean's list, ask the company if it has a good-student discount.
• Encourage your young person to take driver training. Generally, that will qualify him for a driver-training discount.
• If another car is bought for the family, include the car on

your policy. This will entitle you to a multi-car discount on the second car.
• Check with the company about the age at which a young driver passes from the high-premium category to the lower-premium adult category, and remind the company when he reaches this age.
• When buying a car, find out if the car is subject to the "souped-up" car surcharge.
• Check on companies offering the "safe driver" plan. If you have an "accident- or traffic violation-free" driving record, you can realize considerable savings on your auto insurance premiums.
• Remember that there is no best company. Be knowledgeable about the types of coverage available and do some cost comparing among two or three companies.

For many years, our auto insurance system depended largely on the person at fault paying for the damage. The "fault" system has been under criticism as being inequitable and costly in settling claims.

Today, many states have adopted the "no-fault" system, in which injured persons are paid by their own companies up to certain amounts for medical expenses and loss of income, regardless of who is responsible for the accident. In states where the no-fault system has been enacted, a reduction of premium rates has occurred. The U.S. Department of Transportation has recommended that all states adopt a no-fault system. Some Congressmen are urging that the federal government make such a system mandatory throughout the country.

## Life Insurance

Life insurance is financial protection for dependents against economic loss as a result of the breadwinner's death. Because of the dependence on cash and credit by today's families, life insurance is a way through which families can gain protection and financial security.

Life insurance is not a savings plan or an investment plan. Neither is it the best method for building an educational fund for children. Life insurance is often sold for such purposes, but there are better ways of obtaining these objectives than through life insurance.

When the breadwinner dies, a family must face many

financial difficulties. The problems usually come in this order:

• Burial expenses and any medical expenses not covered by health insurance.

• Adequate funds to meet the family's living expenses until the spouse and/or the children can make employment arrangements.

• Educational funds for children.

Regardless of the extravagant claims made about some life insurance policies, there are four basic types of life insurance: term, straight life, limited payment life, and endowment.

Term insurance provides simple protection, whereas the other three have a savings feature. But remember that the basic principle is to gain the greatest protection for the family at the lowest cost should the breadwinner die.

Term insurance is a type of life insurance that provides protection only. As the name implies, the policy covers the holder for a term of 1, 5, 10, 20, or some other pre-set number of years. At the end of the term the coverage stops and the policy has no cash value. It is wise to buy a "renewable term" policy. This allows the policy owner to renew the policy for another term without another physical examination.

Term insurance gives the family the greatest amount of protection for a limited period at the least cost. It generally is best to buy term insurance on a reducing coverage basis so that it can be reduced or terminated as dependents become older and no longer require as much protection.

Term insurance can be increased to the maximum protection as each child is born or can be decreased to no insurance on the breadwinner as the children become economically independent. Several term policies rather than

**245**

one or two large policies can be purchased. This allows the policyholder to increase coverage or to drop policies to best meet his needs. Buying term insurance in this way also allows for convenient distribution of premium dates.

Straight life insurance, also known as ordinary life or whole life insurance, provides for a certain amount of coverage throughout life. It differs from term insurance in that straight life combines a decreasing amount of protection with an increasing amount of savings in the policy. Because of the savings element as well as the protection in the straight life plan, the premium for a certain amount of straight life at a given age is higher than the premium for term insurance.

The premium for straight life remains the same through the length of the policy. In the early years, the policyholder is actually paying more for the cost of protection. The extra portion of the premium is what builds up the savings element of the policy.

In a straight life policy the terms "face value" and "cash surrender value" are often used. The face value is the amount payable at the insured's death. The cash surrender value is the amount of savings that has built up in the policy.

The cash value increases while the policy is in force. The insured may cash the policy in at any time, but this will terminate the policy and the protection stops. If the insured desires, he may borrow the cash value from the company. But when the policy is borrowed from, the coverage is reduced until the loan is repaid.

Limited payment life insurance is comparable to straight life except that the policyholder pays the premiums on the policy in a given number of years. Usually the premiums are for 20 or 30 years, or until the insured reaches age 65.

Premiums for limited payment life insurance at a certain age are higher than premiums for straight life. The reason for the difference is that all the premiums are paid within a given number of years.

After the policy is paid up, it remains in force for the rest of the insured's life, unless he wishes to withdraw the cash value. If the policy's cash value is withdrawn, the coverage stops.

Families that have very high incomes in their early years and whose income may decrease in later years may want to make use of the limited payment life insurance policy. The average family would not possess ample funds and would have difficulty purchasing enough coverage to meet its needs.

The fourth type of life insurance is the endowment policy. Saving is the primary emphasis in an endowment policy, but some protection is also included. The primary purpose is to build up a certain amount of money in a given number of years. Endowment insurance can be purchased on the basis of 10, 15, 20, 25, or 30 years, or mature to cash at a given age. When the endowment policy has reached a point at which the cash savings equal the amount of the face value, the policy matures. (See Table 3 at the end of the book.)

At this point, with the total cash available to the policyholder, the protection portion is zero and the coverage ends.

The premiums are much higher for endowment policies than for other types because of the emphasis placed upon savings.

When purchasing life insurance there are many important considerations other than the four basic types of insurance just discussed. When you and your family are establishing a life insurance program, consider these very important factors:

• Buy the policies that will give the most protection at the least cost.
• Insure the right family members.
• Consider the family's financial needs.
• Buy the insurance from companies that are financially sound and are represented by honest, well-trained agents.

To illustrate the kinds of life insurance needed in particular situations, let's consider some individuals at various stages in the life cycle.

Peter is single and has no dependents. Probably the only life insurance he needs is enough to cover his debts and burial expenses.

Insurance can be purchased at a lower rate during the young years, but by buying while young, Peter will be paying the premiums for a longer period of time. In the end, the amount paid in for premiums is about the same. But he is paying for protection that really isn't necessary.

Suppose that Peter marries Susan, who is a college graduate and is working. Perhaps only enough insurance would be needed to cover their debts and burial expenses.

Later, Susan has quit work and is pregnant with their first

child. They have purchased a home with a small down payment and a 30-year mortgage. The situation regarding life insurance takes on a different aspect. There are dependents who need financial protection. Now the question is not whether they need insurance, but how much?

As the family increases in size, it is essential to add more insurance on the father or the breadwinner to protect the dependents. The time when the children are young and depend upon the family for financial needs is precisely the time when families with modest incomes have difficulty providing enough life insurance on the father to protect the mother and the children.

Families with modest to average incomes should insure the breadwinner or breadwinners first. When considering the amount of insurance for the mother with dependent children, the need for substitute child care should be planned for until the children can care for themselves. The death of a small child would have no effect upon the income of the family. Perhaps a policy to meet funeral expenses would be sufficient for the young child.

Families should consider the other resources available. Social Security benefits are available to most people with dependent children under the age of 18 and to widows when they reach age 62. Also, families should strive toward savings to be used for emergencies and have some stocks or real estate or both that will increase in market value during inflationary times.

As the children become financially independent, the emphasis on family financial security will shift from protection to saving for the retirement years. Every family situation is different, and it is important that each family give adequate thought and study to planning its financial future.

## Homeowner's Insurance

We all hear about property losses but relatively few of us, fortunately, have firsthand experience with them. Each loss is unexpected, and many people have the feeling "it won't happen to me."

The value and importance of your property can be quickly demonstrated if you list all your personal belongings, household goods, and the house itself. Then add up how much it would cost for replacements if they were lost or

damaged. Generally, you accumulate property over the years and don't realize how much you have, nor how it would be missed if it were gone. Inflation probably has substantially increased replacement costs, and any significant loss would hurt financially.

Many steps can be taken to prevent or reduce loss from fire, wind, theft, and other perils, and some losses that may happen will not be large enough to be serious. For substantial losses, insurance is the best method of protection. By paying a relatively small, set payment to an insurance company, homeowners can protect themselves against the possibility of a large and unpredictable loss.

Property owners can insure themselves in several ways. They can build up their protection by buying insurance for most losses separately, or they can buy a package policy that protects against a dozen or more perils. Even with a package policy, additional insurance for special needs can be purchased by paying an extra premium.

When separate insurance coverages are bought, property owners usually start with a standard fire policy that insures the home and contents against fire and lightning. Then for an additional premium they may get extended coverage to include damage from wind, hail, smoke, explosion, riot, vehicles, and aircraft.

Another policy—for burglary and theft protection—is available. Still another, called liability insurance, will protect against losses from lawsuits for injuries suffered by visitors or damage caused to the property of others.

Buying insurance through separate policies may be the best solution for owners of specialized property or those facing certain definite dangers. Also, in some localities package policies may not be readily available or may provide more costly protection than is needed or wanted. The value of some homes and their contents may be less than the minimum amounts of protection that must be bought in package policies. Separate insurance policies are used more for protection in rural areas than in urban communities.

The federal government has cooperated with the insurance industry in making several types of protection available. Flood insurance, for one, generally has been impossible to obtain because of the potential catastrophic nature of this peril in certain areas. Now it is available at low cost through governmental cooperation in about 1,200 communities where there is danger of flooding. To be eligible for governmental participation, the community must pledge to set certain construction standards and to enforce land-use controls in flood-prone areas.

In some cities and high-crime localities, homeowners have had difficulty in getting fire, theft, and vandalism insurance. To meet such needs, private insurers as a group with government cooperation have developed FAIR (Fair Access to Insurance Requirements) Plans.

Property and liability insurance is generally regulated and supervised by states and not the federal government. The obligation of each state is to make certain that insurance companies do not overcharge or discriminate against customers and that companies remain in sound financial condition so as to be able to pay for losses.

If you feel you have been unfairly denied insurance protection or charged excessive premium rates, you should

complain to the state supervisory official, usually called the commissioner of insurance, located in the capital city of your state.

Package policies that protect against losses from a variety of perils have been spreading rapidly over the past two decades. The most familiar package policies are the homeowner's, farmowner's, and renter's policies.

Such policies, as suggested earlier, are not always available, nor are they the best for everybody, but they do have advantages. You usually have only one policy and one premium to worry about, and the wide variety of protection costs less than if the same coverages were purchased in separate policies.

To buy a homeowner's policy you must own and occupy a one- or two-family residence. The policy protects the house and additions to it such as an attached garage. It also insures other structures including toolsheds and detached garages; these latter are called "appurtenant structures" in the policy.

Buildings used for commercial purposes or rented to others (except garages) are not covered.

All household goods and personal property owned or used by the family are protected. Losses to personal belongings and other property are frequently covered whether they occur at home or away. An inventory and photographs of personal property, especially of more valuable items, are helpful in filing a claim in the event of fire, theft, or other loss.

The homeowner's policy specifies some exceptions and conditions under which indemnities for losses may not be paid. For example, pets are not covered, and protection for jewelry and furs is usually limited to $500 or $1,000 unless otherwise specified. Theft of credit cards may be excluded, as well as the loss of boats and trailers when away from the insured premises.

Consult with your insurance agent to avoid any misunderstanding about your coverage. The extra protection you need may be available if you pay an additional premium.

Another coverage included in the homeowner's policy is additional living expense. This pays for the expenses incurred if damage to the house is so severe that it cannot be occupied. It would cover the cost of hotels, motels, and restaurant meals.

There are three types of homeowner insurance policies: basic, broad, and comprehensive.

The basic homeowner's policy usually protects against 11 perils to property: fire and lightning, wind and hail, explosion, riot, aircraft, vehicles, smoke, vandalism, theft, breakage of glass, and loss of property removed from premises endangered by fire or other perils.

The broad homeowner's policy covers seven additional perils: falling objects, weight of ice and snow, collapse of building, sudden and accidental damage to a steam or hot-water heating system or water heater, accidental leakage within a plumbing, heating, or air-conditioning system, freezing of these systems, and accidental injury from artificially generated currents to electrical appliances and wiring (excluding TV and radio tubes).

The comprehensive homeowner's policy covers all perils except earthquake, landslide, floods of various kinds, backing up of sewers, seepage, war, and nuclear radiation.

In buying a homeowner's policy, the property owner decides the amount of coverage he wants on his dwelling. On this basis, the amounts on appurtenant structures, personal property, and additional living expense are automatically determined as 10 percent, 50 percent, and 20 percent, respectively, of the dwelling coverage. For example, if the dwelling is insured for $40,000 the coverage would be $4,000 on appurtenant structures, $20,000 on personal property, and $8,000 for additional living expenses.

A homeowner's policy, besides paying for property losses from such perils as fire and wind, provides liability coverage for family members living in the home. Under the personal liability feature, you are protected against lawsuits from people who believe that you, your family, or your pets are responsible for their injuries or damage to their property. It covers accidents both on and away from the insured property.

For example, if your dog bites a neighbor or a visitor is hurt in a fall and you are sued, the insurance company will pay the legal costs and any damages assessed against you. The minimum personal liability protection offered in a homeowner's policy is $25,000, but larger amounts can be purchased for an additional premium.

Medical payment to others also is a feature of homeowner's insurance. Such payments are made for injuries to other people caused by you, your family, or pets. This coverage is similar to personal liability except that it is designed mainly for minor injuries, and payments may be made regardless of who is at fault. Medical payments to any one person are limited to a specified amount.

A farmowner's package policy that provides basic protection comparable to the homeowner's policy is available to owners of farms in many areas. Any protection needed on the farm service buildings, livestock, and machinery is added to coverages related to the dwelling.

## Insurance for the Renter

A tenant's or renter's policy, similar in many respects to a homeowner's policy, is available for those who live in an apartment or rent a home. (In some cases, such a policy may go by the name of a homeowner's policy). It insures contents of a home and personal possessions of the family against most of the same perils and also provides personal liability protection and medical payments to others.

### Costs

The cost of property and liability insurance to a homeowner or a renter depends on a variety of factors. The value of your property and the amount of protection you want are, of course, basic. Cost also varies with the number of perils protected against and differences in location and condition of property that may increase or decrease the risks of loss. Homes located far from fire departments or hydrants or those with faulty electrical wiring or heating systems would be relatively costly to insure.

Some insurance companies may charge more than others

for the same protection, but competition and state regulation tend to hold premium rate differences to a minimum.

Developing an insurance program at reasonable cost should begin with an appraisal of the perils faced. Consider the financial consequences of damages or losses. Study the various kinds of available insurance coverages and their costs. Select what matches as closely as possible your needs for protection.

Don't overinsure, as you won't be paid more than the replacement cost of any loss regardless of the insurance you carry. Talk with several reputable insurance agents to find the lowest reasonable premium rates. Repairing hazardous wiring, roofs, and chimney conditions may be worthwhile in terms of lower insurance costs.

Insurance under which the property owner himself bears any losses up to the amount of a deductible will provide savings. Many policies already include a deductible of $50, but insurance with larger deductibles is available at lower rates.

Determining the value of your house or other property is often difficult, especially in times of rapid inflation or deflation. Talking with neighbors and others about the going price of houses like yours can be of some help. Real estate tax assessments are usually a specified percentage of market values and may be a guide.

The insurance agent, too, will have useful information on sales prices and construction costs. In fact, someone from the insurance company will probably inspect the property before the policy is approved to check on values and make sure no fire hazards or other conditions make it uninsurable.

What your insurance pays after a loss is spelled out in the policy, and it may not reach the exaggerated levels that you hear or read about. Most policies state that the company will pay "the actual cash value at the time of loss." This means that only the depreciated value is paid.

For example, if a five-year-old TV set is destroyed by fire, you should not expect to recover its original cost of $500, because it is not worth that much. Nor should you expect your insurance to give you the price of a brand-new storm door to replace an old one that has been broken during a windstorm.

By paying an additional premium, however, you usually can get protection for the replacement cost rather than the depreciated value.

With a homeowner's policy, you can receive full payment (except for deductible amounts) for any damage to the dwelling, up to the amount of the coverage, provided it is insured for at least 80 percent of its value. In periods of rising property values and building costs, it is important to maintain this level of protection.

At the time you buy a homeowner's policy, you probably can get an endorsement that automatically increases the protection every three months or so.

Insurance—and your enduring insurance man—can be your best friend in time of need. Take the time to consider the various types of insurance in terms of your family's needs. Just knowing you are protected in case of trouble will help you to enjoy life more.

| TABLE 2 | REQUIRED BY STATE LAW | | AVAILABLE AT POLICY-HOLDER'S REQUEST |
|---|---|---|---|
| | MAY NOT Be Rejected | MAY Be Rejected | |
| ALABAMA | | X | |
| ALASKA | | X | |
| ARIZONA | X | | |
| ARKANSAS | | X | |
| CALIFORNIA | | X | |
| COLORADO | | X | |
| CONNECTICUT | X | | |
| DELAWARE | | X | |
| DIST. OF COL. | | | X |
| FLORIDA | | X | |
| GEORGIA | | X | |
| HAWAII | | X | |
| IDAHO | | X | |
| ILLINOIS | X | | |
| INDIANA | | X | |
| IOWA | | X | |
| KANSAS | | X | |
| KENTUCKY | | X | |
| LOUISIANA | | X | |
| MAINE | X | | |
| MARYLAND † | | | X |
| MASSACHUSETTS | X | | |
| MICHIGAN | | X | |
| MINNESOTA * | X | | |
| MISSISSIPPI | | X | |
| MISSOURI | X | | |
| MONTANA | | X | |
| NEBRASKA | | X | |
| NEVADA | | X | |
| NEW HAMPSHIRE | X | | |
| NEW JERSEY | X | | |
| NEW MEXICO | | X | |
| NEW YORK | X | | |
| NORTH CAROLINA | | X | |
| NORTH DAKOTA | X | | |
| OHIO | | X | |
| OKLAHOMA | | X | |
| OREGON | X | | |
| PENNSYLVANIA | X | | |
| RHODE ISLAND | | X | |
| SOUTH CAROLINA | X | | |
| SOUTH DAKOTA | X | | |

*Table 2 cont.*

| | REQUIRED BY STATE LAW | | AVAILABLE AT POLICY-HOLDER'S REQUEST |
|---|---|---|---|
| | MAY NOT Be Rejected | MAY Be Rejected | |
| TENNESSEE | | X | |
| TEXAS | | X | |
| UTAH | | X | |
| VERMONT | X | | |
| VIRGINIA | X | | |
| WASHINGTON | | X | |
| WEST VIRGINIA | X | | |
| WISCONSIN | X | | |
| WYOMING | | X | |

* Uninsured Motorist Coverage may be rejected on commercially rated vehicles.
† Uninsured Motorist Coverage in Maryland applies only to accidents occurring outside the state.

Table 2. Some states require Uninsured Motorists Coverage as part of all automobile liability policies. Other states allow the policyholder to reject this coverage by giving written notice to the insurance company.

Table 3. The spread between premiums for different types of life insurance is greatest for young insurance buyers.

**TABLE 3**

## ANNUAL PREMIUM RATES PER $1,000 OF INSURANCE

| AGE OF IN-SURED AT ISSUANCE OF POLICY | ORDINARY LIFE | 20-PAYMENT LIFE | 20-YEAR ENDOWMENT |
|---|---|---|---|
| **PARTICIPATING INSURANCE** (ANY DIVIDENDS PAID WILL REDUCE THESE COSTS) | | | |
| 20 | $18.00 | $30.00 | $49.00 |
| 25 | 21.00 | 33.00 | 50.00 |
| 30 | 24.00 | 36.00 | 51.00 |
| 35 | 28.00 | 40.00 | 52.00 |
| 40 | 33.00 | 44.00 | 54.00 |
| 45 | 39.00 | 50.00 | 57.00 |
| 50 | 47.00 | 56.00 | 62.00 |
| 55 | 58.00 | 65.00 | 69.00 |
| 60 | 73.00 | 78.00 | 79.00 |
| 65 | 94.00 | 95.00 | 96.00 |